ROYAL HISTORICAL SOCIETY

STUDIES IN HISTORY

New Series

CARDINAL BENDINELLO SAULI AND CHURCH PATRONAGE IN SIXTEENTH-CENTURY ITALY

Anonymous North Italian draughtsman, *Bust of the Cardinal Bendinello Sauli, after Sebastiano del Piombo* (? sixteenth century) (Devonshire Collection, Chatsworth House). Reproduced by permission of the Chatsworth Settlement Trustees. Photograph: Photographic Survey, Courtauld Institute of Art.

CARDINAL BENDINELLO SAULI AND CHURCH PATRONAGE IN SIXTEENTH-CENTURY ITALY

Helen Hyde

THE ROYAL HISTORICAL SOCIETY
THE BOYDELL PRESS

First published 2009

A Royal Historical Society publication
Published by The Boydell Press
an imprint of Boydell & Brewer Ltd
PO Box 9, Woodbridge, Suffolk IP12 3DF, UK
and of Boydell & Brewer Inc.
668 Mt Hope Avenue, Rochester, NY 14620, USA
website: www.boydellandbrewer.com

ISBN 978-0-86193-301-3

ISSN 0269-2244

A CIP catalogue record for this book is available
from the British Library

The publisher has no responsibility for the continued existence or accuracy of
URLs for external or third-party internet websites referred to in this book,
and does not guarantee that any content on such websites is,
or will remain, accurate or appropriate.

This publication is printed on acid-free paper

Printed in Great Britain by
CPI Antony Rowe, Chippenham and Eastbourne

TO MY MOTHER, BRENDA BATTSON (1931–95)

Contents

List of Illustrations

Frontispiece/jacket illustration: Anonymous North Italian draughtsman, *Bust of the Cardinal Bendinello Sauli, after Sebastiano del Piombo* (? sixteenth century) (Devonshire Collection, Chatsworth House). Reproduced by permission of the Chatsworth Settlement Trustees. Photograph: Photographic Survey, Courtauld Institute of Art.

Acknowledgements

The time spent researching and writing this book was divided between Genoa, Rome and London. Different people in all three centres and elsewhere have helped and my grateful thanks go to Professor Enzo D'Agostino, Fausto Amalberti, Francis Ames-Lewis, Enrico Basso, Piero Boccardo, Josefa Costa, Thomas Dormandy, Francesco Guidi Bruscoli, Donald Green, Peter Humfrey, Philippa Jackson, Bram Kempers, Andrea Lercari, Professor Rocco Liberti, Kate Lowe, Paolo Rossi, Eleonora Saita and Carlo Taviani.

Marchese Cattaneo Adorno kindly made the Sauli archives in Genoa available to me and Maddalena Giordano provided expert knowledge of the inventory. The reading room personnel in the various libraries and archives I consulted were all very helpful, but special mention must be made of the support and friendship of the *sala studio* staff of the Archivio Segreto Vaticano, the Biblioteca Apostolica Vaticana and the Archivio di Stato in Genoa and Rome. They made the lonely life of an independent scholar a lot more fun. Thank you.

My advisory editor, Steven Gunn, has helped enormously, both in correcting my prose and in helping me to see the bigger picture and Christine Linehan has been an extremely patient editor. My biggest debt of gratitude, however, is to Roy Hyde.

Helen Hyde
November 2008

Abbreviations

ACR	Archivio Capitolino di Roma
ADGG	Archivio Durazzo Giustiniani, Genoa
ASG	Archivio di Stato di Genova
ASI	Archivio Storico Ingauno
ASL	Archivio di Stato di Locri
ASR	Archivio di Stato di Roma
ASS	Archivio di Stato di Siena
ASV	Archivio Segreto Vaticano
BAV	Biblioteca Apostolica Vaticana
BCIS	Biblioteca Comunale degli Intronati di Siena.
BUG	Biblioteca Universitaria di Genova
ASI	*Archivio Storico Italiano*
ASLSP	*Atti della Società Ligure di Storia Patria*
ASRSP	*Archivio della Società Romana di Storia Patria*
DBI	*Dizionario biografico degli italiani*
RIS	*Rerum Italicarum Scriptores*

Figure 1. Bendinello Sauli *quondam* Pasqualotti and his descendants

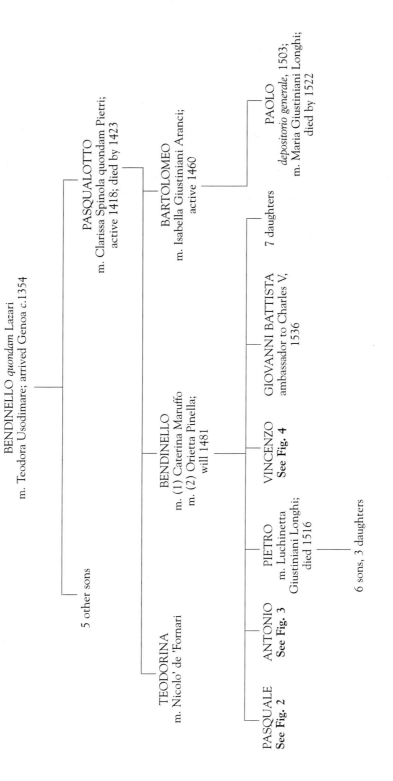

BENDINELLO *quondam* Lazari; arrived Genoa c.1354
m. Teodora Usodimare

PASQUALOTTO
m. Clarissa Spinola quondam Pietri;
active 1418; died by 1423

5 other sons

BARTOLOMEO
m. Isabella Giustiniani Aranci;
active 1460

PAOLO
depositorio generale, 1503;
m. Maria Giustiniani Longhi;
died by 1522

TEODORINA
m. Nicolo' de 'Fornari

BENDINELLO
m. (1) Caterina Maruffo
m. (2) Orietta Pinella;
will 1481

GIOVANNI BATTISTA
ambassador to Charles V,
1536

7 daughters

PASQUALE
See **Fig. 2**

ANTONIO
See **Fig. 3**

PIETRO
m. Luchinetta
Giustiniani Longhi;
died 1516

VINCENZO
See **Fig. 4**

6 sons, 3 daughters

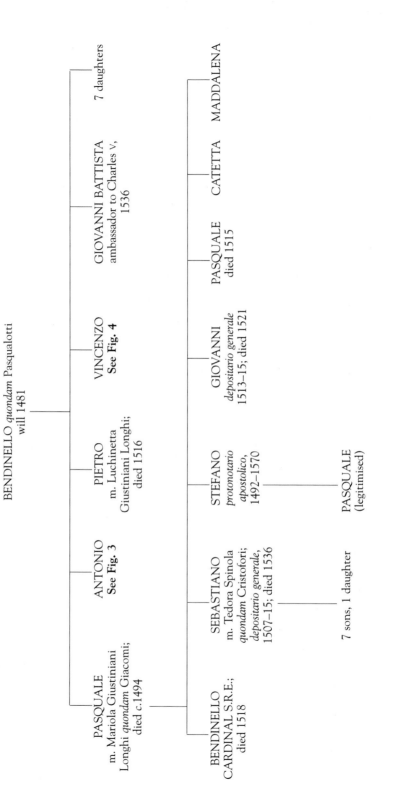

Figure 2. Pasquale Sauli *quondam* Bendinelli and his descendants

BENDINELLO *quondam* Pasqualotti
will 1481

PASQUALE
m. Mariola Giustiniani
Longhi *quondam* Giacomi;
died c.1494

ANTONIO
See Fig. 3

PIETRO
m. Luchinetta
Giustiniani Longhi;
died 1516

VINCENZO
See Fig. 4

GIOVANNI BATTISTA
ambassador to Charles V,
1536

7 daughters

BENDINELLO
CARDINAL S.R.E.;
died 1518

SEBASTIANO
m. Tedora Spinola
quondam Cristofori;
depositario generale,
1507–15; died 1536

STEFANO
*protonotario
apostolico*,
1492–1570

GIOVANNI
depositario generale
1513–15; died 1521

PASQUALE
died 1515

CATETTA

MADDALENA

7 sons, 1 daughter

PASQUALE
(legitimised)

Figure 3. Antonio Sauli *quondam* Bendinelli and his descendants

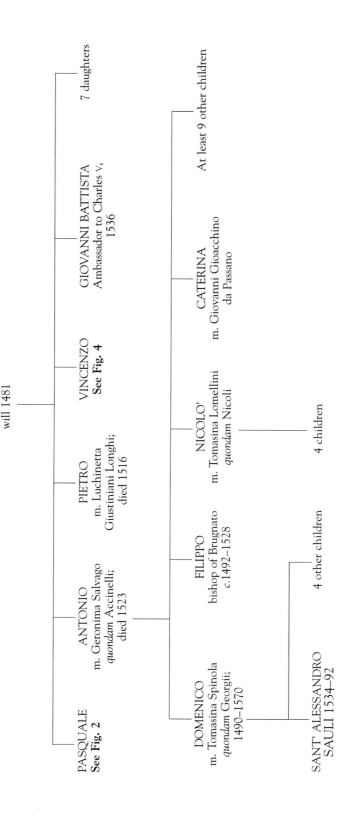

Figure 4. Vincenzo Sauli *quondam* Bendinelli and his descendants

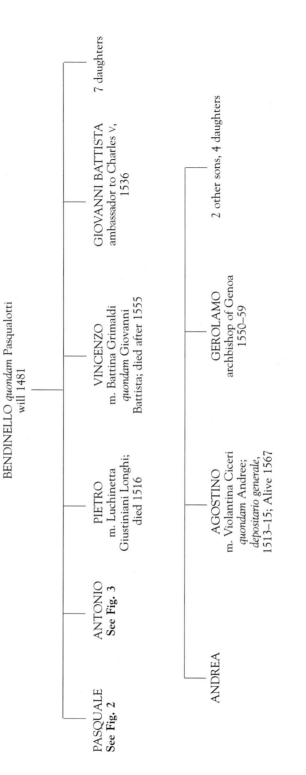

BENDINELLO *quondam* Pasqualotti
will 1481

PASQUALE
See **Fig. 2**

ANTONIO
See **Fig. 3**

PIETRO
m. Luchinetta
Giustiniani Longhi;
died 1516

VINCENZO
m. Battina Grimaldi
quondam Giovanni
Battista; died after 1555

GIOVANNI BATTISTA
ambassador to Charles V,
1536

7 daughters

ANDREA

AGOSTINO
m. Violantina Ciceri
quondam Andree,
depositario generale,
1513–15; Alive 1567

GEROLAMO
archbishop of Genoa
1550–59

2 other sons, 4 daughters

Introduction

Bendinello Sauli was born in Genoa in about 1481 into a wealthy family of merchants. His ecclesiastical and curial career began in 1503 and he attained the cardinalate in 1511. By early 1518 he was dead, stripped of all but the appearance of rank.[1]

The call by Gian Giacomo Musso in 1958 for a monograph dedicated to this 'remarkable figure' went unanswered and this is, to date, the first in-depth study of Sauli's life and career.[2] Monographs on cardinals were, and remain, unfashionable but this is not the only probable cause for his neglect: the view of Genoa as a backwater of the Renaissance may well have led those qualified to investigate Sauli's life to disagree with Musso's assessment.[3]

In fact Sauli has suffered from mixed reviews to the present day. He is either an angel or a demon depending on the commentator, whose stance generally reflects his opinion of the event which caused Sauli's downfall, disgrace and death: his implication in 1517 in the plot to murder Leo X. Assessments vary, from remarking on 'his many outstanding qualities of mind and body which he had acquired by his own personal virtue ... a lively and intelligent disposition' and his 'possessing every type of virtue' to noting that 'he was an ambitious and envious man', 'he had the soul of a factious baron

[1]   The spelling of Sauli's Christian name varies but the form 'Bendinello', which is to be found in all Genoese family documents, is used throughout this book.
[2]   G. G. Musso, 'La cultura genovese fra il quattrocento e il cinquecento', *Miscellanea di storia ligure*, i, Genoa 1958, 121–87 at p. 166 n. 45. For Sauli see H. Hyde, 'From devotion to damnation: the Sauli as men of the Church in the early *cinquecento*', *Devotio* i (2000), 41–72; J. Jungic, 'Prophecies of the angelic pastor in Sebastiano del Piombo's "Cardinal Bandinello Sauli and three companions"', in M. Reeves (ed.), *Prophetic Rome in the high Renaissance*, Oxford 1992, 345–70; and B. Kempers, 'The canonical portrait of a cardinal: Bendinello Sauli, Raphael and Sebastiano del Piombo', in M. Gallo (ed.), *I cardinali di Santa Romana Chiesa: collezionisti e mecenati*, ii, Rome 2001, 7–21. The latter two concentrate upon the portrait of *Cardinal Bendinello Sauli and three companions* (Samuel H. Kress Collection, National Gallery of Art, Washington).
[3]   The few studies of cardinals of this period include P. Paschini, 'Tre illustri prelati del Rinascimento: Ermolao Barbaro, Adriano Castellesi, Giovanni Grimani', *Lateranum* n.s. xxiii (1957), 11–207 at pp. 45–130; D. S. Chambers, *Cardinal Bainbridge in the court of Rome, 1509 to 1514*, Oxford 1965; K. J. P. Lowe, *Church and politics in Renaissance Italy: the life and career of Cardinal Francesco Soderini, 1453–1524*, Cambridge 1993, and 'Questions of income and expenditure in Renaissance Rome: a case study of Cardinal Francesco Armellini', in W. J. Sheils and D. Wood (eds), *The Church and wealth* (Studies in Church History xxiv, 1987), 175–88; and relevant *DBI* entries. For the current neglect of Genoa see H. Hyde, 'Genoa: "urbem ... cuius similem non habet orbis universus"', *Bulletin for the Society of Renaissance Studies* xviii (Oct. 2000), 1–7.

rather than that of a priest', or even 'a totally insignificant personality'.[4] Such a wide range of opinions is not in itself remarkable but to pass judgement on Sauli purely on the basis of his involvement or otherwise in the plot is to do him an injustice, not least because so little was known about Sauli the cardinal when these judgements were passed. More needs to be known of the context within which the plot occurred and the events leading up to it. The aim of this monograph is thus twofold: through a detailed study of Sauli's life and career to provide not only some idea of the man himself but also about the Church and Italy during the early *cinquecento* and the dynamics of power and patronage which governed the life of a Renaissance cardinal and his family.

The Sauli and Genoa

Sauli came from a socially and politically ambitious family which employed a combination of money, political influence, marriage and artistic patronage to become, some ten years after the cardinal's death, a force in the new Genoese ruling class. The first members of the Genoese branch of the Sauli left Lucca and arrived in Genoa at the beginning of the fourteenth century and the progenitor of the second line of the family (that of Cardinal Sauli) had settled in the city by 1354.[5] By that date the People's Republic (1339–1528) had been established: headed by a doge, it was marked by factional fighting and instability, often resulting in domination by foreign powers such as France or Milan. Although much has been made of the hostility between the two dogal factions, the Adorno and the Fregoso, this was far from being the only cause of internal bickering in Genoa. More important for the Sauli (and in their case also better documented) was the competition for political office in the city's councils and the social prominence accorded to certain families.[6]

---

[4] A. Ciaconii, *Vitae et res gestae pontificum romanorum et SRE cardinalium*, Rome 1630, 1385; BAV, MS Vaticani Latini 9167, fo. 526r; E. Rodocanachi, *Histoire de Rome: le pontificat de Jules II, 1503–13*, Paris 1928, 126–7; A. Ferrajoli, 'La congiura dei cardinali', *Miscellanea della Reale Società Romana di Storia Patria*, vii, Rome 1920, i–355 at p. 98

[5] H. Hyde, 'Early *cinquecento* "popolare" art patronage in Genoa, 1500–1528', unpubl. PhD diss. Birkbeck College London 1994, i. 124 n. 4; Biblioteca Civica Berio, Genoa, sezione conservazione, raccolta locale, MS m. r. IX. 5, iv, fo. 386.

[6] The complex contemporary Genoese political scene is best analysed in R. Musso, 'Lo "stato cappellazzo": Genova tra Adorno e Fregoso (1436–64)', *Studi di storia medioevale e di diplomatica* xvii (1998), 223–88 at pp. 224, 232, 249–52. For the fluidity of the support given to the Adorno and Fregoso see A. Pacini, 'Ideali repubblicani, lotta politica e gestione del potere a Genova nella prima metà del cinquecento', in S. Adorni Braccesi and M. Ascheri (eds), *Politica e cultura nelle repubbliche italiane dal medioevo all'età moderna, Firenze, Genova, Lucca, Siena, Venezia: atti del convegno (Siena 1997)*, Rome 2001, 189–236 at p. 200, and for the support of the Sauli at pp. 206–7; cf. BUG, MS C. IX.19/21, iii, fo. 144v.

The method whereby eligible citizens were elected to the governing councils pitted the *nobili* (a term which had originally denoted those who took part in government and was used to distinguish them from the governed) and the *popolari* against each other in the distribution of offices.[7] But the 'inherent hatred' between these two groups, noted by the contemporary chronicler (and Sauli intimate) Agostino Giustiniani, derived not just from political but also from economic and social competition.[8] Indeed, the *nobili* were socially dominant: gathered into *alberghi*, or groups of families who took the same name, their power lay in their ties of blood and their day-to-day proximity, with most members of an *albergo* living in a specific area around the *domus magna* of the clan, its square, loggia and often the clan's own church or *parrocchia gentilizia*.[9] It was through the *alberghi* that appointment to half of the seats on the different councils of the republic was made. Yet if the *nobili* were socially homogenous, the *popolari* were anything but. They were based in different areas of the city and came from different social and economic backgrounds (for the most part the rich mercantile and artisan bourgeoisie). Subdivided as they were into *mercatores* and *artefices*, they were appointed to civic offices according to the district in which they lived. They rarely formed *alberghi*, and when they did these were more often temporary groupings based on commonly-held business interests rather than on blood ties.[10] In turn this militated against the establishment of dynastic symbols such as the *domus magna* and the *parrocchia gentilizia*.

How did this situation reflect on the Sauli and what, if anything, could they do to improve their position? They were classified as *mercatores* and, as members of the *popolari*, they were part of the ruling class, but their power and influence, especially at a social level, were strictly limited. Yet there is clear evidence of concerted efforts by the family to raise their social and political profile and to show themselves the equals of any other family. This began with the first branch of the family, yet it was the money and influence of Cardinal Sauli's grandfather, Bendinello *quondam* Pasqualotti (d. 1481)

---

[7] G. G. Camajani, *Il 'Liber nobilitatis Genuensis' e il governo della repubblica di Genova fino all'anno 1797*, Florence 1966, 3–4. For the division of offices and its permutations see J. Heers, *Gênes au XVe siècle: activité économique et problèmes sociaux*, Paris 1961, 602, 606, and Pacini, 'Ideali repubblicani', 195, 198–9, and 'I presupposti politici del "secolo dei genovesi": la riforma del 1528', *ASLSP* n.s. xxx/1 (1990), 7–422 at pp. 29–30.

[8] A. Giustiniani, *Castigatissimi annali con la loro copiosa tavola della eccelsa & illustrissima repubblica di Genoa, da fideli & approvati scrittori, per el reverendo Monsignore Agostino Giustiniani Genoese vescovo di Nebio accuratamente racolti*, Genoa 1537 and anastatic edn 1981, c. 258r. For the divisions between the two groups see cc 253v, 257v, 258v. See also A. Borlandi, '"Janua, janua italiae": uno sguardo al quattrocento genovese', *ASI* cxliii (1985), 15–38 at p. 28.

[9] J. Heers, *Le Clan familial au moyen âge*, Paris 1974, 85–90, 149.

[10] Idem, *Gênes*, 582.

(see Fig. 1), that were employed openly to demonstrate the family's ambitions.[11]

The family acted on two fronts. In an attempt to attain political prominence they used their economic expertise (gained through their banking and mercantile activities) to obtain positions in the administration of the public debt known as the *Casa di San Giorgio* and in governmental offices involved in the city's finances such as the *ufficio della moneta*. They also vied for power as members of the *anziani* and for prestige as representatives of the republic on diplomatic missions. Bendinello's sons, in particular Antonio (d. 1523) (see Fig. 3), Pietro (d. 1516) and Vincenzo (c. 1467–mid 1550s) (see Fig. 4), were also protagonists of the (initially anti-*nobiliare*) *popolare* revolt of 1506–7 and Antonio, followed by other members of the family, was then involved in the political reform process of the following decades which aimed to promote union and equality amongst the Genoese.[12] At the same time they also employed their vast wealth to make a series of socially advantageous marriages (into both *nobile* and wealthier *popolare* clans) and to pursue what can only be described as a systematic imitation of the artistic patronage of the *nobili*.[13]

The Sauli had little alternative but to imitate the patronage of the *nobili*: the reign of a Genoese doge was often short-lived and bloody leaving little time for, or interest in, the arts. The most powerful symbol of social predominance was the *parrochia gentilizia*. These, although limited in number, were an overt manifestation of the privileged status of the *albergo* which, in a situation almost exclusive to Genoa, had sole rights over the church.[14] It was thus not always possible for the *popolari* – as was indeed the case for the Sauli – to become patrons of their neighbourhood church and they had to seek chapels in other churches, many of which were also patronised by these same *nobili*. This was not necessarily a disadvantage *per se*: the Sauli turned to the church of San Domenico and from 1316 members of both branches of the family were buried in the cloister, but these humble beginnings were transformed in 1467 when Bendinello *quondam* Pasqualotti seemingly profited from his own reputation, and the expansion of the body of the church in the mid-*quattrocento*, to join an elite of patrons (which included various *nobili*) and build a chapel dedicated to the Annunciation.[15] Yet his ambitions lay on a much larger scale.

---

[11] Genoese notarial documents of the period use the term 'quondam' to denote the relationship of 'son of the late'. The term is used throughout this book.

[12] C. Taviani, '"Franza populo e fora lo gatto": una rivolta cittadina nelle guerre d'Italia: Genova 1506', unpubl. PhD diss. Perugia 2004, 1, 15, 41, 46–8, 52, 58, 81; Hyde, 'Early cinquecento', ii, appendices 2.3, 2.1, 2.4; Pacini, 'I presupposti politici', 199–200.

[13] ASG, MS 494, fo. 23.

[14] M. Moresco, *Le parrochie gentilize genovesi*, Turin 1901, passim and at p. 57.

[15] Hyde, 'Early cinquecento', i. 143–5.

In his will of 16 October 1481 Bendinello blatantly imitated the *nobili* and laid the financial basis for the dynastic celebration of the Sauli through the foundation of their own *parrocchia gentilizia*, S. Maria and SS Fabiano and Sebastiano (now known as S. Maria Assunta di Carignano). This was to be built after sixty years when a complicated investment in the *Casa di San Giorgio* matured. The splendour, size and magnificence that he detailed in his will were more than met by the architect Galeazzo Alessi when construction of the church began in the mid-*cinquecento*.[16] The claim to social equality promulgated by the elder Bendinello was then continued by his sons in their rich, ambitious endowments of chapels in different churches both in and outside Genoa.[17] When Vincenzo Sauli became patron of the main altar of the church of the Benedictine-Cassinese monastery of San Girolamo della Cervara in the early *cinquecento* he provided Gerard David's *Cervara altarpiece*[18] and also the (now lost) surrounding tapestries and altar frontals.[19] The commission was of a scale and expense rarely encountered in Genoese patronage and again reflected the Sauli desire for prestige and commemoration.

But to the younger Sauli the erection of S. Maria Assunta must have seemed a distant dream. Sixty years was a long time to wait and in reality little had changed in Genoa. The family was prominent – in 1506 Jean d'Auton listed the Sauli as amongst the 'great houses' of Genoa – but effectively powerless.[20] They chose again to publicise their ambitions through a further, audacious, act of artistic patronage. On 14 August 1515 several members of the family (including Cardinal Sauli and his brothers) registered a joint holding in the *Casa di San Giorgio*, the profits of which were to pay for the celebration of a daily mass in the now destroyed 'chapel or oratory' of SS Fabiano e Sebastiano, founded in Carignano by the family in the same year and of which they held the *iuspatronatus*.[21] The very foundation of the oratory confirmed the Sauli's desire to have their personal place of worship and was a clear imitation of the *parrocchie gentilizie*: even the main *Altarpiece of Sts Fabian and Sebastian*[22] by the Pavian artist Lorenzo Fasolo (c. 1463–c. 1518), was modelled on the *Altarpiece of Sts Sebastian, John the Baptist and*

---

[16] M. Bologna (ed.), 'L'archivio della famiglia Sauli di Genova', *ASLSP* n.s. xl/2 (2001), 11–661 at p. 38; ADGG, Archivio Sauli, no. 299, fos 1v, 2r–v.

[17] Hyde, 'Early *cinquecento*', i. 173–96.

[18] Now divided and to be found in the Palazzo Bianco, Genoa; the Metropolitan Museum of Art, New York; and the Louvre, Paris.

[19] H. Hyde, 'Gerard David's *Cervara altarpiece*: an examination of the commission for the monastery of San Girolamo della Cervara', *Arte Cristiana* lxxxv (1997), 245–54.

[20] *Chroniques de Jean d'Auton*, ed. P. L. Jacob, Paris 1834, i. 4.

[21] ASG, Archivio del Banco di San Giorgio, Colonne San Lorenzo 1516, 610, fo. 476v; Archivio Sauli, no. 13, unfoliated; Hyde, 'Early *cinquecento*', i. 349.

[22] Private collection.

Francis [23] by Filippino Lippi which stood in the church of S. Teodoro, whose patrons were the *nobile* Lomellini.[24]

In October 1528 the Sauli gained their reward: under the *reformationes novae* they, with four other *popolare* families (who had also been active participants in the revolt and the ensuing attempts at political reform), became heads of five of the twenty-eight *alberghi* which made up a single order of ruling citizens, called, ironically, *nobili*.[25] The active participation of the Sauli in political life and the public image of the family promoted through their patronage fulfilled the 'dignity of life' required to have been shown by those who were included in the *alberghi*, and perhaps more particularly, by those who headed them.[26] Undoubtedly the singular achievement of the elevation to the cardinalate of Bendinello Sauli *quondam* Pasquali enhanced their standing. He was the first member of a genuine Genoese *popolare* family to become a cardinal: the only earlier example, Cardinal Paolo Fregoso (1480–98), had served as doge twice before receiving his cardinalate when his nephew, Battista Fregoso, was head of the republic.[27] Cardinal Sauli himself benefited from family connections, but in a different way. But how did the Sauli begin to make their influence felt within the papal Curia and finally secure the cardinalate for Bendinello?

The Sauli and Rome: the breakthrough into papal finances

They did so by joining the ranks of the papal bankers ('mercatores curiam romanam sequentes') and by lending their financial wealth and support to three popes: Innocent VIII (1484–92), Julius II (1503–13) and Leo X (1513–21). Undoubtedly they turned their attention to Rome in the hope of profit, and, presumably, of social climbing.[28] The position of banker was prestigious and, as Peter Partner notes, 'the bankers moved the cogs which made the great Roman machine rotate'.[29] In the *caput mundi* they might attain the pre-eminence which was denied them in Genoa and they might also bring further 'honour and profit' to their own house, and their native city, by the

---

23 Palazzo Bianco, Genoa.
24 Hyde, 'Early *cinquecento*', i. 354–5, 358–66.
25 Pacini, 'I presupposti politici', 42, 202, 256, 269; Hyde, 'Early *cinquecento*', i. 201.
26 Camajani, *Il 'Liber'*, 7.
27 M. Cavanna Ciappina, 'Fregoso, Paolo', *DBI* l (1998), 427–32, passim. The dates in brackets which follow the first citing of a cardinal refer to the length of his cardinalate.
28 P. Hurtubise, 'L'Implantation d'une famille florentine à Rome au debut du XVI siècle: les Salviati', in S. Gensini (ed.), *Roma capitale: (1447–1527), Pisa and San Miniato 1994: atti del IV convegno di studio del centro studi sulla civiltà del tardo medioevo, 27–31 Ottobre 1992, San Miniato (Pisa)*, Pisa 1994, 253–71 at p. 268.
29 P. Partner, *Renaissance Rome, 1500–1559: a portrait of a society*, London 1976, 148.

acquisition of a cardinal's hat for a member of their family, as was often the case with papal bankers.[30]

The highest position within the administration of papal finances to which a lay banker could normally aspire was that of *depositario generale*, to whom all monies due to the *camera apostolica* were paid and who executed all payments of papal money, on the instructions of the cardinal *camerlengo* (chamberlain). He was 'the foremost papal banker'.[31] Bankers, including the *depositario generale*, aided the papacy by providing loans and credit on interest with repayment either in cash or through assignments of cameral revenues (either spiritual or temporal); by importing goods necessary to the upkeep of the papal court; by collecting spiritual revenues; and by the rental (*appalto*) of customs duties and incomes due from Rome and the Papal States.[32] The Genoese were far from new to papal banking; under the impecunious Innocent the Centurione and other families are listed in banking records.[33] In the case of the Sauli the wealth required for the provision of credit to the papacy had been gained through their wide-ranging business activities which were largely based on overseas trade with, amongst other places, Chios and the East, Lyons, London, Bruges and Spain.[34] On 24 January 1486 Andrea Cicero (*c.* 1460–1520/8), Alessandro Sauli (d. 1509) from the first branch of the family and their associates (namely the heirs of Bendinello *quondam* Pasqualotti) took over a loan to the *camera* from Gerardo Usudimare, the Genoese *depositario generale* to whom the Sauli were related by marriage, for 3,500 ducats.[35]

On 8 April 1486 they firmly established themselves as important financiers by lending the *camera* the significant sum of 19,550 ducats, receiving as security the jewels and mitre of Paul II.[36] Four additional smaller loans,

---

30 'honore e utile': Genoese *anziani* and *balia* to the Genoese orators to Julius II, 20 Nov. 1506, ASG, Archivio Segreto 2707/C; B. McClung Hallman, *Italian cardinals, reform and the Church as property*, London 1985, 135.

31 For a fuller explanation see C. Bauer, *Studi per la storia delle finanze papali durante il pontificato di Sisto IV*, Rome 1928, 9–10. See also P. Partner, 'Papal financial policy in the Renaissance and Counter-Reformation', *Past and Present* lxxxviii (1980), 17–62 at p. 19, and F. Guidi Bruscoli, *Benvenuto Olivieri: i mercatores fiorentini e la camera apostolica nella Roma di Paolo III Farnese (1534–1549)*, Florence 2000, 87.

32 Guidi Bruscoli, *Benvenuto Olivieri*, p. xxi.

33 M. Cassandro, 'I banchieri pontifici nel XV secolo', and M. Bullard, 'Fortuna della banca medicea a Roma nel tardo quattrocento', in Gensini, *Roma capitale*, 207–34 at p. 219, 235–52 at p. 245; ASR, Camerale I, mandati camerali 851, fos 5v, 7v–9r, 21r, 35v–38r, 56r, 248v; 852, fos 55r, 170r, 280r.

34 Hyde, 'Early *cinquecento*', i. 128–38; Camerale I, mandati camerali 853, fo. 87v; ASG, Notai Antichi, 950, no. 96, 21 June 1493.

35 ASV, Camera Apostolica, Diversa Cameralia, 44, fos 218r–v; ASG, MS 494, fo. 24r; Notai Antichi, 1353 ter, no. 78, 25 May 1492.

36 Cam. Ap., Div. Cam. 44, fos 263r–265v; Camera Apostolica, Introitus et Exitus, 512, fo. 72v; Camerale I, mandati camerali 851, fo. 184v; ASV, Armadio. XXXIX, 19, fo. 378r.

totalling over 7,000 ducats, were made that year.[37] Innocent's financial situation did not improve and on 19 December 1486 Cicero-Sauli and eight other merchants signed a contract with the *camera* for the farming of the Church's spiritual incomes, the *appalto degli spirituali*.[38] Cicero-Sauli were at the head of this group which was to loan the papacy 216,000 ducats over four years and receive the spiritual revenues from which they would reimburse themselves.[39] They provided 19,500 of the 54,000 ducats lent annually to the pope and were thus his most important creditors and continued to be so when the *appalto* was then revised.[40] It is striking that Cicero-Sauli, relatively new to dealings with the papal court, felt able and inclined to contribute a bigger holding to the *appalto* than prestigious banks such as that of the Medici who were shortly to be related to Innocent through the marriage between Franceschetto Cibo and Maddalena de' Medici. They obviously felt that the gains in influence to be made outweighed any potential risk, but risk there clearly was: although they made their last loan payment on 31 December 1492, on 23 January 1493 repayments under Alexander VI to the Sauli began at only 45 per cent of face value.[41] Losses were thus indeed sustained, but their extent is far from clear given the lack of clarity in the records.

Cicero-Sauli also provided other loans to the papacy, of which the larger and more clearly identifiable include more than 17,000 ducats loaned in 1487, approximately 10,000 ducats loaned in 1488–90 and a spate of smaller loans in 1491.[42] They were thus prominent both within and outside the context of the *appalto*. In a short period they had become high-profile financial supporters of the papacy, but their gains in prestige almost certainly exceeded any profit they had hoped to make. Cicero-Sauli were bought out, with the approval of the bank's other associates, on 12 April 1492 by Paolo Sauli *quondam* Bartholomei who replaced them in the Curia and took over all of the firm's dealings.[43]

---

[37] Cam. Ap., Intr. et Ex. 514, fos 23v, 25v, 34v; Div. Cam. 45, fos 72v, 73v–74r, 76r–77r, 91v–92r.
[38] Ibid. Div. Cam. 49, fos 123r–133v, cited at length in M. Bullard, 'Raising capital and funding the pope's debt', in J. Monfasani and R. Musto (eds), *Renaissance society and culture: essays in honor of Eugene F. Rice Jr.*, New York 1991, i. 23–32, passim.
[39] M. Bullard, 'Farming spiritual revenues: Innocent VIII's "appalto" of 1486', in A. Morrogh (ed.), *Renaissance studies in honor of Craig Hugh Smyth*, Florence 1985, i. 29–42 at p. 31, and 'Raising capital', 29.
[40] Idem, 'Raising capital, 35, and 'Farming', 36–7.
[41] Cam. Ap., Intr. et Ex. 524, fos 33r, 101r, 105r; Camerale I, mandati camerali 855, fos 12v, 41r; Bullard, 'Farming', 37.
[42] Cam. Ap., Div. Cam. 45, fos 112r–113r, 131v–132v, 179v–180v; Camerale I, mandati camerali 852, fos 21r, 22v, 62r, 93r, 102v; 853, fos 94v, 186r; 854, fos 82v, 97v, 106v; Cam. Ap., Intr. et Ex. 514, fos 71v, 95v, 119r; 516, fo. 5r; 504, fos 135v–38r; 522, passim and fo. 22r.
[43] Notai Antichi, 1353 ter, no. 78, 25 May 1492; Cam. Ap., Intr. et Ex. 522, fos 61r ff, 168r.

The election of Alexander VI on 11 August 1492 meant swift removal from the spotlight. With the transfer of the *depositeria generale* to the Sienese firm of Spannocchi, and the gradual rise of that firm's associate, Agostino Chigi, and other Sienese bankers, Paolo figures only sporadically in papal accounts during the Borgia pontificate and there is no mention of his bank in the records between March 1494 and February 1497. This all changed again with the election of Cardinal Giuliano della Rovere as Julius II on 1 November 1503 and his appointment of Paolo as *depositario generale*. For Julius, Paolo was a natural choice: he and Antonio Sauli, with della Rovere's encouragement, had helped to finance the Italian expedition of Charles VIII in 1494 and since January 1496 part of Julius' own deposits had been banked with Paolo's branch at Lyons and another part had been held from the time of his cardinalate until his elevation to the papacy by Antonio Sauli and associates.[44]

Proximity to the pope and the supply of credit meant that Paolo could gain access to other lucrative sources of papal income – the *dogane*, the *tesorerie* and the salt tax. He and the Genoese Grimaldi and associates purchased the important salt tax (*salaria urbis, patrimonii, campanie et maritime*) on 22 November 1503 for five years.[45] As was often the case with the renting of tax farms, an anticipatory loan (to be repaid through the farm's income during the period of the the rental) was required. Sauli and the Grimaldi were to lend (or anticipate) the sum of 10,000 ducats and in 1504 the Grimaldi lent a further 1,500 ducats. Loans were also requested at the time of purchase of all the other tax farms which the Sauli later gained, both under Julius and under Leo.[46] On 20 June 1505 Paolo then signed a contract for the rental of the *dohane pecudum urbis et provincie et patrimonij* (grazing and pasture duties) for five years.The *dogana* had previously been held by Agostino Chigi.[47]

Paolo's time as *depositario generale* was surprisingly short. On 25 September 1507 Vincenzo Sauli and his nephew Sebastiano (d. 1536), the brother of Bendinello *quondam* Pasquali, are recorded for the first time as *depositarii generali* and also took over the outstanding rental periods on the salt tax and the *dogana* previously held by Paolo.[48] The call on their finances was

[44] *Memoirs of Philip de Commines, lord of Argenton*, ed. A. R. Scobie, London 1855, ii. 94. For the differing sums involved see Giustiniani, *Castigatissimi annali*, cc 249r–v, and B. Senaregae, *De rebus genuensibus commentaria ab anno MCDLXXXVIII usque ad annum MDXIV*, ed. E. Pandiani, *RIS* xxiv/8, Bologna 1937, 34. See also Cam. Ap., Intr. et Ex. 536, fo. 49v, 20 May 1505; 535, fo. 41v, 24 May 1504. These were the remains of Julius' holdings as a cardinal (1,500 and 1,299 ducats respectively) and were paid into the papal accounts.

[45] Cam. Ap., Div. Cam., 62, fos 55r–70r.

[46] Intr. et Ex. 535, fos 5v, 41r, 51r, 90r.

[47] Div. Cam. 62, fos 118v–123v; Intr. et Ex. 535, fo. 100r; 536, fo. 9v.

[48] Camerale I, mandati camerali 857, fo. 113v; Cam. Ap., Intr. et Ex. 543, fo. 97r; ASG, MS 10, fo. 198v; Hyde, 'Early *cinquecento*', i. 234; ii, appendices 2.1, 2.3, 2.4; Guidi

also suitably rewarded: in either 1508 or 1509 the contract for the *salaria urbis* was renewed and on 12 May 1510 the treasury of Perugia, Umbria and Spoleto, that is, the responsibility for running the finances of these provinces and the exaction of all money due to the *camera apostolica*, was sold to Sebastiano (despite the fact that earlier in the year it had apparently been sold to the Chigi and Sigismondo Chigi had provided a loan to Julius on the strength of it) for five years.[49] On 26 May 1510 Vincenzo and Sebastiano were rewarded with a second tenure of the *dohana pecudum urbis* to run for five years and on 4 September Sebastiano purchased the rights to the incomes of the treasury of Città di Castello.[50] Julius' military campaigns against Ferrara and Bologna in 1510 and 1511 increased the papacy's need for money and, in addition to their normal provision of credit, on 2 March 1511 the Sauli lent Julius 10,000 ducats as part of a larger loan of 20,000 ducats.[51] Their devotion was rewarded: on 10 March 1511 Bendinello Sauli was elevated to the cardinalate at Ravenna; the Sauli had, to all intents and purposes, bought his cardinal's hat.

There were, of course, other bankers present and active in the Curia during the della Rovere pontificate – Florentines such as the del Bene, the Altoviti, the della Casa and others never completely disappeared, while the Sienese Chigi and Ghinucci and the Bolognese Crescenzio families held other, generally less important, *dogane* and, with other bankers, at times supplied loans to the papacy. Yet there can be little doubt of the importance of the Sauli: they held the main *tesoreria* and *dogana*, supplied important loans and were the only banking family in this period to obtain a cardinalate for a relative.[52]

Julius died on 21 February 1513 and Giovanni de' Medici was elected as Leo X on 11 March 1513. A change of pontiff also saw a change in the formation of the bank: the brothers Sebastiano and Giovanni Sauli (d. 1521) and their cousin Agostino, the son of Vincenzo, were the new *depositarii generali*.[53] With the election of a Florentine pope the Sauli's situation was no longer so favourable. Relations between the pope and his bankers were far from easy and the extravagant Leo was soon in financial difficulties: by 1514 the Sauli were being threatened with removal from office if they did not pay

Bruscoli, *Benvenuto Olivieri*, 144, 182; M. Caravale, *La finanza pontificia nel cinquecento: le province del Lazio*, Camerino 1974, 59, 68; Notai Antichi, 2049, 2 May 1536.
[49] Cam. Ap., Div. Cam. 62, fos 213r–215r; Intr. et Ex. 548, fo. 19r; ASR, Camerale I, Tesoreria di Perugia et Umbria, 29, reg. 114, fos 1v, 2r.
[50] Cam. Ap., Div. Cam. 62, fos 234r–237v, 246r–248r. The latter superseded Div. Cam. 58, fos 96v–97r. See Caravale, *La finanza*, 41.
[51] Cam. Ap., Intr. et Ex. 549, fo. 42r; 550, fo. 125r.
[52] Ibid. 535, fos 4r, 11v, 14v, 16v, 46v, 49v, 50v; 536, fo. 17r; 547, fo. 7v; 548, fo. 81r; 549, fos 28r, 55v, 59v, 60r, 119v; 550, fos 46v, 121v.
[53] Ibid. 551, fo. 83r, 1 Apr. 1513; fo. 104r, 30 June 1513; Cam. Ap., Div. Cam. 63, fos 205v–206r.

a list of monthly salaries.[54] Vastly increased anticipatory loans were required before the rental of their *dohane* and *tesoreria* were confirmed, but on 10 October 1513 the *dohane pecudum* was renewed from 1 October 1515 and the treasury of Perugia from 1 January 1516, each for a further five years.[55] On 15 July 1513 Giovanni Sauli was awarded the lucrative treasury of the Romagna, yet Leo was fickle: in December 1514 he removed Giovanni and awarded the treasury to his relative, Jacopo Salviati.[56]

Leo may initially have maintained the Sauli as *depositarii generali* because he was grateful to Cardinal Sauli who, with the other young cardinals, had helped in his promotion, but by the autumn of 1513 the campaign of Filippo Strozzi (a Florentine and a Medici relative to boot) to gain the position had begun in earnest.[57] By May 1514 Leo had decided to award it to Strozzi after he had recompensed Cardinal Sauli.[58] On 24 July 1515, little more than a month after Strozzi had signed the contract to take over the post, Sebastiano, Agostino and Giovanni were ordered by Leo to pay Bendinello 1,000 ducats in a one-off payment as a gift.[59] The same day, less than two years after the previous renewal, the Sauli were granted the *dohane pecudum* and the *tesoreria* of Perugia to run from October 1520 and January 1521 for five years, but this time with no increase in the anticipatory loans.[60] These seem to have been pay-offs. It can surely be no coincidence that they are amongst the last references to the Sauli as *depositarii generali* and that by the end of the year Strozzi was firmly in post. Yet these two favours were small when compared to the power and influence that they had lost: stripped of the post of *depositarii generali* and of the treasury of the Romagna, the Sauli were left simply as holders of the *dohane pecudum* and the *tesoreria* of Perugia. From late 1515, although still active as bankers in Rome, they no longer appear in the papal accounts. The family's prestige and position at the Curia now lay entirely in the hands of Cardinal Sauli.

It is clear that the Sauli were ambitious and that having once started their campaign for prominence within Genoa they then turned their attention to Rome and the Curia, a smaller, more socially mobile environment where money could work wonders. When Sauli himself moved to Rome in 1503 on

---

[54] Cam. Ap., Div. Cam. 63, fos 186v–187v; M. Bullard, *Filippo Strozzi and the Medici*, Cambridge 1980, 109.

[55] Cam. Ap., Div. Cam. 63, fos 147v–148v; Bullard, *Filippo Strozzi*, 75 n. 48; Caravale, *La finanza*, 42, 44; Cam. Ap., Intr. et Ex. 551, fo. 57v; Camerale I, Tesoreria di Perugia e Umbria, 29, reg. 116, fo. 2r.

[56] Cam. Ap., Div. Cam. 63, fo. 90r; Intr. et Ex. 551, fo. 25r; Huturbise, *L'Implantation*, 254.

[57] Bullard, *Filippo Strozzi*, 77; F. Petrucelli della Gattina, *Histoire diplomatique des conclaves*, Paris 1864–6, i. 492; Vat. Lat. 3920, fo. 3r.

[58] Bullard, *Filippo Strozzi*, 85, 86.

[59] For the signing of the contract by Strozzi see ibid 101. See also Cam. Ap., Div. Cam. 65, fo. 61v; Camerale I, Tesoreria di Perugia e Umbria, 29, reg. 116, fo. 7r.

[60] BAV, Armadio XXXVII, 27, fos 808r–809r.

the election of Julius he would have found that the two cities shared some features in common, but essentially he found himself in a different political and social ambience. The threat of domination by foreign powers was not unique to Genoa: the territorial claims of France and Spain, and indeed of certain Italian states such as Venice, affected the peninsula as a whole. But whereas the Genoese at times invited foreign control in order to restore peace to a strife-torn city and were in no real position to resist foreign influence, the pope was one of the major players on the international scene, ready to contest, either via negotiation and compromise or through direct action, any invading force which threatened the freedom and independence of the Church. Sauli had thus joined a powerful elite at the fulcrum of European events.

In Genoa the reign of the doge was often short and dramatic and the city was frequently in turmoil. The dynamics of political power were often called into question. In Rome, the pope was a ruler who could do as he pleased – the cardinals were his advisors but he often chose to ignore them – and he generally enjoyed a longer reign than that of a Genoese doge. Although external threats ensured a constantly changing series of alliances (and wars) between the papacy and France, Spain and the Holy Roman Empire as circumstances dictated, the inner environment, namely that of the Curia, was, in theory, more stable. Yet whilst gaining and keeping the pope's favour meant that a papal favourite had the chance to prosper, losing it meant that prosperity (through curial advancement, the accumulation of benefices or promotion to the cardinalate) and career prospects then waned. Favour could be won by means of such banal realities as the supply of money from relatives when it was required, by sharing common roots, by backing the right candidate for election in the conclave, by supporting the pope's political aims, by sharing the pope's own interests and by, it must be supposed, being the sort of person the pope liked to have around him. Whatever the reason, papal favour was essential and Sauli's career demonstrates how this valuable commodity could be gained, and lost.

The strength of allegiances within Genoa still requires further close study: the impression gained from an examination of Sauli tactics in the late *quattrocento* and early *cinquecento* is that the family *per se* was more important than any other domestic alliances and that the family functioned on a political and social level as a close-knit unit. To a certain extent this was true in Rome: the glory of one member reflected upon another. With the Sauli in command of papal finances, other members of the family prospered and once Bendinello achieved the cardinalate, honours followed, for example for his cousin and brother, Filippo and Stefano Sauli. When the fortunes of some members changed, through no fault of their own, others were compensated, as was the case when the Sauli ceased to be *depositarii generali*. Yet in Rome broader alliances came into play: cliques could form within the college of cardinals based upon age, political inclinations or perhaps shared interests, but essentially a cardinal owed his allegiance to the pope who elevated him, to the foreign powers who may have supported his elevation, and to his *patria*. Sauli's Genoese origins, and the essentially pro-French stance of the Sauli family, were to prove critical in the furtherance (and at times hindrance) of his career, and indeed in the saving of his life. The Sauli entered papal finances through their Genoese connections and later became the *depositarii generali* under a Ligurian pope who rewarded them by promoting Sauli, one of eight Ligurians to be elevated under Julius and the only Genoese to be so honoured. Their demise began under a Florentine pope.

The fortunes of Bendinello Sauli and his family depended upon patronage, and whether extended by the pope, by the king of France or by Cardinal Sauli himself, patronage in all its forms is a central theme of this book. In part this is because these are the better-documented areas of his life; all Sauli's personal papers, with the exception of two letters, have disappeared and any account must depend on notarial documents, account books, contemporary accounts by third parties and later commentators to gain a picture of Sauli the cardinal. There are benefits to this: it helps the reader to gain a better understanding of the dynamics of Sauli's career, while an examination of the patronage that Sauli himself bestowed also allows an examination of the image that he wished to project. Yet a cardinal was not just a patron: he was also a churchman and no study of a cardinal's career is complete without research into this aspect of his role. The way in which Sauli and his cousin fulfilled their ecclesiastical duties (which in turn often meant the bestowal of patronage) will show how the spiritual and temporal concerns of a benefice could be successfully combined. Against the background of the Fifth Lateran Council (1512–17) and moves towards spiritual renewal within the Church, the involvement of the Sauli in reform will also be examined. Finally, having established how much Sauli gained through patronage, exactly how, and why, he lost it all through his implication in the plot to murder Leo will be the subject of the final chapters of this book.

PART I

THE SAULI AS MEN OF THE CHURCH

1

Politics and Money:
The Career of Cardinal Sauli

Remarkably few documents concerning the early life of Bendinello Sauli have survived. The first member of the second branch of the family to be dedicated to a career in the Church, he was probably born in about 1481, the eldest of the five sons of Pasquale Sauli *quondam* Bendinelli and Mariola Giustiniani Longhi *quondam* Giacomi, a member of the largest Genoese *popolare* family (*see* Fig. 2).[1] As the eldest son, he would normally have been expected to carry on the family business and there is evidence that his early years were spent in learning to do just that. On 14 July 1492 a very young Bendinello was in Rome to help deliver cloths to the *camera apostolica* on behalf of Paolo Sauli for the *appalto degli spirituali* and on 1 December 1499, having availed himself of the *venia aetatis* and thus declaring himself to be legally competent and an adult over the age of fourteen, he acted on behalf of himself and his brothers to arrange the rental of a property below their house near the Porta Sant'Andrea in Genoa.[2]

Bendinello's expertise in trade and finance was apparently valued by the Genoese Republic: in 1498 he was a member of the *ufficio della moneta*, an *anziano* in 1499 and in 1500 a member of the *ufficio mercanzie* (the body which controlled mercantile activities and arbitrated in business disputes) and of the *ufficio clavigeri* (holders of the keys to the chest containing Genoa's most holy relic, the *sacro catino*, but also responsible for the comune's treasure chests).[3] This involvement in trade seemingly continued throughout his life: in a letter of 1515 the humanist Raffaele Brandolini linked the cardinal and Sauli banking activities and noted Bendinello's success in the Curia in the

---

[1] 'Cardinal de Sauli, zenoese, … anni 32': C. Marcello to A. Marcello, 7 Mar. 1513, in M. Sanuto, *I diarii di Marino Sanuto (1496–1533)*, ed. M. Allegri, N. Barozzi, G. Berchet, R. Fulin and F. Stefani, Bologna 1879–1902, xvi. 32. On 19 May 1517 the contemporary diarist Sebastiano di Branca Tedallini described Sauli as 'de anni 30': *Il diario romano 3 Maggio 1485 al 6 Giugno 1524*, ed. P. Piccolomini, RIS xxxiii/3, Città di Castello 1907, 370. See the will of Pasquale Sauli, Notai Antichi, 950, no. 96, 21 June 1493, in which frequent reference is made to 'Bendinello filio suo primogenito', and Notai Antichi, 1284, no. 532, 27 Aug. 1515, where Bendinello's mother is named as 'Mariola filia quondam domini Jacobi Justiniani uxor quondam domini pasqualis Sauli'.
[2] Cam. Ap., Intr. et Ex. 522, fo. 92v; Notai Antichi, 1004.
[3] ASG, MS 10, fos 86, 165, 198; Biblioteca Civica Berio, Genoa, sezione conservazione, raccolta locale, MS m.r. IX, 2, 25, fo. 446v; MS m.r.i.c. 2.25, ii, fo. 446. I am grateful to Dr Enrico Basso for his help with the *venia aetatis* and the *clavigeri*.

early years, writing that 'you offered people your name and faith regardless of inconvenience, and thus became universally popular' and praising his good 'reputation as a businessman'.[4] On 17 March 1517 Marino Giorgi, the Venetian ambassador, described him as 'Sauli from Genoa, who practises trade like his relatives, and is a good merchant'.[5] It thus seems likely that Bendinello lent money when necessary, or perhaps arranged loans via other members of his family. This should come as no suprise: creating a good impression in the Curia could prove expensive if one wanted the right dress, entertainment or place to live and other cardinals also benefitted from outside financial investments, whether in property or other areas of commerce.[6]

Yet Bendinello also attended university in some form or another – in the earliest surviving Vatican documents in which he is mentioned he is given the title of 'magister' – and this would seem to indicate that at some point it was decided that the Church or at least the Curia, rather than trade, was to be his career.[7] This may have occurred as a result of the election of Julius and the appointment of Paolo Sauli as *depositario generale* when it would have been clear to the Sauli that the chances for promotion for a family member within the Church were now high, but it is equally conceivable that this change of direction evolved naturally and was related to deteriorating physical health. There is evidence that in later life Sauli was lame: the 1516 'will' of Hanno, the elephant sent to Leo X by the king of Portugal in 1514, leaves various parts of the elephant's anatomy to different cardinals and Sauli is bequeathed 'the bone marrow of my legs … to extend his shorter leg'. In the *pasquinata* 'In Leonem et cardinales' of early 1517, in which the cardinals are given attributes which are the opposite of reality, Sauli is described as being able to walk quickly.[8] There is a chronic condition known as Perthes which is a malformation of the femoral head, often leading to stiffness and reduced movement in the hip and affected leg which then manifests a limp or can be wasted in appearance. It develops in childhood or adolescence and increases in severity the later it strikes.[9] Either scenario may explain why an eldest son entered the Church.

Others were also keen that Bendinello should dedicate himself to the

---

[4] 'nemini tuum nomen, tuam fidem vel magno cum incommodo non benignissime praestitisti unde perfectum est: ut unicuique charus gratusque tuo merito putareris' and 'inter mercatores fidem': BCIS, MS K VI 73, fos 24v, 23r respectively.

[5] *Relazioni degli ambasciatori veneti al senato*, ed. E. Alberi, ser. ii, volume iii, Florence 1846, iii. 58.

[6] For Cardinal Francesco Soderini see Lowe, *Church and politics*, 192–225, and for Cardinal Francesco Armellini, 'Questions of income', 185.

[7] ASV, Registra Lateranensi 1129A, fo. 238r, 19 Dec. 1503.

[8] V. Rossi, 'Testamento dell'elefante', in *Scritti di critica letteraria: dal Rinascimento al Risorgimento*, Florence 1930, iii. 223–4, 236, 238; G. A. Cesareo, 'Pasquino e pasquinate nella Roma di Leone X', *Miscellanea della R. Deputazione romana di storia patria* xi (1938), 94.

[9] I am grateful to Roy Hyde and D. Green for their suggestions on this point.

Church, recognising, as Kate Lowe notes, that Rome was 'one of the major centres of the European political system' and important influence could thereby be gained.[10] From the beginning of the pontificate of Julius II the Genoese government assiduously, and with increasing urgency, promoted Bendinello's elevation to the cardinalate. On 20 November 1506 the Genoese *anziani* and the *ufficio di balia* instructed the republic's orators to 'especially recommend the Reverend messer bandinelo [sic] sauli for the honour of his family which is devoted to His Holiness and for the good social standing and virtue of the aforesaid messer bandinello. And you will use your greatest skill in this as you see fit and will do everything possible to help messer band-inello'.[11] His talents, position and potential influence both as a cleric and as a relative of the *depositario generale* were clearly recognised by the Genoese government, but almost five years were to pass before their hopes were realised. Bendinello Sauli's cardinalate then lasted seven short years.

The wait for the cardinalate

On the election of Julius II, Bendinello travelled to Rome and soon began to receive signs of the pope's favour.[12] On 19 December of that year he was given his first known benefice when he was appointed commendatory abbot of the prestigious abbey of San Siro in Genoa.[13] On 29 October 1504 he received the Genoese church of San Giacomo di Carignano *in commenda*.[14] In 1505 he was given a number of smaller benefices in the dioceses of Genoa and of Seville and Palencia in Spain, the latter, according to Peter Partner, indicating a position of some influence.[15] The end of that year saw the clearest sign thus far of Julius' preferment: on 1 December 1505, in a long and stormy

---

[10] Lowe, *Church and politics*, 1.

[11] 'ricomandereti specialmento el Reverendo messer bandinelo sauli sia per le bone condicione e virtu del detto messer bandinello. E in questo con quella maior destrezza che a voi parira/ fareti aldetto messer bandinello ogni favore possibile': Genoese *anziani* and *balia* to the Genoese orators to Julius II, 20 Nov. 1506, ASG, Archivio Segreto 2707/C, no. 51. The first recorded instance is that of Philippe de Cleves and the *anziani* to the Genoese orators, 5 Feb. 1504, ibid. no. 16.

[12] 'Ad urbem primo Julij secondi invictissimi pontificis anno profectus es': BCIS, MS K VI 73, fo. 24r.

[13] Reg. Lat. 1129A fos 238r–240r; L. Staffetti, 'Il "Libro di ricordi" della famiglia Cybo pubblicato con introduzione, appendice di documenti inediti, note illustrative e indice analatico da Luigi Staffetti', *ASLSP* o.s. xxxviii (1908), pp. vii–615 at pp. 390, 496. Not all volumes of the *registri lateranensi* have survived for the early *cinquecento* and twelve benefices given to Bendinello are in lost volumes. Of these seven are in the first three years of Julius' reign. Some of these can be reconstructed by consulting the Vatican *resignationes* series, but the exact dates of the conferral of the benefices still remain unclear.

[14] Notai Antichi, 1158, nos 164, 217; ASG, MS 839, fo. 71.

[15] Reg. Lat. 1158, fos 93r–v; 1161, fos 195r–199r; 1186A, fos 325r–327v; P. Partner, *The pope's men: the papal civil service in the Renaissance*, Oxford 1990, 13.

secret consistory, the pope tried, and failed, to make him one of ten new cardinals, all of whom have been described as having close dealings with Julius. Whilst the appointment of candidates such as Antonio Ferreri, Julius' *maestro di casa*, was accepted, that of Sauli was rejected by the existing cardinals.[16] The reason for this remains unclear, but Raffaele Brandolini noted in 1515 that Bendinello had eventually achieved the cardinalate despite 'no little jealousy and disparagement'.[17] This episode constitutes an interesting, if somewhat rare, example of the college of cardinals managing to thwart, at least in part, the pope's wishes. Julius was forced to compromise on the number of new cardinals. The sacrifice of Bendinello indicates that he was of less importance to the pope than candidates such as Leonardo Grosso della Rovere (a papal relative), Sigismondo Gonzaga (from the ruling family of Mantua) and personal favourites such as Francesco Alidosi.

However, the fact that Julius had attempted to elevate Bendinello to the purple after a mere two years in the Curia demonstrates that the Sauli and Bendinello himself did possess a certain amount of clout. Of course he came from the pope's *patria*, Liguria, with which the pope strongly identified and furthermore was a member of a family which Julius knew intimately: he owned a palace in Genoa; Julius' money was held with two Sauli banks while he was a cardinal; and he had encouraged the Sauli and other Genoese to finance the Italian expedition of Charles VIII of France.[18] The Sauli were also pro-French (perhaps, like many Genoese merchants, as a result of their business interests in France) and in that period Julius enjoyed good relations with Louis XII (1498–1512).[19] Indeed the creation of 1505 was viewed by Julius himself as promoting cardinals favourable to France. He had already elevated one French cardinal (François Guillaume de Clermont, d. 1541) at the beginning of his reign, another (Robert de Challand) in the December elevation and would soon include more.[20] But perhaps most important, Paolo Sauli was the papal *depositario generale* and confirmation of the importance of Paolo's influence, certainly at the beginning of Bendinello's ecclesiastical career, comes from the advance of large sums of money by Paolo at the same time as the conferral of a benefice on Bendinello. His appointment to the *commenda* of San Siro had been preceded on 4 December by the loan of 8,000 ducats on the *salaria urbis* held by Paolo and the Grimaldi and on 31 October 1504, two days after Bendinello received San Giacomo di

16 J. Burckhard, *Liber notarum ab anno* MCCCCLXXXIII *usque ad annum* MDVI, ed. E. Celani, *RIS* xxxii/1, Città di Castello 1906, 498; C. Shaw, *Julius II: the warrior pope*, Oxford 1993, 173.

17 'nec minima invidorum obtrectatione': BCIS, MS K VI 73, fo. 12r.

18 Shaw, *Julius II*, 194, 206–7

19 Senaregae, *De rebus*, 149–50 n. 6; D. Goiffrè, *Gênes et les foires de change: de Lyon à Besançon*, Paris 1960, 33, 127, 133, 187–91.

20 Lowe, *Church and politics*, 176; C. Eubel and G. Van Gulik (eds), *Hierarchia Catholica medii et recentioris aevi sive summorum pontificum, S.R.E. cardinalium, ecclesiarum antistitum series*, 2nd edn, Munster 1913–2001, iii. 10.

Carignano, Paolo and the Grimaldi lent the pope 2,000 ducats in cloth on the same *salaria*.[21] In December 1505 Paolo Sauli was owed 15,656 florins by the *camera* and the cardinalate could certainly have been viewed as more than adequate compensation for this. In fact Paolo was repaid on the very day that Bendinello failed to become cardinal.[22] Certainly some consolation for Julius' failure to elevate Bendinello was needed, and was given: on 25 December 1505 he received a parcel of benefices in the diocese of Toledo which brought a very healthy income of 700 florins, and in January 1506 he was granted a further benefice in Spain.[23]

The year 1506 saw the consolidation of Bendinello's position with the award of an expectancy (a benefice, already occupied, which would come to the awardee on the holder's death); the acquisition of benefices in the dioceses of Seville, Cordoba and Mondovi; and his appointment to the see of Malta on 5 October, when Julius attempted to impose Bendinello as his own nominee over that of the king of Spain.[24] During this time the *popolare* revolt, in which the Sauli were important players, was underway in Genoa. This rebellion was initially against the *nobili* and eventually against the French (although at that point not necessarily with the full consent of the Sauli); the promotion of Bendinello may be viewed as a sign of Julius' support for the rebels (Giustiniani, indeed, stated that some believed that Julius himself had instigated the revolt).[25]

At the end of that year Bendinello was given a number of parish churches in the diocese of Seville with an income totalling 230 ducats.[26] The next two years witnessed the resolution of a quarrel over a benefice in Toledo and Bendinello either resigned benefices to benefit his *famigliari* and others, or helped the same people to gain new benefices.[27] A further, more concrete, promotion was certainly in the wind: a Genoese notarial document of 5 August 1508 describes Bendinello as bishop of Gerace, although he was only actually promoted to this bishopric (which was joined with that of Oppido) on 23 February 1509. The total income of the joint benefice was a mere 400 ducats per year but Bendinello made the most of this.[28] In this

---

[21] Cam Ap., Intr et Ex. 535, fos 5v, 90r.

[22] Ibid. 538, fo. 166r.

[23] Reg. Lat. 1172, fos 289v–291r; 1195, fos 137v–139r.

[24] ASV, Registra Vaticana 889, fos 355r–357r; 917, fos 103v–105r; 'Le due spedizioni militari di Giulio II tratte dal diario di Paride Grassi bolognese', ed. L. Frati, *R. deputazione di storia patria per le provincie di Romagna* i (1886), pp. xxxiii–363 at p. 58; R. Pirri, *Sicilia sacra*, Palermo 1733, ii. 911; Shaw, *Julius II*, 221–2; Arm. XXXIX, 24, fos 475v–476v, 506v–507r; 25, fo. 352r.

[25] Giustiniani, *Castigatissimi annali*, c. 258v; Taviani, '*Franza populo*', 75–6, 85, 88.

[26] Reg. Vat. 913, fos 50r–52v.

[27] Ibid. 971, fos 303v–306r; ASV, Camera Apostolica, Resignationes, 11, fos 121v, 163r, 166v; Reg. Lat. 1200, fos 139r–140v.

[28] Eubel, *Hierarchia*, iii. 243. For this premature promotion, however, see Notai Antichi, 1160, no. 198. Later documents in the same *filza* revert to his correct title as bishop *electus* of Malta: Reg. Vat. 943, fos 63r–68r.

and the following year, however, he received only one further benefice (the documents for which are lost) and resigned others.[29] Once again political loyalties may have influenced papal favour: Franco-papal relations soured in late 1509 with the collapse of the League of Cambrai and the French victory over Venice at Agnadello. France was now the main threat to papal independence. It can surely be little coincidence that fewer benefices were forthcoming for the pro-French Sauli and that he was in fact absent from the Curia during this period, visiting Genoa and possibly Gerace. Relations between Julius and Cardinal Francesco Soderini (1500–24), another known supporter of France, also declined rapidly during this time.[30]

The cardinalate

Although Sauli did not come from one of the great, politically influential, Italian families and seemingly lacked powerful friends to support his rise within the Church, he did have the support of the Genoese government and his family had wealth. As was the case for many who gained the purple, home support and money talked. The fiscal generosity of the *depositarii generali*, and the pleas of the Genoese government, finally reaped their rewards when Bendinello was appointed to the cardinalate at Ravenna on 10 March 1511, again despite the protests of the existing cardinals. One week later he was granted the title of cardinal-deacon of Sant'Adriano.[31] On his elevation he duly resigned the venal offices in the Curia that he had purchased during his years in Rome, namely the posts of *magister registri cancellarie, secretarius, scriptor litterarum apostolicarum* and *abbreviator de parco minori*.[32]

Given their struggle for social prominence within Genoa, the satisfaction of the Sauli at Bendinello's promotion must have been immense; Paolo Giovio, a member of Sauli's household, later recalled Bendinello's own pleasure with more than a touch of irony.[33] Sauli humbly thanked the Genoese govern-ment for 'your letters, your recommendations to His Holiness' which had also helped in his promotion.[34] Undoubtedly political considerations had also come into play. It is probable that Julius saw the Sauli, holders of the papal *depositeria* and now relatives of a cardinal, as useful advocates for his interests in Genoa whilst the city was under French control. Sauli's cardi-nalate followed shortly after the papal attempts of 1510 to persuade the

[29] Cam. Ap., Resignationes 10, fo. 239v; 12, fo. 287r; ASV, Inventory 347, fo. 160v.

[30] Lowe, *Church and politics*, 63–4.

[31] ASV, Archivio Concistoriale, Acta Miscellanea, 3, fo. 30.

[32] T. Frenz, *Die Kanzlei der Päpste der Hochrenaissance (1471–1526)*, Tübingen 1986, 301; cf. Reg. Lat. 1190, fos 135r–136r.

[33] P. Giovio to Cardinal Rodolfo Pio da Carpi, 26 Dec. 1551, in *Paolo Giovio: lettere*, ed. G. G. Ferrero, Rome 1956, ii, no. 389, at pp. 214–15.

[34] 'vestras litteras, commendationem vestram de nobis apud eius Sanctitatem': Bend-inello Sauli to Genoese government, 17 Mar. 1511, Archivio Segreto, 2816.

Genoese to rebel against the French. It was not the only political appointment: Christopher Bainbridge was elevated at the same time to encourage Henry VIII against the French; Matthaeus Schinner was promoted as a clear thank-you for Swiss support against France; Denis Hay has also described the elevation of Alfonso Petrucci from the ruling family of Siena as politically motivated.[35] The perceived power of the cardinalate and potential influence of individual cardinals were such that their own governments desired proximity to the pope and the pope himself hoped for gratitude and obedience from the governments concerned.

Although the news of Sauli's elevation was greeted with joy in Genoa, Giustiniani noted that 'the governor did not allow the usual celebrations for his elevation, a decision resented by the populace'.[36] The stance taken by the French governor seems inexplicable: Genoa was under French rule and the Sauli were, with the exception of the later moments of the *popolare* revolt of 1506–7 when the momentum of the revolt was beyond the control of *popolari* merchants, pro-French.[37] Indeed, in 1507 Julius had written to Louis XII to plead for mercy towards the family after the *popolare* revolt and had described them as 'most loyal and dedicated to your crown'.[38] In January 1510 he had described the family as 'good men, but still subjects of the king of France'.[39] Cardinal Nicolò Fieschi (1503–24), the senior Genoese cardinal, was similarly pro-French and was to be a French candidate for the papacy in the conclave of 1513.[40] Sauli's illness in October 1511, after dining with the pope and other cardinals, had even raised the suspicion of poison.[41] Yet the absence of authorised celebrations indicates the lack of French support for his candidature to the cardinalate. Did the French, perversely, think that Sauli was too close to Julius at this time? Whatever the reason, this was a temporary hiccup and Sauli's relations with the French throne prospered again: his appointment to important benefices in Milan in later years met with French approval and Francis I did his best to forestall Leo's fury when the plot to murder the pope, and Sauli's involvement in it, was uncovered in 1517.

At the time of Sauli's elevation there were thirty-three cardinals. Raffaele Riario (1477–1521) was the only survivor from the pontificate of Sixtus IV and Giovanni de' Medici (later Leo X) and Federico San Severino (1489–

---

[35] Shaw, *Julius II*, 252–4; Chambers, *Cardinal Bainbridge*, 36; D. Hay, 'The Renaissance cardinals: Church, state, culture', *Synthesis* iii (1976), 35–46 at p. 38.
[36] Giustiniani, *Castigatissimi annali*, c. 267r.
[37] Taviani, 'Franza, populo', 85, 88.
[38] Arm. XXXIX, 25, fo. 243r.
[39] Shaw, *Julius II*, 252; Chambers, *Cardinal Bainbridge*, 125.
[40] A. Cevolotto, 'Fieschi, Nicolò', *DBI* xlvii (1977), 503–6 at p. 504; Goiffrè, *Gênes*, 12.
[41] B. Bibbiena to Cardinal Giovanni de' Medici, 5 Oct. 1511, in *Epistolario di Bernardo Dovizi da Bibbiena*, ed. G. L. Moncallero, Florence 1955–65, i, no. 88 at p. 265; *protonotario* Lippomano to H. Lippomano, 6 Oct. 1511, *Diarii di Sanuto*, xiii. 87.

1516) from that of Innocent VIII. Most had been creations of Alexander VI but time had whittled down the number of Spaniards appointed by the Borgia pope and in March 1511 the college was dominated by the eighteen Italians with only seven French, seven Spanish and one Hungarian. Julius had himself boosted the number of Italians by promoting seven Ligurians (although two had later died), not including Sauli, and had added five French cardinals (reflecting his pro-French policy at the time of their creations) and two Spaniards, although one from each camp died before 1511.[42] The total number of cardinals rose to forty-one with the promotion of March 1511, five of whom were Italian, one English and one Swiss. Most of the Italians at that time were resident in Rome, but, with the exception of those few cardinals who took part in the French-sponsored Council of Pisa convoked in that year (they were absent from Rome, and deprived of their rank, until 1513), the situation with regard to the French and Spanish cardinals is far from clear. Other cardinals were at times absent from the Curia either on official papal business, because they chose to reside in their country of birth or because political circumstances often led foreign cardinals, or those Italians whose political alliances were not viewed favourably by the pope, to leave the Curia. Residence in Rome guaranteed proximity to the pope and the chance to gain or maintain papal favour, and Sauli,with brief exceptions, stayed in Rome in the following years.

Sauli thus joined a predominantly Italian princely elite, one which included representatives of important Italian families, such as the Medici, Gonzaga, d'Aragona, Fieschi and d'Este, but also newcomers with no political or social pedigree like himself and Adriano Castellesi (1503–18). He would have had common links with the Ligurians but would have lacked the intimacy of the papal *nipoti* or those who had served Julius during his cardinalate. Kate Lowe believes that the loyalty of a cardinal lay in three possible directions: to the pope who appointed him, to his political supporters, whether his own family (if one of the ruling Italian dynasties) or the foreign power which had supported his promotion, or to the religious order to which he belonged.[43] Despite the lack of French enthusiasm for his promotion Sauli undoubtedly enjoyed an intermittently cordial relationship with France, but his main loyalties must have been to his family, to his *patria* and above all to Julius.

This perhaps explains why, his pro-French inclinations notwithstanding, Sauli continued to received favours from Julius after his elevation. In May 1511 he received the *commenda* of a monastery in Otranto, in June the award of a pension of 1,000 ducats on two monasteries and finally, in October, the *commenda* of the monastery of San Simpliciano in Milan.[44] He was also awarded the important titular church of Santa Maria in Trastevere *in*

---

[42] Eubel, *Hierarchia*, iii. 10–11.
[43] Lowe, *Church and politics*, 49.
[44] Reg. Lat. 1253, fos 79r–81v; Reg. Vat. 960, fos 74v–77v; Reg. Lat. 1258, fos 361v–362v.

commenda on 29 October, which he then held until it was formally awarded to him in 1516 on the death of Cardinal Marco Vigerio (1503–16).[45] In addition to these, the last benefices that Bendinello received from Julius, on 12 January 1512 he was formally promoted to cardinal-priest, and granted the church of Santa Sabina, previously held by the schismatic French cardinal René de Prie.[46]

Julius died on 21 February 1513. Bendinello Sauli had risen to prominence during his pontificate as a result of papal generosity and the influence of his family's wealth, his shared *patria* and a good dose of politics. From the very beginning of the della Rovere pontificate he had been a member of the pope's household: the conferral of the abbey of San Siro of 19 December 1503 is addressed to him as 'Genoese cleric, our familiar and notary', clarified in documents of 10 June and 12 November 1504 as '*protonotario* of the apostolic see' and thus presumably one of the *prothonotharii sopranumerari* or *titolari*, an unpaid post with the same privileges as the *prothonotarius partecipans* which he later purchased on 13 June 1509.[47] On 20 July 1505 he is described as 'our chamberlain' ('cubicularius noster'), an important and intimate papal servant.[48] In a document of 20 November 1506 he is a 'domestic prelate' ('prelatus domesticus'), one of a number of *cubicularii* who, although not sleeping in the pope's bedroom, recited the hours with him, helped him to retire, dealt with various secretarial matters and other household details and helped officiate at mass and other holy offices.[49] At an early stage in his career, he thus had close contact with the pope.

But what of his personal relations with Julius? Raffaele Brandolini was perhaps overstating the case when he wrote to Sauli in 1515 that 'you restrained the great and brilliant – yet certainly difficult and slippery – character of Julius II by your moderation or your prudence or your clemency, or by all these at once'.[50] Yet there is some evidence that he was a papal intimate. Sauli accompanied Julius and much of the Curia on the expedition against Bologna in 1506 and was with him when he entered the city on 11 November.[51] On 22 March 1511 he and five other cardinals accompanied Julius to Cervia.[52] Proximity to Julius is also indicated by a letter from

---

[45] Eubel, *Hierarchia*, iii. 66; Reg. Vat. 1066, fos 197r–199v.

[46] Reg. Vat. 969, fos 422v–423r.

[47] Reg. Lat. 1129A, fo. 238r; Cam. Ap., Intr. et Ex. 546, fo. 55r; Notai Antichi 1158, nos 164, 217.

[48] Reg. Lat 1161, fo. 195v; G. Moroni, *Dizionario di erudizione storico-ecclesiastica da S. Pietro sino ai nostri giorni compilato dal cavaliere Gaetano Moroni romano primo aiutante di camera di Sua Santità Gregorio XVI*, Venice 1840–61, xix. 6, 9.

[49] Reg. Lat. 1200, fos 138v, 248v; Moroni, *Dizionario*, xix. 12.

[50] 'Julij II Pontificis maximi animum maximum quidem, ac splendidissum: sed certe difficilem, ac lubricum, tua vel modestia, vel prudentia, vel mansuetudine, vel his simul omnibus retinuisti': BCIS, MS K VI 73, fo. 12r.

[51] 'Le due spedizioni', 93.

[52] Ibid. 255.

Bernardo Dovizi da Bibbiena to Giovanni de'Medici of 13 March 1512 in which Medici's letter was read to the pope 'in the presence of Cardinals Sinigaglia (Vigerio) and Sauli'.[53] We know that he was resident in the Vatican Palace, and probably continued to be so for a short period after his elevation to the cardinalate, briefly becoming one of what are known as the 'palatine cardinals', confirming his closeness to Julius. But there can be little doubt that the level of intimacy was not as great as that between the pope and the papal *nipoti* or cardinals Vigerio or Alidosi when alive. His career is thus indicative of, if not of great personal intimacy with Julius, then at least of Julius' esteem for him and dependence upon his family's financial capabilities and potential influence within Genoa.

Cardinal Sauli and Leo x

Yet if Julius was generous towards Bendinello during his pontificate – the abbeys of San Simpliciano and San Siro in Genoa alone supposedly yielded an annual income of 2,500 ducats – even greater riches came his way under Leo x.[54] Giovanni de' Medici was elected pope on 11 March 1513 as a result of the votes of the younger cardinals, Sauli seemingly chief among them.[55] Allegiances within the college were multi-layered, formed on the basis of age, the pontiff under which the cardinal in question was elected, the shared *patria* of the different cardinals and personal interests.[56] Why Sauli threw in his lot with de' Medici and with the younger cardinals (not all of whom had been elevated by Julius), rather than support French candidates such as the Genoese, albeit *nobile*, Fieschi or the ambitious fellow Ligurian Raffaele Riario who was the candidate of the Holy Roman Emperor, remains a mystery and was to prove in the long term to be a costly mistake. However, in the short term, Sauli flourished: Leo duly maintained the Sauli as *depositarii generali* for a further two years and from 19 March 1513 there follows a long list of benefices (ten alone in the first year of Leo's pontificate which included the bishopric of Albenga) and a proliferation of favours towards

---

[53] Bibbiena to Cardinal de' Medici, 13 Mar. 1512, *Epistolario*, i, no. 151 at p. 463.

[54] For their joint income see Ferrajoli, *La congiura*, 52 n. 4. This could not be verified: Ferrajoli's reference could not be traced.

[55] 'Ut nostri huius Pontificis creationi, non opibus et copijs, non honorum, ac dignitatum pactione: sed virtute, sed integritate, sed innocentia, sed acerimmo servandae, ac tuendae Christianae reipublicae desiderio affueris. Atque ita affueris ut iuniorum maxime suffragiis ac studiis, quorum authoritate, et gratia es nemini secundus, res celerrime conficeretur': BCIS, MS K VI 73, fo. 25r; P. Giovio, *Le vite di Leone Decimo, et d'Adriano Sesto sommi pontefici, et del Cardinal Pompeo Colonna, scritte per Mons. Paolo Giovio vescovo di Nocera, e tradotte per M. Lodovico Domenichi*, Florence 1549, 192.

[56] Lowe, *Church and politics*, 49.

members of his family and his *famigliari*.[57] An examination of the *registri vaticani* and the *registri lateranensi* for the first year of Leo's pontificate highlights the fact that of all the young cardinals who contributed towards Leo's election – d'Aragona, Petrucci, Gonzaga, Farnese – only Luigi d'Aragona (1494–1519) received more generous treatment in 1513.

In 1514 Bendinello received *in commenda* a parish church in the diocese of Vicenza, a parish church in Corsica, the monastery of San Dionigi outside Milan and a pension on the fruits of the priory of San Marco in the diocese of Asti.[58] In 1515 a dispute over a previous benefice was settled and he received separately a canonry, prebend and archdiaconate in the diocese of Leon in Spain and two monasteries in Otranto.[59] The following year he was in Genoa for almost two months and the year as a whole was far less lucrative. Furthermore, his family had now ceased to hold the papal purse strings: apart from the resignation of some benefices to settle disputes he was merely confirmed, in July, to Santa Maria in Trastevere, which he had held *in commenda* since 1511. In April 1517 he earned a pension of 4,000 ducats through the resignation by himself and his brother, Stefano, of San Simpliciano to the Benedictine-Cassinese congregation, and also seems to have benefitted from the redistribution of benefices after the death of Cardinal Sisto Gara della Rovere (1507–17).[60] His disgrace in that year, through his involvement in the plot to murder Leo, saw the rapid redistribution of almost all his remaining benefices.

There can be little doubt of the importance this pope attached to Cardinal Sauli. Giovio described him as 'greatly intimate with Leo' and evidence survives of what was a reasonably close relationship until Sauli's disgrace.[61] The pope and cardinal seemingly shared a love for the same social pursuits. Both were ardent hunters: on 20 May and 11 October 1513, Leo went to his hunting lodge at Magliana with a small number of cardinals including Sauli

---

[57] For Sauli's appointment to Albenga on 5 Aug. 1513 see Reg. Lat. 1281, fos 216r–218r. The other benefices included the division between thirteen cardinals of 2,000 ducats: Reg. Vat. 994, fos 232v–234v; the retention of an annual pension of 500 ducats on the fruits of the *mensa* of Malta: 1003, fos 241r–243r; a canonry and prebend in San Lorenzo, Lodi: 1000, fos 155r–158v; an annual pension on the fruits of some benefices in Toledo: 999, fos 277r–279v; the retention of small benefices at Mondovi: 1038, fos 18r–21r; a canonry and prebend in Corsica: Reg. Lat. 1283, fos 141r–143r; benefices in the dioceses of Oppido and Messina: 1301, fos 133v–137v; a pension on Santa Maria di Chiaravalle in the diocese of Milan: 1283, fos 155v–158r; the *commenda* of the abbey of San Benedetto in the diocese of Salerno: 1301, fos 256v–258v; and the chaplaincy of an altar in the diocese of Utrecht: 1276, fos 8v–11v.
[58] Reg. Vat. 1029, fos 16r–18r; 1004, fos 75r–77r; 1016, fos 12v–15v; ACR, Archivio Urbano, sezione 66, protocollo 13, fo. 106r.
[59] Reg. Vat. 1047, fos 296r–298v; Cam. Ap., Resignationes 16, fos 146r–v; Reg. Vat. 1070, fos 251r–253r; Archivio Urbano, sezione 66, protocollo 14, fo. 166v.
[60] Reg. Vat. 1080, fos 157r–161r; Archivio Concistoriale, Acta Vice Cancellarii, 2, fo. 26r.
[61] Giovio, *Le vite*, 270.

and in mid-September 1516 he was one of those cardinals who accompanied Leo to Viterbo for hunting.[62] He and the pope also enjoyed festivities: on 16 June 1514 Sauli was one of a select group of cardinals who went to Florence to celebrate, incognito, the return of the Medici and on 22 August he was one of seven cardinals at the marriage of Leo's niece to the lord of Piombino.[63]

Leo also knew how to take make the most of Sauli's political leanings and apparently numbered him amongst his political advisors. In 1513 he was one of the cardinals present at the Lateran Council appointed to discuss the problem of the Pragmatic Sanction, and when Leo X and Francis I of France met at Bologna in December 1515 it was Sauli who, with Cardinal Giulio de' Medici (1513–23), 'were the only two cardinals whom the pope sent to his majesty' before the entry into the city on 11 December. Cardinals de' Medici, Bibbiena, Sauli and Cibo dined with the king before he met the pope – the group was thus composed of two Florentine and two Genoese papal intimates; the absence of the Genoese Nicolò Fieschi is striking. This group kept the king company throughout the visit.[64] In September 1516, in the uneasy period preceding the ratification of the Treaty of Noyon between Francis I and Charles V of Spain, Sauli was consulted twice by the Venetian orator on the actions of the Spanish orator, French intentions towards Verona and his opinion of the pope's attitude.[65]

Undoubtedly Sauli was not on an equal footing with Florentine cardinals such as Bibbiena who was, as the Genoese government had noted in 1514, 'continually close to His Holiness' during the early years of Leo's pontificate or with Giulio de' Medici with whom relations soured in the last year of Sauli's life, but signs of preferment continued and made Sauli's ultimate betrayal of the pope's trust difficult to accept.[66]

---

[62] BAV, MSS Barberini Latini 2683, fo. 169r. Sauli is not specifically mentioned but he had returned to Rome with Cardinal Carvajal shortly before a letter from L. Suares to Cardinal Petrucci of 22 Oct. 1516: BAV, Codici Registri Latini 387, fo. 184r.

[63] Vetor Lippomano to Venetian government, 20 May 1513; 12, 15 Oct. 1513; 14 June 1514, Diarii di Sanuto xvi. 295; xvii. 217; xviii. 278.

[64] Copy of papal letters, 3 June 1513, ibid xvi. 360. For the Pragmatic Sanction and the problems involved in the papal conferral of benefices in France and French territory see Moroni, Dizionario, lv. 31; Antonio Grimani and orators to Venetian government, 11 Dec. 1517, Diarii di Sanuto, xxi. 372; Giovio to M. Sanuto, 15 Dec. 1515, Paolo Giovio: lettere, i, no. 2 at pp. 84–5; L. von Pastor, The history of the popes, 3rd edn, London 1949–60, vii. 136; Barb. Lat. 2683, fo. 142r.

[65] Venetian orator in Rome to Venetian government, 5 Sept. 1516, Diarii di Sanuto, xxii. 542; Pastor, History of the popes, vii. 159, 160.

[66] O. Fregoso to Genoese ambassadors, 2 May 1514, Archivio Segreto 2707/C, no. 105.

The role of the cardinal

Whatever the degree of intimacy with the reigning pope, a cardinal had certain duties to fulfil. Barbara McClung Hallman has described cardinals as the 'veritable "hinges" of the church', there to advise the pope where appropriate in consistories, to take part in the government of the Church but also to represent their families and place of birth, promoting both whenever possible, in addition to carrying out their ecclesiastical duties.[67] Mention of Sauli in the consistorial records are unexceptional and he held no important office such as that of legate or governor, except for the governorship of Colle Scipione in the Papal States which he gained when lots were drawn in the conclave of 1513:[68] this town has proved impossible to identify with any certainty, perhaps indicating its lack of importance.

Sauli's role as a protector of Genoese interests was already evident as early as 1506 when the city's ambassadors were to give him a (lost) letter from the *anziani* and, on the departure of the ambassadors, Genoese concerns were to be placed in the hands of Vincenzo Sauli, or, in his absence, those of a certain Franco or '*messer* Bendinello'.[69] This role continued and expanded after his elevation to the cardinalate, as can be seen by the letters addressed to him and Cardinal Fieschi by the various offices of the Genoese republic and by their own letters to the Genoese. Sauli was young – he had become cardinal at approximately thirty years of age – and lacked the experience and status of Fieschi (who was also cardinal-protector of the Dominican order). Clearly Sauli was the 'junior' cardinal. Despite Sauli's almost continuous presence in Rome, it is Fieschi who is more frequently mentioned in the letters of the Genoese ambassadors on their visit to Rome of 1514 and Fieschi who was badgered by the Genoese orator at Bologna in December 1515 about Genoese problems with Savona, although ironically it is Sauli who is repeatedly the first to inform the orator of French replies to Savonese requests – an indication, perhaps, of his intimacy with the French camp. Yet Sauli, Fieschi and, after 23 September 1513, Cardinal Innocenzo Cibo (1513–50), worked together to try to promote Genoa's affairs, although Cibo, described as a good Genoese by the ambassadors in 1514, seems at times to have been sidelined by the other two cardinals.[70]

If the Genoese turned to the cardinals for advice in times of crisis – for example in June 1512 when Giano Fregoso, with papal backing, was about to rid Genoa of the French, and the Genoese were anxious about their

---

[67] McClung Hallman, *Italian cardinals*, 4.
[68] Unsigned report of March 1513, Sanuto, *Diarii*, xvi. 81; Cam. Ap., Div. Cam. 63, fos 6r–v, 21 Mar. 1513.
[69] *Anziani* to the orators, 16 Dec. 1506, Archivio Segreto 2342.
[70] N. Oderico to O. Fregoso and the *anziani*, 11, 19, 23, 25 Dec. 1515, ibid. 2177, fos 713r, 716r, 718r; G. B. Lasagnia to O. Fregoso and the *anziani*, 23, 30 May 1514, ibid. 2342.

extensive business interests in France – at times the Genoese cardinals were, perforce, the pope's mouthpiece, expressing his wishes and intentions towards Genoa. In reply to the letter from the Genoese *pacificatori* the cardinals gritted their teeth and wrote that Julius had sent Giano Fregoso and that 'His Holiness' wish and will is that the said *messer* Jano be admitted to the city and peacefully and unanimously accepted.'[71] At other times they were little more than a papal shortcut, a means of avoiding sending information via the papal bureaucrats, as when in 1516 Fieschi, Sauli and Cibo wrote at Leo's request to update the Genoese government on the longstanding dispute between two Genoese merchants then being heard in the *sacra rota*.[72] For both cardinals and government, the 'service and honour' of Genoa was paramount and they pressed the pope with Genoese concerns, especially in times of danger to Genoa – indeed their account of Genoese worries prior to the arrival of Giano Fregoso evoked Julius' disdain.[73] When, later in the same year, the arrival of Cardinal Gurk (the emperor's representative) occasioned the sending of Genoese ambassadors, they were told that when they reached the outskirts of Rome they were to send a messenger to Fieschi, Sauli (and the Savonese cardinals), who were to arrange an audience with Julius. The ambassadors were in everything 'to be directed by our aforesaid two cardinals' who were to advise them and act 'with their singular prudence and the charity they bear towards their homeland'; they even advised the ambassadors on the clothes they should wear.[74]

Similarly, members of his family turned to him to help promote their interests. The careers of Stefano and Filippo Sauli demonstrate how a cardinal could benefit his own. Yet politics and personal and family advancement were not the only concerns of a cardinal. Sauli, with Fieschi, also sought the pope's help in the reform of Genoese monasteries such as San Defendente, the unification of churches and the awarding of indulgences, including the plenary indulgence granted to the Dominican church of Santa Maria di Castello – of which members of his family were fond – through his intervention in 1514.[75] In Rome a cardinal's ecclesiastical duties included accompa-

---

71 Letter from *pacificatori*, 21 June 1512, Goiffrè, *Gênes*, 13–14; 'lo desiderio et volunta sua esser chel prefato messer Jano sia admesso et acceptato pacificamente et di bono et unanimo accordio': Cardinals Fieschi and Sauli to *pacificatori*, 24 June 1512, Archivio Segreto 2805.
72 Fieschi, Sauli and Cibo to O. Campofregoso and *anziani*, 10 Mar. 1516, Archivio Segreto 2805.
73 'servitio et honore': Cardinals Fieschi and Sauli to Genoese government, 24 June 1512; Hyde, 'From devotion to damnation', 46–7; Cardinals Fieschi and Sauli to *balia*, 30 June 1512, Archivio Segreto 2805.
74 'vi faciati capo de li prefati reverendissimi nostri doa Cardinali' and 'per le singolare prudentie loro e carita verso questa patria': G. Fregoso and *anziani* to L. Fregoso, S. Fieschi, Q. Cavalo and H. Doria, 30 Nov. 1512, Archivio Segreto 2707/C, no. 102.
75 *Officialium monachorum reformandarum* to Julius II, Cardinals Leonardo Grosso della Rovere, Fieschi and Sauli, 22 Sept. 1511, ibid 1958bis; *Officialium monachorum reformandarum* to Cardinals Fieschi and Sauli, 22 Sept. 1511, ibid; doge and *anziani* to

nying the pope at official ceremonies, receiving newly promoted cardinals, attending the vigils and funerals of dead cardinals, participating in the Fifth Lateran Council and following religious observances. But he also had obligations towards his *commende*, his bishoprics, his titular church and the other benefices which – in Sauli's case – he had so avidly collected. Exactly what type of churchman was Cardinal Sauli?

Genoese cardinals, 10 Sept. 1515, ibid. 1830, fo. 10v; Biblioteca Civica Berio, Genoa, sez. conservazione, raccolta locale, MS m.r.III. 1, 19, fo. 62v.

2

Cardinal Sauli: 'Gubernator Utilis et Ydoneus'?

Barbara McClung Hallman defines an ecclesiastical benefice as 'a sacred office, with or without the care of souls, to which a permanent income is attached'.[1] The fact that benefices were used by popes as the principal source of rewards 'encouraged churchmen to view benefices first as income and only secondarily as sacred offices'.[2] How true was this for Cardinal Sauli and, if true, did it necessarily mean that his benefices suffered?

During his fifteen-year ecclesiastical career Sauli held at least thirty-eight benefices, ranging from parish churches to bishoprics and his titular churches.[3] Given this relatively large number in such a short career (and the dearth of documentary material for many of the smaller ones) if any insight is to be gained into how Sauli administered his benefices, and the care he gave to them, then some selection, based on the size and importance of the holding and the survival of sources, is clearly called for. An examination of the administration of two of his *commende*, the abbeys of San Siro in Genoa and San Simpliciano in Milan; of Gerace and Oppido, one of his two bishoprics; and of his titular church, Santa Sabina, should provide a fairly coherent assessment of Cardinal Sauli as churchman.

A few initial points need to be made. There is no doubt that, despite his family's wealth, the income from his benefices was important to Sauli: on at least five occasions he was involved in disputes, and gave up his rights with great reluctance, on one occasion pressing home his advantage on the election of Leo X almost five years after the settlement of a dispute.[4] Secondly, he always leased out his major benefices in what were sometimes detailed (and revealing) lease agreements, giving the administration of the bene-fice to relatives and/or businessmen in exchange for an annual sum. This was regarded as commonplace and acceptable during the period in ques-

---

[1]   McClung Hallman, *Italian cardinals*, 17. In this period the phrase 'gubernator utilis et ydoneus' is often to be found in letters of appointment to benefices as being what the benefice in question required. See, for example, Reg. Vat. 1004, fo. 75r.

[2]   McClung Hallman, *Italian cardinals*, 17.

[3]   For the difficulty in establishing the exact number of benefices held by churchmen, and the income involved, see Lowe, *Church and politics*, 186. This figure was reached by counting the packages of lesser benefices awarded on the same day as a single benefice.

[4]   For the resurrected dispute see Reg. Vat. 975, fos 31r–32; 1004, fos 150r–151v; for the other disputes see Reg. Lat. 1200, fos 248r–250v; Reg. Vat. 971, fos 303v–306v; Cam. Ap., Resignationes 12, fo. 287r; and Reg. Vat. 1007, fos 33r–35v.

tion.[5] Thirdly, he was a Curia cardinal, resident in Rome and leaving the city
for only brief periods. This meant that all benefices with the care of souls
attached were initially taken in his name by a proctor and then administered
by a proctor and/or a *vicario generale* appointed by Sauli. His choice of *vicario
generale* is often in itself interesting, revealing Sauli's concerns for his benefices; the use of intermediaries does not necessarily mean that his interest in
the running of the benefice in question was negligible. Fourth, he was often
appointed *in commenda* to run monasteries or abbeys and it was accepted that
he, like previous holders, did not reside there. Much damage was wrought,
both spiritually and temporally, by appointments *in commenda* as was officially, albeit for the most part ineffectively, recognised in the reform bull
Supernae dispositionis arbitrio of 5 May 1514. It is worth bearing in mind that
in some cases Sauli may well have been awarded a benefice that had been
poorly run in the past and that his efforts to rectify any damage may well
have come too late.[6]

The abbey and convent of San Siro, Genoa

On 19 December 1503, less than two months after the beginning of the della
Rovere pontificate, Bendinello Sauli received *in commenda* the Benedictine
abbey of San Siro at Genoa. It is his first known ecclesiastical benefice and,
given its importance, was a provocative move by a confident Julius who
wished to demonstrate the esteem in which he held the Sauli.[7] San Siro
had been Genoa's cathedral until that role passed to San Lorenzo, and the
iuspatronatus of the abbey belonged to the powerful Genoese Cibo family to
whom it paid a tribute.[8] Parishioners of San Siro included the influential
Vivaldi, Lomellini, Spinola, Adorno, Centurione, Gentile and De Franchi
families.[9]

Previous commendatory abbots had included Giovanni Battista Cibo,
later Innocent VIII, and Cardinal Lorenzo Cibo Mari, on whose death the
benefice had fallen vacant. The Cibo family were duly horrified at the nomi-
nation of Sauli and as soon as the news arrived in Genoa they acted. On
23 February 1504 three members of the family met in front of a public notary
to state that the *commenda* was now vacant and that the *iuspatronatus* and
thus the right of appointment belonged to them; they had chosen Cardinal

[5] McClung Hallman, *Italian cardinals*, 69.
[6] D. Hay, *The Church in Italy in the fifteenth century*, Cambridge 1977, 74–5; J. C. Olin,
The Catholic Reformation: Savonarola to Ignatius Loyola, New York 1992, 57.
[7] Reg. Lat. 1129A, fos 238r–240r.
[8] ASG, MS 839, fo. 287. For the history of San Siro see C. Da Prato, *Genova: chiesa di
San Siro: storia e descrizioni*, Genoa 1900, and L. De Simoni, *Le chiese di Genova: storia,
arte, folclore*, Genoa 1948, ii. 215–24.
[9] Archivio Sauli, no. 705, fos 1r, 2r, 3r, 5r–v.

Giovanni de' Medici.[10] A proctor in Rome was to promote their choice and ensure that the apostolic letters were made up, but the Cibo were too late and Julius would not be moved. The necessary documents had already been drawn up on 19 January 1504 and Sauli moved quickly to defend his rights. On 2 March 1504 Sauli's proctor, Benedictus Campanarius, presented the documents to Lorenzo Fieschi, the archbishop of Genoa's *vicario generale*, who then undertook to execute them.[11]

San Siro was a benefice which Sauli held almost to the end of his life and is thus an interesting case study. The first notice of his involvement in the abbey's affairs is dated 24 May 1504 when Sauli granted permission to one of the brothers to study outside the convent for two years.[12] This is written *manu propria* and, coming so shortly after he took possession of the convent, indicates that a *vicario generale* had not yet been appointed to take charge of the convent for him. On 4 April 1505 Sauli remedied this situation by appointing Giacomo Anselmo.[13]

The powers of the *vicario generale* were not limited merely to the spiritual affairs of San Siro; in the surviving documents the temporal affairs of the convent are the more dominant. By the eleventh century the convent was already rich, deriving its income from land and property holdings in the city of Genoa itself and to the east of the city, in Asti and Alessandria and Chiavari. It also had at least three churches under its jurisdiction.[14] Indeed notarial acts for much of Sauli's *commenda* are mostly rental agreements for these property holdings, all undertaken by the *vicario* or Sauli's proctor. The question of exactly whom he appointed to run the temporal affairs of San Siro is rather complicated and eventually required Sauli's personal intervention. From August 1506 Anselmo had apparently worked in tandem with Giovanni Battista de' Balanchiis, a chaplain of San Giorgio in Genoa, but some problems obviously came to light. By October 1506 Anselmo had 'freely' resigned San Giovanni in Piscina in the diocese of Tortona, a church under San Siro's jurisdiction which he had previously been awarded for his role as *vicario*, and this was given to Agostino Sauli *quondam* Simoni on the following day.[15] Sauli was present in Genoa in the summer of 1507 – probably because of his family's involvement in the *popolare* revolt – and whilst there he took the opportunity to review the situation at San Siro and was obviously dissatisfied with what he saw. On 7 July 1507 he personally

[10] Notai Antichi, 1158, no. 55.

[11] Ibid. no. 67, 2 Mar. 1504.

[12] ASG, Archivio Segreto, Abbazia di San Siro, Pergamena di San Siro 692.

[13] The original document for the appointment of Anselmo is missing, but was drawn up in Rome by the notary Paolo de Landucci on the above date and is cited in all the subsequent documents in which Anselmo acts for Sauli.

[14] S. Origone, 'Il patrimonio immobiliare del monastero di San Siro di Genova (secoli x–xiii)', *Studi genuensi* x (1973–4), 3–14 at pp. 6, 7.

[15] Notai Antichi, 1159, nos 223, 259.

replaced Anselmo, and any other proctors, with Hieronimo de Vernatia, a chaplain of Santa Maria delle Vigne in Genoa.

De Vernatia had already gained some experience in the administration of the goods of San Siro. On 26 July 1505 Vincenzo Sauli, who had been acting as Bendinello's agent in collecting the monies and incomes due to the convent and had dealt with all disputes regarding them, appointed de Vernatia to take over from him.[16] On 28 January 1506 Vincenzo similarly appointed de Vernatia to obtain the income and profits from the convent's shares in the *Casa di San Giorgio* and sell them if necessary. By 19 December of that year de Vernatia had also taken charge of the rental of San Siro's properties.[17] On 7 July 1507 he then took over complete control of the running of the benefice in Sauli's absence.[18] De Vernatia was evidently held in high esteem by the Sauli, but also within Genoa: in the 1507 document he is described as a chaplain of the cathedral and he also acted for the nuns of San Sepolcro at Sampierdarena. In 1512 he was also appointed *vicario generale* of the bishopric of Brugnato and in 1516 was to obtain money owing to the deanery of Santo Stefano di Lavagna for Filippo Sauli. By 1517 he was described as Sauli's *famigliare* and *continuus commensalis*.[19]

To return to the abbey itself: with the exception in 1506 of a slightly unseemly quarrel with Pietro de' Mari over the spoils of a late brother, Sauli, as commendatory abbot, showed concern for the spiritual and temporal welfare of his flock.[20] In late 1506 the convent contained only seven brothers and in January 1507, in the face of the disapproval of the existing brothers, Sauli approved the transfer of Fra Pietro Lercario, an Augustinian, to San Siro. Lercario had asked to join the Benedictines because of his particular devotion to the order but had not specified which convent. The pope's decision to send him to San Siro demonstrates that the need to increase numbers there must have already been signalled by Sauli and that Julius considered the convent a suitable choice for a devout brother.[21] The number of brothers was to fall further. The Genoese revolt had been particularly bloody and a papal brief of 2 May 1508 noted that there were then no brothers in the convent at all and that Sauli wished to receive some so that the holy office could be celebrated. Julius accordingly approved the transfer there of three (inexplicably Franciscan) friars.[22] Not only had the existing brothers apparently fled (although they eventually returned), but the convent had suffered considerable damage to its buildings and Sauli recognised the need

---

[16] Ibid. 1158, no. 225.
[17] Ibid; 1159, no. 321.
[18] Ibid. 1159, no. 118.
[19] Ibid.; 1161, nos 282, 309, 18 Nov. 1510, 29 Nov. 1511; 1165, no. 50, 25 Feb. 1517.
[20] ASR, Collegio de' Notai Capitolini, 60, fo. 19r.
[21] See Notai Antichi, 1159, no. 293, 2 Dec. 1506, which includes the transcription of Julius' letter to Lercario dated 24 Oct. 1506, and no. 16, 25 Jan. 1507.
[22] Arm. XXIX, 26, fo. 527r.

to restore the convent, gaining papal permission on 9 August 1508 for the income of fourteen ducats per year from twenty *luoghi* in the *Casa di San Giorgio* belonging to a former brother of San Siro to be used for the repair of the convent (most specifically the sacristy) and the purchase of necessary vestments and ornaments. The convent was obviously short of money: from 1508 to 1514 there is a marked increase in the number of rentals of its property.[23] On 14 May 1509 Sauli decided to act further and, again with the aim of helping the convent, he abolished the rent on a house near San Siro and instructed the occupants to inscribe one and a half shares in the *Casa di San Giorgio* in the name of the convent and for the convent's use.[24] He thus guaranteed the convent a reliable source of income.

Sauli could not avoid contact with the Cibo and gave in to their wishes regarding the chaplaincy of certain altars on 26 June 1505, 11 July 1508 and 16 October 1512.[25] Indeed, on 3 October 1509 he was in Genoa and 'wishing as far as possible to avoid scandal' settled problems regarding three chaplaincies and the holders' duties in strong terms and in favour of the Cibo.[26] The only notice that we have of Sauli's intervention in the convent's affairs after 1512 is on 18 February 1516 when he ordered that a new brother, Gregorio de Solario, be received into the convent.[27] All remaining documentation for the rest of Sauli's *commenda* is in the form of rental agreements drawn up by de Vernatia. Most probably there were no further problems at the convent that required Sauli's intervention; it is unlikely that additional documents have been lost as most of the convent's affairs were dealt with by the Genoese notary Baldassare de Coronato, whose *filze* remain remarkably intact.

Naturally, when possible, he promoted the interests of his own family and household: in addition to the conferral of San Giovanni in Piscina on Agostino Sauli he also arranged for the conferral of the parish church of San Marcellino, whose collation lay with the commendatory abbot, to a Secundino Celexie, his *famigliare* and *continuus commensalis*.[28] Giovanni Sauli, the cardinal's brother, also acted as banker for the convent.[29] Following his disgrace Sauli was replaced as commendatory abbot on 29 June 1517 by, ironically, Cardinal Innocenzo Cibo.[30] In his administration of San Siro, Sauli emerges as one who, while protecting his family's interests, intervened when necessary for the good of the abbey. Yet it is of interest that he seemed to do little personally to benefit San Siro financially. In August 1508 he

[23] Ibid. 28, fo. 445r–v; Notai Antichi, 1160, nos 1, 2, 3 passim.

[24] Collegio de' Notai Capitolini, 1914, fo. 40r.

[25] Archivio Segreto, Abbazia di San Siro, Pergamena di San Siro, 693; Notai Antichi 1158, nos 186, 188; 1161, nos 253–4; Arm. XXXIX, 26, fos 493r–494r.

[26] 'Nos volentes quantum possimus scandalis obviare': Notai Antichi, 1413, nos 326, 327.

[27] Ibid. 1164, no. 69, 18 Feb. 1516.

[28] Ibid. 1158, no. 213, 22 July 1505.

[29] Ibid. 1162, no. 258, 19 May 1512.

[30] ASG, MS 839, fo. 295.

gained papal approval to use what was essentially the convent's money to repair the damage caused during the *popolare* revolt, and his attitude did not change: the inventory of the contents of the sacristy, drawn up on 25 July 1517 by Nicolò Pinelli, does not list any articles as having been presented by Sauli whereas four separate gifts from his predecessor, Cardinal Cibo, are cited.[31] This was not always to be the case in his other major benefices.

San Simpliciano, Milan

On 5 October 1511 Bernardo Bibbiena informed Cardinal de' Medici that Sauli had been granted San Simpliciano in Milan, with an income of 2,000 ducats.[32] He proved to have been well-informed: Sauli was in fact awarded the church and convent of San Simpliciano on 13 October 1511.[33] This was another prestigious benefice: San Simpliciano was one of the four churches founded by Sant'Ambrogio and lay outside the city walls. In 881 it had passed to the Benedictines but became a *commenda* in the mid-*quattrocento*.[34] After the death of its most famous *commendatario*, Gian Antonio Negri, there were four more commendatory abbots, all 'people of high standing', but few documents survive for the period in question.[35] That it was conferred upon Sauli was proof of his favour with Julius II, and also with the rulers of Milan, the French.

Cardinal Sauli acted swiftly to protect his, and the convent's, interests: unable to reside in person he leased the convent and its lands and goods to Hieronimo Adorno on 21 November 1511.[36] This meant that he had chosen to ignore the lease agreement drawn up on 7 November 1508, and valid for nine years, between the previous *commendatario*, Cardinal Leonardo Grosso della Rovere (1503–20), and Bartolomeo and Filippo Doria (de Auria) and associates. A quarrel rapidly ensued and on 22 October 1512 settlement was reached in Milan between Giovanni Sauli, as the cardinal's representative, and the two Doria and others, including a certain Michele de Provano. A further five-year rental was agreed which Sauli ratified on 15 December 1512. The agreement is reasonably detailed but, with the exception of the money to be paid for the brothers' expenses, is mostly concerned with what

[31] Notai Antichi, 1477.
[32] Bibbiena to Cardinal de' Medici, 5 Oct. 1511, *Epistolario*, i, no. 88 at p. 268..
[33] Reg. Lat. 1258, fos 361v–362v.
[34] M. T. Fiorio (ed.), *Le chiese di Milano*, Milan 1985, 125.
[35] C. Baroni, *S. Simpliciano abbazia Benedettina*, Milan 1934, 92; P. Puccinelli, *Zodiaco della chiesa milanese*, Milan 1650, 102.
[36] The original document is now lost but is cited in Archivio Urbano, sezione 66, protocollo 20, fo. 55v.

the lessee could and could not do and the financial responsibilities of both parties. Future improvements were also, in theory, agreed.[37]

It is difficult to arrive at any conclusions about the value of the rent to be paid given the lack of documentation on the size of the benefices leased in the early *cinquecento*, but the 1,700 ducats to be given to Sauli each year seem to have been at the root of the original disagreement and obviously still rankled. On 30 June 1513 Vincenzo and Sebastiano Sauli were appointed as *conductores* (lessees) of the abbey, to lease all the fruits, possessions, lands and incomes for a period of nine years to begin on 11 November 1513 and at the more substantial rent of 2,100 ducats *per annum* for the first three years.[38] The new agreement represented not just an increase in income for Cardinal Sauli but also a change in outlook. One could almost think that he or, as seems more likely, Giovanni Sauli, had seen the abbey and its possessions in the meantime and was determined to do more for it.

The lease document is particularly detailed. It to some extent reveals the abbey's possessions and the extent of its jurisdiction: Vincenzo and Sebastiano were to lease lands, properties, possessions, waters, aqueducts, dovecotes, vegetable gardens and fish ponds both inside and outside the walls of Milan, in the Milanese *ducato* and in the bishopric of Como. Cardinal Sauli was to obtain papal approval for the lease within three months and pay all expenses.[39] The agreement naturally deals with the rights of the lessees and the responsibilities of Cardinal Sauli but also with the safekeeping of the convent's goods and the welfare of the brothers. Vincenzo and Sebastiano were to make an inventory of all goods and possessions at the beginning of the lease and to ensure that at the end all were returned in the same, pristine, condition.[40] Special emphasis was placed on the trees, both fruit-bearing and otherwise, which were to be detailed in the inventory and none were to be topped or felled or a penalty of five ducats per tree was to be paid, thus indicating that the trees were an important source of income for the convent.[41] The condition of the convent was to be maintained and even improved: Sauli was to provide the wood to repair or rebuild certain bridges; de Provano and Bartolomeo Doria were to be recompensed for improvements they had made and Vincenzo and Sebastiano could make any useful and necessary improvements to the sum of 2,000 Milanese pounds (approximately 500 ducats). All buildings and outbuildings belonging to the abbey were to be maintained and the supply of materials was established.[42]

Vincenzo and Sebastiano were to treat the brothers 'honourably' and to

---

[37] ASR, Notai del Tribunale, AC 7151, fos 228r–233r: copy of the original document drawn up in Milan.
[38] Archivio Urbano, sezione 66, protocollo 20, fos 49v–56v at fo. 50v.
[39] Ibid. fos 50r, 51v.
[40] Ibid. fo. 51v.
[41] Ibid.
[42] Ibid. fos 52v–53r, 54r.

allow them to ride in certain areas when they pleased. They were also to ensure that six masses were celebrated in the sacristy of the church or face a fine of fifty ducats; additional masses were to be celebrated in two of the other churches that belonged to the convent.[43] The maintenance of these churches was to be ensured and they were to be kept covered. Like previous *conductores* they were to pay the brothers' expenses.[44] The lease agreement thus protected the interest of both parties, did its best to protect the assets of the convent and the brothers themselves and to promote the celebration of the holy office. McClung Hallman believes that lease agreements 'must have been detrimental'.[45] Although Sauli took steps in this agreement to protect the property and the brothers, and indeed later paid for some repairs from rental income, there is some evidence that San Simpliciano was temporally and spiritually exhausted by the end of the Sauli *commenda*.[46] Yet given that the abbey had been *in commenda* for almost sixty years (and, given the improvements he authorised, Sauli seems to have realised that there were problems), responsibility may well not have lain with him.

But were all the provisions he made in vain? On 24 December 1513 Vincenzo and Sebastiano, not wishing to move to Milan, appointed Carolo de' Fornari and Domenico Sauli (1490–1570) (*see* Fig. 3) as their proctors to manage their lease of the abbey and its possessions for the next four years. This document deals solely with the fiscal and legal powers of de'' Fornari and Domenico.[47] Did the omission of Bendinello's earlier provisions reflect the fact that, in the meantime, on 3 October 1513, Cardinal Sauli had relinquished the *commenda* of the abbey, which then was awarded by Leo (presumably at Sauli's instigation) to Sauli's brother Stefano, a twenty-one-year-old student at Bologna and perhaps a less than assiduous *commendatario*?[48] Transfer of benefices within a family was not uncommon: Cardinal Fieschi resigned the bishopric of Fréjus to his nephew in 1511 and the arch-bishopric of Ravenna to another nephew in 1517; Cardinal Soderini resigned the bishopric of Volterra to his nephew Giuliano in 1509; and in 1498 and 1503 Cardinal Oliviero Carafa (1467–1511) resigned the *commenda* of a convent and the archbishopric of Naples to two different nephews. Cardinals obviously felt the need to keep the wealth and prestige of rich benefices within the family.[49]

There is no further news of San Simpliciano until 20 April 1517 when the

---

[43] Ibid. fo. 54v.
[44] Ibid. and fo. 55r.
[45] McClung Hallman, *Italian cardinals*, 77.
[46] Archivio Sauli, no. 730, fo. 40r.
[47] Notai Antichi, 1283, no. 664.
[48] Reg. Vat. 1000, fo. 248v.
[49] Ibid. 998, fos 232r–234v; Cevolotto, 'Fieschi', 504; K. J. P. Lowe, 'Un episcopato non esaminato: analisi delle relazioni tra il vescovo di Volterra e la sua diocesi prima della Riforma', *Rassegna Volterrana* lxv–lxvi (1989–90), 107–25 at p. 107; F. Petrucci, 'Carafa, Oliviero', *DBI* xix (1976), 588–96 at pp. 592, 594.

pope accepted Stefano's resignation of the abbey and Cardinal Sauli's resignation of the income and the *regressus* (the right to take the benefice back on its falling vacant): San Simpliciano was to join the strict Benedictine-Cassinese congregation, apparently for the good of the convent.[50] Although Stefano was later to show signs of deep spirituality, his youth and inexperience may have told. In 1517 only six brothers were left and of these two were sent to San Dionigi, also held by Cardinal Sauli, and the rest received pensions.[51] The fact that two of the brothers were sent to San Dionigi indicates that, spiritually at least, this convent, which Sauli had held since July 1514, was in a healthy condition.[52]

There can be no doubt that the absorption of San Simpliciano into the Benedictine-Cassinese congregation benefited the convent: the new regime carried out extensive restoration of the church and extended the convent's buildings, which seem to have been in a ruinous condition. Enrico Cattaneo believes that the unification originated in what he calls the Sauli family's reformist tendencies and this does seem possible. The reform of the convent appears to have gained its initial impetus from the intervention of Francis I who wrote to Leo in September 1516 for this express purpose, but given the close relations between Sauli and Francis in this period as witnessed by the meeting at Bologna and later events, it is possible that the letter was written at Sauli's behest.[53] Even if this were not the case, Sauli's concern for the convent as expressed in the lease agreement with Vincenzo and Sebastiano would not have allowed him to oppose the move and the pill was certainly sweetened by the award of a very generous annual pension – 4,000 ducats, to be paid by four churches – which passed to Stefano on his death and was apparently paid off in 1525.[54]

Bishop of Gerace and Oppido

Apostolic dispensations had been granted to enable Sauli to hold both San Simpliciano and San Dionigi. As was common, and yet illegal at the time,

[50] 'ipsumque Monasterium Sancti Simpliciani in spiritualibus et temporalibus salubrius regeretur et gubernaretur': Arch. Concist., Acta Vicecanc. 2, fo. 26r; Reg. Vat. 1080, fo. 157v.
[51] Reg. Vat. 1080, fo. 159r; E. Cattaneo, 'Istituzioni ecclesiastiche milanesi', *Storia di Milano*, ix, Milan 1961, 509–720 at p. 594; Baroni, *San Simpliciano*, 92.
[52] Reg. Vat. 1004, fos 75r–77. This important church and convent were destroyed in 1793. Sauli also made repairs to this convent's holdings (Reg. Lat. 1333, fos 287v–289r) and resigned San Dionigi on 1 Aug. 1517: Cam. Ap., Resignationes 17, fo. 253v.
[53] Cattaneo, *Istituzioni ecclesiastiche*, 540; C. Mauri, *Storia e descrizione delle chiese distrutte ed esistenti in Milano e dintorni*, Milan 1857, 58; S. Latuada, *Descrizione di Milano, ornata con molti disegni in rame dalle fabbriche più cospicue, che si trovano in questa metropoli*, Milan 1737–8, v. 272; Baroni, *San Simpliciano*, 93.
[54] Reg. Vat. 1080, fo. 157v; Puccinelli, *Zodiaco*, 37.

Sauli was a pluralist, the holder of two or more incompatible benefices.[55] From 1513 he also held two bishoprics: Gerace and Oppido, and Albenga, although these were minor holdings when compared to those of other cardinals such as Francesco Soderini (at least six bishoprics, although he generally held only two at one time) and Jean de Lorraine (eleven bishoprics).[56] Indeed, McClung Hallman believes that 65 per cent of cardinals during the period 1512–19 practised pluralism in bishoprics but 'life-styles or reputations do not distinguish pluralists from non-pluralists, nor do reformers stand out from non-reformers in the matter of bishoprics'.[57]

On 23 February 1509 Sauli was translated from the bishopric of Malta to that of Gerace and Oppido in Reggio Calabria which he held until 19 November 1517 when he resigned it in favour of the Medici favourite Cardinal Francesco Armellini (1517–28).[58] Although Enzo D'Agostino believes that the bishopric was awarded to 'worthy clerics', financially it was a poor resource: if the rental value of San Simpliciano was a healthy 2,100 ducats *per annum*, that of Gerace and Oppido was considerably less: between 650 and 800 ducats.[59] Sauli was awarded the bishopric *in episcopum et pastorem* but administered it through *vicarii generali*, although no concrete evidence survives to support the names of those listed by the later (Genoese) bishop, Ottaviano Pasqua.[60] A document dated 18 September 1515 sheds no further light on the situation: on that date Sauli's brother, Giovanni, who is cited as lessee of the incomes of Gerace and Oppido, appoints as his proctor his cousin, Filippo Sauli, who was to lease the incomes in Giovanni's name for three years and was also to act as *vicario*.[61] This would have been a positive move: Filippo was a reforming bishop who in his own see, Brugnato, cared attentively for his flock, although no record survives of him in connection with Gerace. However, the provisions of this document are unlikely ever to have come into effect. Cardinal Sauli was related, via his grandfather, to the Maruffo family and by 22 February 1515 Luca Maruffo had secured the lease of the fruits of the bishopric. Sauli, in documents of

---

55 McClung Hallman, *Italian cardinals*, 18.
56 Lowe, *Church and politics*, 184–5. Sauli was appointed bishop *in administrationem* of Albenga, near Genoa, on 5 Aug. 1513 but held the see for only four years. The little surviving archival evidence about his time there can be found in Reg. Lat. 1281, fos 216r–218r; Notai Antichi, 1162, nos 178, 180; 1406, 15 Feb. 1514; 1163, no. 283; 1164, no. 66; 1285, no. 717; Archivio Sauli, no. 707 unfoliated, entry, Apr. 1517; Archivio Urbano, sezione 66, protocollo 21, fo. 113r; 13, fos 109v–110r; ASI, Archivio Comunale di Albenga, I, consilium 1514, fos 18r, 29r, 64r, 138v, 172v; Archivio Raimondi 40, fos 34v–35r, 150v; 10, 28 Sept., 8 Oct. 1515; Reg. Vat. 1206, fos 363r–365r; Arch. Concist., Acta Vicecanc. 2, fo. 58v.
57 McClung Hallman, *Italian cardinals*, 21.
58 Reg. Vat. 943, fos 63r–68r; 1105, fos 75r–76v; Arch. Concist. Acta Vicecanc. 2, fo. 58v.
59 E. D'Agostino, *I vescovi di Gerace-Locri*, Chiaravalle 1981, 90.
60 O. Pasqua, *Vitae episcoporum ecclesiae Hieracensis*, Naples 1754, 298.
61 Archivio Urbano, sezione 66, protocollo 14, fo. 166v.

23 and 24 August 1516, having been satisfied with this earlier lease (possibly Maruffo had then sublet the fruits to Giovanni Sauli) agreed to renew it for three years beginning on 23 February 1517 at an annual (increased) price of 800 cameral ducats.[62]

Whoever governed the bishopric in Sauli's name was far from idle and benefited the bishopric in various ways, demonstrating that Sauli was, in fact, an active bishop, in contrast to his predecessor Giacomo Conchilles (1505–9).[63] All the sources rely once again on Pasqua who notes that Sauli succeeded in wresting ultimate control of the bishopric from the archi-episcopal see of Reggio Calabria and placing it in his own hands, some-thing that few other bishops had succeeded in doing.[64] The Greek rite still survived in this remote part of Italy, most specifically in the convent of San Pantaleo, but Sauli ensured that the Latin rite prevailed. He is also believed to have founded the Dominican convent of Santa Maria della Palomba at Messignadi in about 1513.[65] Pasqua also ascribes to Giovanni Capoferro, whom he believed to be one of Sauli's *vicarii*, the restoration of San Teodoro and Santa Maria de Ferro, but it is impossible to ascertain whether he was acting under Sauli's aegis given that he had previously been *vicario* under Conchilles and was active in the diocese under later bishops.[66]

Perhaps Sauli's most important contribution to the bishopric was what can be interpreted (from a passage of obscure Latin in Pasqua) as the rebuilding of the side naves of the cathedral and the decoration of them with his coat of arms.[67] Pasqua also notes that he restored the chapel of the Madonna dell'Itria in the *soccorpo* of the church and founded the church of the Annun-ziata.[68] D'Agostino firmly dates the latter to 1524 and ascribes it to Capoferro and, seemingly on the basis of this, then also ascribes to him the restoration of the Cappella dell'Itria in the catacombs, whereas other scholars ascribe it to Sauli.[69] A later restoration of 1613 destroyed any surviving physical evidence but if it is accepted that Sauli was the author of the restoration a

---

[62] Ibid. 28, fos 73r–75r. The previous lease payment had initially been 650 ducats. The details are confirmed and slightly amended in Notai Antichi, 1522bis, no. 126, 24 Aug. 1516.

[63] For Conchilles see D'Agostino, *I vescovi*, 89.

[64] Pasqua, *Vitae*, 297.

[65] Ibid.; D'Agostino, *I vescovi*, 91; C. Zerbi, *Della città, chiesa e diocesi di Oppido Mamer-tina, e dei suoi vescovi: notizie cronistoriche*, Rome 1876, 219; R. Liberti, *Diocesi di Oppido-Palmi: i vescovi dal 1050 ad oggi*, Rosarno 1994, 34.

[66] Pasqua, *Vitae*, 298.

[67] 'utraque testudine, praeter mediam, in qua familiae Sauliae spectantur insignia, sua opera, ac impensa Ecclesiam maiorem exornavit': ibid; A. Oppedisano, *Cronistoria della diocesi di Gerace*, Gerace 1934, 528–9; D'Agostino, *I vescovi*, 91. The cathedral was seri-ously damaged during the earthquakes of 1744 and 1783.

[68] 'Sacellum conceptionis B. Mariae in catacumbis pulcriorem reddidit, ipsius Virginis imagine introeuntibus ad dexteram prope altare antiquitus sita, in medio locata': Pasqua, *Vitae*, 298.

[69] D'Agostino, *I vescovi*, 91; cf. Oppedisano, *Cronistoria*, 528, and G. Occhiato, 'Il

slight insight can be gained into the success of the work from later descriptions drawn up during episcopal visits. In 1541 the Cappella dell'Itria was described as 'decorated with the usual ornaments and vestments' and in 1552 as 'well repaired and decorated'.[70] All this was achieved during his mere eight years as bishop, a considerable achievement if one considers that it took Cardinal Soderini thirty-one years as bishop of Volterra to rebuild a castle, found a *monte di pietà*, establish a charitable *fraternità* and donate three choral books, and that Cardinal Lorenzo Cibo Mari was archbishop of Benevento for eighteen years and in that time donated only an *ostensorio* and an organ to the cathedral.[71]

Thus, despite the dearth of contemporary documents, a reasonably clear picture of Sauli's dealings with Gerace emerges: as was accepted (and expected), he leased the incomes and appointed *vicari generali*, but he did not neglect the bishopric. He contributed to the physical upkeep and embellishment of the main ecclesiastical asset, the cathedral. Later assessments of him have been kind: Pasqua described him as 'as a good man, and innocent' (a reference to his later disgrace); Antonio Oppedisano believed that Cardinal Sauli 'ruled the diocese wisely for eight years' and Candido Zerbi agreed that he 'left of himself and of his works, some questionable, but not unhappy, memories'.[72]

Cardinal of Santa Sabina

Sauli held three titular churches, Sant'Adriano, Santa Sabina and Santa Maria in Trastevere. On his appointment to the cardinalate in 1511 he was made cardinal deacon of Sant'Adriano ai Fori, holding it for a mere nine months – and with no surviving documents or trace of his intervention – until his promotion to cardinal priest of Santa Sabina in early 1512. Santa Sabina was built in the fifth century during the papacy of Sixtus III (432–40) and passed to the Dominicans in 1218. St Dominic lived there until his death in 1221.[73] It was, and remains, the Lenten station for Ash Wednesday when it is visited by the pope. The church and convent are situated on the Aventine hill and were thus, in the *cinquecento*, somewhat isolated. Little is known of Sauli's involvement in the day-to-day affairs of the church and

soccorpo', in S. Gemelli (ed.), *La cattedrale di Gerace: il monumento, le funzioni, i corredi*, Cosenza 1986, 101–26 at p. 102.

[70] 'ornatam ornamentis ac paramentis solitis': ASL, Fondo Gerace, Fondo del Tufo, 1, fo. 22r; 'bene reparatam et ornatam': 1bis, fo. 7r.

[71] Lowe, *Church and politics*, 14–19, and 'Un episcopato', passim; F. Petrucci, 'Cibo Mari, Lorenzo', *DBI* xxv (1981), 275–7 at p. 276.

[72] Pasqua, *Vitae*, 298; Oppedisano, *Cronistoria*, 528; Zerbi, *Della città*, 223.

[73] R. Beny and P. Gunn, *The churches of Rome*, London 1981, 61; M. Armellini, *Le chiese di Roma dalle loro origini sino al secolo XVI*, Rome 1887, 582–6.

convent other than that he gave a total of nineteen ducats to the convent in 1516.[74] However there is later evidence of his patronage.

The oldest reference to Sauli's contribution is that of Ugonio who, writing in 1588, noted the restoration of the cloister and frescoes of the life of St Dominic which he believed were commissioned by Sauli approximately eighty years earlier.[75] In 1703 Carlo Bartolomeo Piazza merely added to Ugonio's description that the cloister was 'embellished everywhere in the wall spaces of the arches with the life of St Dominic'.[76] An eighteenth-century manuscript source then states that Sauli had the (wooden) roof of the (north) wing of the cloister vaulted and his coat of arms fixed in the middle of the vault.[77] In 1912 Joachim Berthier, basing his argument on physical examination of the cloister, believed that Sauli's restoration and the frescoes were limited to the north wing of the cloister.[78] It thus seems that Sauli began to restore the cloister and completed one wing but restoration of the other wings was finally completed, with the help of later titular cardinals, in 1588.[79] If, as Ugonio believes, the frescoes did extend to the whole cloister, then they may well have been damaged when the rest of the roof was replaced.

By 1755 all that was left of the paintings was a fresco of the Virgin accompanied by Santa Sabina and a kneeling Cardinal Sauli. The paintings had been covered up in the eighteenth century and also pierced to make niches at certain points.[80] However, Berthier uncovered some of the frescoes and was able to reconstruct part of the original cycle. He described how in the wall spaces beneath each arch there was a life-size saint or person associated with Santa Sabina, including cardinals and brothers; their names were given below and each figure was framed by two large painted vases of flowers. Lower down were episodes from the life of St Dominic, with special reference to

---

[74] Archivio Sauli, no. 730, fos 27r, 72r. The first payment was on 30 January when seven ducats were given for the celebration of Lent. The second payment, of twelve ducats, was on 26 June 'pro pensione mansionis fratrum'.

[75] P. Ugonio, *Historia delle stationi di Roma che si celebrano la quadragesima di Pompeo Ugonio: all'illustrissima et eccell. Sig. Camilla Peretti: dove oltre le vite de santi alle chiese de quali e' statione, si tratta delle origini, fondazioni, siti, restaurazioni, ornamenti, reliquie,et memorie di esse chiese, antiche e moderne*, Rome 1588, c. 13v.

[76] C. B. Piazza, *La gerarchia ardinalizia di Carlo Bartolomeo Piazza della Congregazione degli Oblati di Milano*, Rome 1793, 435.

[77] 'fece fare il volto ad un'ala del chiostro medesimo a dirittura della sudetta Imagine, in segno di che nel mezzo del volto si vede lo stemma gentilizia della sua stripe scolpito in pietra': Vat. Lat. 9167, fo. 274v; J. Berthier, *L'Église de Sainte-Sabine à Rome*, Rome 1910, 536.

[78] J. Berthier, *Le Couvent de Sainte-Sabine à Rome*, Rome 1912, 6.

[79] A. Munoz, *Il restauro della basilica di Santa Sabina*, Rome 1938, 42; Berthier, *Le Couvent*, 6.

[80] 'l'imagine della Beata Vergine con quella di S Sabina da un lato, e dall'altra [sic] il Ritratto del Cardinale genuflesso': Vat. Lat. 9167, fo. 274v; Jungic, 'Prophecies', 356; Berthier, *Le Couvent*, 6.

his time in Rome; buildings and churches of *cinquecento* Rome formed the background.[81]

When were these works commissioned? Berthier, without citing any documentary evidence, implies that the date was 1518: writing in 1910, after noting that Sauli was deprived of his rank and then reinstated in 1518 (*sic*), he describes how he was disgusted by life and 'withdrew to Santa Sabina, of which he became one of its most distinguished benefactors and was buried there'. In 1912 he firmly fixed the date as 1518 and this was accepted by most later scholars. There is, however, no evidence to support the theory of a stay at the convent: Berthier had simply confused two names: Sauli was in fact briefly exiled by Leo to Monterotondo, a town in the territorial region of Sabina.[82] Indeed, strangely, Berthier chooses to ignore a seventeenth-century manuscript which he quotes as recording, albeit in a later hand and thus after 1678, that in '1512: the vault of the cloister is begun by Cardinal Sauli in c. 1512, as shown by his coat of arms'.[83] It is of course possible that the work was begun after Sauli's death on 29 March 1518 at the instigation of his family to serve as a memorial to him (he was buried in the church). There was a precedent for this: the Fifth Lateran Council had decreed that a cardinal should donate to his titular church, either during his lifetime or after his death, enough money to maintain a priest or to undertake repairs to the church.[84] This reform was (on at least one occasion) taken seriously: on 26 August 1516, at the funeral of Cardinal Vigerio, holder of Santa Maria in Trastevere, Paris de' Grassis, the papal master of ceremonies, somewhat inaccurately reminded Vigerio's executors of the recent reform and they duly complied.[85] Equally, given the description of the frescoes, they could have been commissioned to celebrate Sauli's appointment to Santa Sabina, making the date of 1512 perfectly acceptable. Why only one wing of the cloister was completed is unclear and to date no surviving concrete proof of the dates when these works were commissioned has been traced.

Although Sauli's patronage of Santa Sabina was not on the same scale as that of Cardinal Carvajal (1493–1523) at Santa Croce in Gerusalemme or as that of Cardinal Oliviero Carafa at churches in Rome as diverse as San

---

[81] Berthier, *Le Couvent*, 7.

[82] Idem, *L'Église*, 519, and *Le Couvent*, 6.

[83] Idem, *L'Église*, 524, citing a manuscript entitled 'Memorie riguardanti il nostro convento di Santa Sabina dal 1412 al 1678'. This is a later *resumé* of a manuscript of 1647 entitled 'Relatione della chiesa e convento di S Sabina di Roma raccolte da varii scrittori e scritture antiche con l'aggiunta delle vite de' santi Alessandro papa e martire, Eventio e Theodulo preti e martiri e delle sante Sabina martire e Serafia vergine e martire fatte l'anno del Signore 1647' now in the Biblioteca comunale at Macerata and published by E. Rodocanachi as *Una cronaca di Santa Sabina sull'Aventino*, Città di Castello 1898. It fails to detail Sauli's patronage.

[84] G. D. Mansi, *Sacrorum conciliorum nova et amplissima collectio*, anastatic edn, Graz 1960–1, xxxii. 878.

[85] Barb. Lat. 2683, fo. 167v.

Lorenzo fuori le Mura, Santa Maria della Pace and Santa Maria in Aracoeli, it is clear that, regardless of when the work at Santa Sabina was commissioned, and whoever devised and executed the fresco programme, a large sum of money was involved.[86] Sauli, or his family, clearly felt some degree of devotion to his titular church. Santa Sabina was part of the reformed Dominican Lombard congregation and Sauli had a close relationship with his cousin, Agostino Giustiniani, who was a member of that congregation. Within Genoa the Sauli also had strong links with the reformed Dominican convent of Santa Maria di Castello.[87]

Some indication of the spiritual well-being of Sauli's titular church is demonstrated by the fact that in 1516 Cardinal Fieschi, titular cardinal of the nearby Santa Prisca, cardinal-protector of the Dominican order and a devout churchman, asked the brothers of Santa Sabina to celebrate Sunday mass in his church.[88] Furthermore, the pope's *magister sacri palatii* and Sauli's confessor, Fra Silvestro de Prierias, 'despite having a living quarters in the apostolic palace, nevertheless always insisted on living in the convent of Santa Sabina' during his stay in Rome from 1516 onwards.[89] That this famous name, associated nowadays with the papal refutation of Luther's theses, the *In presumptuosas Martini Luther conclusiones de potestate pape dialogus* of 1518, was linked to Sauli should not be a surprise. He was recognised as a good man, of great authority, and would have been an excellent choice as Sauli's confessor.[90] He too was a member of the reformed Dominican Lombard congregation and a friar with an illustrious career behind him, some of which was spent in Genoa: from 1507 to 1508 he had been prior of Santa Maria di Castello where he had preached the Lenten sermons in 1507, a period during which Sauli visited the city.[91] In late 1515 he was appointed *magister sacri palatii* by Leo, a role described by Michael Tavuzzi as 'the pope's personal theological counsellor'.[92] Santa Sabina is unlikely to have been a suitable residence for a man of recognised piety if the convent were wallowing in spiritual decay; indeed, during the period of Prierias's stay (1516–21), the convent enjoyed 'a well-ordered and reasonably prosperous existence'.[93]

Thus Sauli restored the cathedral at Gerace and benefited the benefice in other ways; he had building and decorative work done in the cloister of

---

[86] G. Fragnito, 'Carvajal, Bernardino Lopez de', *DBI* xxi (1978), 28–34 at p. 33; M. Hollingsworth, *Patronage in Renaissance Italy from 1400 to the early sixteenth century*, London 1994, 294; Petrucci, 'Carafa', 595.

[87] M. Tavuzzi, *Prierias: the life and works of Silvestro Mazzolino da Prierio, 1456–1527*, London 1997, 3, 79.

[88] Rodocanachi, *Una cronaca*, 14; Tavuzzi, *Prierias*, 73.

[89] Vat. Lat. 9451, fo. 107v.

[90] ASV, Archivum Arcis, Armadio I–XVIII, 5042, fo. 10v.

[91] Tavuzzi, *Prierias*, 6, 16, 47.

[92] Ibid. 76.

[93] Vat. Lat. 9451, fo. 107v; Tavuzzi, *Prierias*, 79.

Santa Sabina; tried to ensure that his lessees ran San Simpliciano to benefit his own interests and those of the brothers; and intervened when necessary at San Siro. This is a far cry from the general view that in this period richer benefices 'were viewed almost entirely either as pieces of property or as sources of income to be milked by the upper echelons of the clergy. No spiritual exertion was required'.[94] Comparison with other cardinals is difficult for several reasons: the scarcity of studies of how they functioned in their benefices, the differences between the benefices in question and the near impossibility of establishing the condition they were in when the holder took possession. However, it could well be that Sauli was not an exception and that further research into the administration by cardinals of their benefices may throw up some surprising conclusions. Overall it is probably fair to say that the picture of Sauli and his benefices is a healthy one for the period: in the prime of his life, when there can have been no thought of *pro remedio animae suae*, he was a far from inactive churchman, one, indeed, who looked after his own interests, yet who also protected the interests of his flock.[95] His attitude is perhaps summed up by a document of 3 September 1515 when he appoints Lorenzo de Gallis de Pontremulo as his proctor to San Nicolò di Casole and SS Angeli degli Greci in the diocese of Otranto. De Gallis was called to 'visit and reform in his name' and not simply to lease the fruits of the benefice.[96] In the early sixteenth century, even before Luther, reform was in the air: a cardinal must have had to take a stance on it. Where did Cardinal Sauli stand?

---

[94] Lowe, *Church and politics*, 186.
[95] For the patronage of Cardinal Ascanio Maria Sforza (1484–1505) see M. Pellegrini, *Ascanio Maria Sforza: la parabola politica di un cardinale-principe del rinascimento*, Rome 2002, ii. 630–3.
[96] 'ad visitandam et riformandam nomine suo': Archivio Urbano, sezione 66, protocollo 14, fo. 167r.

3

The Sauli and Early Cinquecento *Reform*

The death of Cardinal Sauli in 1518 precluded any possible sympathy on his part for Lutheran tendencies; discussion of his interest, if any, in reform must thus centre on a school of thought which had developed earlier and is now known as Catholic Reform. It aimed to reform the Church from within whilst maintaining the Church's teachings and authority. This reforming trend, if such it can be called, was spurred on by the advent of Protestantism and culminated in the Council of Trent (1543–63).[1]

There can be little doubt that there were many aspects of ecclesiastical life which required renewal: corruption, pluralism, absenteeism, nepotism and simony were rife; priests were often barely literate and rarely models of proper ecclesiastical behaviour, and monastic houses had fallen into spiritual and physical decay. The reform of some monastic orders such as the Benedictines and Dominicans had enjoyed limited success, but other measures, whether attempts at local reform by individual prelates, calls for change from popular preachers, the writings of scholars such as Erasmus or even the reform bulls of the Fifth Lateran Council as a whole achieved little. But that is not to denigrate their aims: to encourage internal reform, for the most part by promoting greater religious vigour and an increased sense of morality and charity. This was supported seemingly not only by Sauli, but also by his brother Stefano and his cousin Filippo through their support for the *Compagnia del divino amore* and their later relations with a network of key reformers.

Cardinal Sauli and reform

Although John Symonds believed that 'we have the right to count Cardinals Sauli and Fregoso among thinkers of the same class', it is not clear why he chose to group these two cardinals together, not least because Fregoso was consciously operating as a reformer at a later date and thus within a different context, but also because there is a clear and documented case to be made for Fregoso, whereas, with the exception of one specific case study, the same cannot be said of Sauli.[2]

---

[1] Olin, *Catholic Reformation*, p. xi; M. Mullett, *The Catholic Reformation*, London 1999, 1–2; C. F. Black, *Italian confraternities in the sixteenth century*, Cambridge 1989, 5; cf. R. de Maio, *Riforme e miti nella Chiesa del cinquecento*, Naples 1973, 14–15.

[2] J. A. Symonds, *Renaissance in Italy: the Catholic reaction*, London 1920, i. 59. Federico

Sauli – a pluralist and absentee bishop – manifested a certain degree of religious concern towards his benefices, but this should not seem out of place, even in a cardinal in Medicean Rome: in Genoa the Sauli were clearly a devout and religious family. The cardinal's father, Pasquale Sauli *quondam* Bendinelli, was recognised by his fellow Genoese as an upstanding individual. In 1483–4 he was involved in the foundation and endowment of the *monte di pietà* in Genoa in order to expiate the illicit gains his late father had made through financial speculation.[3] In 1491 he was a member of the *ufficio delle virtù*, a body which oversaw the moral welfare of the city and whose members led good lives, setting an example to other Genoese.[4] For three years, beginning in 1491, Pasquale was also a member of the *ufficio della misericordia*, helping the needy in their homes.[5] Indeed, his will of 21 June 1493 confirms his pious inclinations, containing an unusually large number of bequests to churches and convents; a genuine sense of compassion towards the poor permeates the document.[6]

Furthermore, three of Cardinal Sauli's uncles were patrons of churches renowned within Genoa for their piety and devotion. Vincenzo Sauli was the patron of the main altar of the Benedictine-Cassinese abbey of San Girolamo della Cervara and two other uncles showed a strong attachment to a symbol of religious reform within Genoa, namely the church of Santa Maria di Castello, a part of the reformed Dominican Lombard congregation since 1442. In 1523 Luchinetta Giustiniani Longhi, the wife of the late Pietro Sauli, endowed the chapel of St Mary Magdalen, which had been built according to her late husband's wishes with the generous bequest of sixteen *luoghi* in the *Casa di San Giorgio*. Other chapels in the church typically benefited from sums ranging from as little as three to between six or seven *luoghi*.[7]

In his first will, made in 1517, Antonio Sauli, the father of Filippo Sauli, asked to be buried in the church in the friars' own monument and in their habit, leaving the friars the sum of five hundred *lire*. He left the same sum to the recently reformed Benedictine convent of Santa Caterina di Genova.[8] In his second will, of 26 May 1522, his burial place had reverted to his father's chapel in San Domenico, but both San Domenico and Santa Maria

Fregoso (1480–1541) was bishop of Salerno, Gubbio and Urbino and later made cardinal: G. Brunelli, 'Fregoso, Federico', *DBI* l (1998), 396–9.

3   Hyde, 'Early *cinquecento*', i. 158–9, 174; G. Giacchero, 'Frate Angelo da Chivasso padre della casana genovese', in *Storia dei genovesi*, iii (1988), 179–96 at p.188.

4   L. Belgrano, *Vita privata dei genovesi*, Genoa 1880, 436.

5   ASG, MS 10, fo. 178r.

6   Notai Antichi, 950; Hyde, 'Early *cinquecento*', i. 176.

7   Archivio Parrocchiale di Santa Maria di Castello, Genoa, 'Colonne di San Giorgio: S Maria di Castello', fo. 119r. For the other legacies see R. A. Vigna, *Illustrazione storica, artistica ed epigrafica dell'antichissima chiesa di Santa Maria di Castello in Genova*, Genoa 1864, 211–12.

8   Notai Antichi, 1285, no. 520, 22 Mar. 1517.

di Castello were to receive five *luoghi* in the *Casa*. Both wills contained generous bequests benefiting the needy.[9] Concern for those less fortunate was seemingly shared by many of the Sauli: Antonio, like Cardinal Sauli, was one of the family members who endowed the Oratorio di SS Sebastiano e Fabiano in 1515. A clause was included in the endowment that should the celebration of a daily mass prove in time to be no longer feasible then the income from the *luoghi* was to be used in charitable works to benefit the poor.[10]

This all echoes the ethos of a movement with which the Sauli were linked, and which is perhaps one of the most outstanding examples of the values of Catholic Reform in the early *cinquecento*, the *Compagnia del divino amore*, the first branch of which was founded in Genoa on 26 December 1497 by Ettore Vernazza (d. 1524). Dominated by the influence of Vernazza's 'spiritual mother' Santa Caterina Fieschi-Adorno (1450–1510), with emphasis on helping the sick and poor, this was predominantly a lay association with a maximum of forty members whose activities and membership were secret but centred on religious vigour through prayer, confession, the taking of communion and charity. The poor and sick were to be cared for 'to root and plant charity in their hearts'.[11] In Genoa this concept of charity manifested itself through, amongst other good works, the foundation of the *Ospedale degli incurabili* in 1500.

In 1511 Vernazza went to Rome to ask for papal intervention in his attempts to take over the convent of San Colombano, near the *incurabili*.[12] This trip was to prove of vital importance for Vernazza's involvement in charitable works in the Holy City: struck by the number of sick to be seen on the streets he founded a Roman branch of the *Compagnia del divino amore*. If Vernazza had not previously known Cardinal Sauli, then he must have had contact with him in Rome during this time: the Genoese cardinals would have been the reference point for all visiting Genoese with important business with the Curia, but, given the surviving evidence it seems unlikely that Sauli was a member of the Roman *Divino amore*. However, by 1515 Vernazza had reformed the *Ospedale di San Giacomo in Augusta* in Rome which then became the *Arcispedale di San Giacomo degli incurabili* in the *motu proprio* of 19 July 1515.[13] This venture received significant support from the Curia,

---

9 Ibid.; 1288, no. 116.

10 ASG, Archivio del Banco di San Giorgio, Colonne San Lorenzo 1516, 610, fo. 476v.

11 D. Solfaroli Camillocci, *I devoti della carità: le Confraternite del Divino Amore nell'Italia del primo cinquecento*, Naples 2002, 12; A. Bianconi, *L'opera delle Compagnie del 'Divino Amore' nella Riforma Cattolica*, Città di Castello 1914, 26; Black, *Italian confraternities*, 6–7; P. Paschini, *La beneficenza in Italia e le 'Compagnie del Divino Amore' nei primi decenni del cinquecento: note storiche*, Rome 1925, 16.

12 C. da Langasco, *Gli ospedali degli incurabili*, Genoa 1938, 79; Notai Antichi, 1161, no. 273, 22 Aug. 1511.

13 Opinions differ as to the date of the foundation of the Roman *compagnia* but it is likely

Cardinal Sauli's involvement being noted in a letter written by Battistina Vernazza, Ettore's daughter, in 1581. She describes her father's efforts to 'build an *Ospedale degli incurabili*: and Cardinal Sauli was in favour of this and told him, "Whenever you have no money, come to me"'.[14]

A concrete patronal link between Sauli and Vernazza does exist: it is known that he gave the *ospedale* ten and then forty ducats as alms on 7 April and 10 December 1516.[15] Further details of his patronage, if any, are not forthcoming due to the loss of the registers of the *ospedale* for much of the years 1516–18 and of the Sauli bank books for 1517–18; the sums Sauli gave in 1516 do not, at first glance, reflect the generosity implicit in Battistina's words. However, the surviving documents, which detail the funding of the *ospedale* during Sauli's lifetime, paint a clearer picture. The most generous patron was the pope who, in 1515, gave twenty-five ducats per month whilst the other cardinals who supported the venture (including the Ligurian cardinals Riario, Vigerio and Fieschi) each gave less than Sauli in the following year.[16] Indeed, if donations for 1516 remained at the same level as those for 1515 then Sauli would have been the *ospedale*'s second most important patron: only Leo showed greater generosity. Da Langasco described Cardinal Sauli as the 'main benefactor of the early stages' of the *ospedale,* but since that prize clearly lies with Leo X it is perhaps fairer to say that Sauli was a generous supporter of Vernazza, a support continued by his family, albeit in a much reduced form, after his death: Agostino Sauli gave two ducats as alms for Christmas in 1519.[17]

Cardinal Sauli was not the only member of his family to lend his patronage to Vernazza. By late February 1515 Vernazza had returned to Rome where he then lived in the house of the cardinal's brother, Sebastiano.[18] There he returned to his original occupation, that of notary, and drew up some (unrelated) documents for Sebastiano and the Sauli. Those which survive date from 16 August 1516 and continue until 22 May 1517; it can surely be no coincidence that the last document is dated just three days after the

to have slightly predated the reform of the Roman *ospedale* of 1515: Solfaroli Camillocci, *I devoti*, 75–7 at p. 76 for the problematic list of members. See also Langasco, *Gli ospedali*, 95, 110.

[14] The original is lost, but it was published in B. Vernazza, *Opere spirituali*, Verona 1602, iv. 1–11, and is also reproduced in Bianconi, *L'opera*, 63–71. See Langasco, *Gli ospedali*, 98.

[15] Archivio Sauli, no. 730, fos 40r, 227r. The ten ducats that Solfaroli Camillocci believes that Sauli gave upon the foundation of the hospital were in fact given by 'cardinal Adriano' and although Sauli briefly held the titular church of Sant'Adriano, this name in contemporary documents always refers to Cardinal Adriano Castellesi and not to Sauli: ASR, Ospedale di San Giacomo degli Incurabili, 1145, fo. 5v; cf. Solfaroli Camillocci, *I devoti*, 83.

[16] Ospedale di San Giacomo, 1145, fos 3v, 7v–8r.

[17] Da Langasco, *Gli ospedali*, 122; Ospedale di San Giacomo, 1146, fo. 15v.

[18] For the date see Solfaroli Camillocci, *I devoti*, 79.

arrest of the cardinal.[19] Battistina records that when the cardinal was lying close to death, i.e. in February/March 1518, his mother, Mariola Giustiniani, came to Rome and summoned Vernazza from Naples to be at her son's bedside. Vernazza declined, ostensibly pleading problems with the *incurabili* in Naples.[20] This is, however, debatable. Vernazza was in Rome on 10 and 30 December 1517 and a final document in Vernazza's Genoese notarial *filza*, dated 3 February 1518 and drawn up in Cardinal Sauli's Roman residence of that time, is obviously for the most part in another hand, but the (cancelled) brief synopsis of the document's contents, the statement of where it was drawn up and the identity of the witnesses is in Vernazza's hand. Did he in fact return to Rome to say goodbye to his benefactor to whom he felt 'great obligation' or did he, given that the Neapolitan *incurabili* did not even exist at this time, indeed never leave his side?[21]

There was also Sauli support for the *Compagnia* in Genoa. Late in his life, Antonio Sauli agreed to back one of Vernazza's long-treasured ventures. Battistina wrote that her father had asked Antonio, 'a man of great importance', to provide tutors in various trades to prevent, to use a modern term, juvenile delinquency in the city. Antonio accepted, but died in 1523 before further action could be taken.[22]

There are thus clear links between the Sauli and the *Compagnia* during the cardinal's own lifetime. He was a generous patron of the *ospedale* and undoubtedly Sebastiano Sauli would not have housed Vernazza in Rome without the cardinal's consent. This implies a certain degree of sympathy on Sauli's part with Vernazza's aims and although his personal patronage came to an end with his death, other members of his family were to continue to lend financial support to the *divino amore*.

Gregorio Cortese and the Sauli

Vernazza was not the only reformer of this and later periods known to the Sauli family. Both Filippo and Stefano Sauli were close to Gregorio Cortese (1480/3–1548), a scholar and important monastic reformer who was later to become a key player in pre-Tridentine Catholic reform. Cortese was a Benedictine and the tutor of his early years was the same Severo Varini who is reported to have later held discussions on theology with Cardinal Sauli. He studied law at Bologna and Padua and, after a brief career in the household

19 Notai Antichi, 1522bis, nos 125–8.
20 Bianconi, *L'opera*, 66.
21 Archivio Sauli, no. 731, fo. 67r; no. 707 unfoliated; Da Langasco, *Gli ospedali*, 92; Notai Antichi, 1522 bis, no. 135; Bianconi, *L'opera*, 65–6. For the later foundation of the Naples hospital see Solfaroli Camillocci, *I devoti*, 82, 83.
22 Bianconi, *L'opera*, 69.

of Cardinal Giovanni de'Medici and at the Curia, joined Santa Giustina di Padova, part of the reforming Benedictine-Cassinese congregation.[23]

In July 1516 he was transferred, with other brothers, from the monastery of San Benedetto Polirone to that of St Honorat on the island of Lérins, by then also part of the Benedictine-Cassinese congregation. The aim was to reform St Honorat (which had been held in commenda for the last fifty years and was in a state of spiritual ruin) through humanist studies.[24] It quickly gained a reputation as a centre for academic pursuits, fulfilling Cortese's ambition to make it 'a thriving study centre and a meeting place for scholars in search of an oasis of tranquillity'.[25] In 1518 or 1519 the Belgian humanist Christophe de Longueil (c.1488–1522) visited St Honorat and was followed by Stefano Sauli, initially incognito. This was the first, but not the last, indication of an interest in 'Christian humanism' on Stefano's part. So impressed was he that he planned to stay for three years but was dissuaded by de Longueil and returned to Padua, whence he sent Cortese Greek texts published in Venice; the Sauli in Rome also sent texts.[26] In autumn 1519 Cortese fell ill and went to Genoa where he was cared for by the Sauli, remaining there for the winter of 1519 and much of 1520. He forged or renewed friendships with, amongst others, Filippo Sauli and Benedetto Tagliacarne (known as Teocreno) (1480–1536) an early humanist member of Cardinal Sauli's circle and subsequently an intimate of Ottaviano and Federico Fregoso and then tutor to the children of Francis I. He also came into contact with the Compagnia del divino amore.[27] In 1522, when once again in the city, Cortese

[23] Gregorii Cortesii monachi Casinatis SRE cardinalis omnia quae huc usque colligi potuerunt, sive ab eo scripta, sive ad illum spectantia, Pavia 1774, i. 13; G. Fragnito, 'Cortese, Gregorio', DBI xxix (1983), 733–40 at p. 733, and 'Il cardinale Gregorio Cortese (1483?–1548) nella crisi religiosa del cinquecento', Benedictina (1983), 129–71 at pp. 140, 145.

[24] F. C. Cesareo, Humanism and Catholic Reform: the life and work of Gregorio Cortese (1483–1548), New York 1990, 70–1.

[25] Fragnito, 'Il cardinale', 151.

[26] The only scholar to place this visit in January of 1519 is T. Simar in his Christophe de Longueil, humaniste, 1488–1522, Louvain 1911, 59, See Fragnito, 'Il cardinale', 152; A. Cataldi Palau 'Catalogo dei manoscritti greci della Biblioteca Franzoniana (Genova) (Urbani 2–20)', Bollettino dei classici: Accademia dei Lincei, supplement viii (1990), 1–120 at p. 21. For the correspondence between Sauli and Cortese see Gregorii Cortesii, i. 20–1; ii, nos 24, 25, 28–30, 35, 38–9, 46, 49, 50, 90 at pp. 54–8, 61–6, 73–4, 82, 85–7, 141 respectively, especially nos 29–30.

[27] Fragnito, 'Il cardinale', 153; Gregorii Cortesii, ii, no. 38 at pp. 73–4; Cam. Ap., Resignationes 10, fos 141r, 142v. For Tagliacarne see P. Jourda, 'Un Umaniste italien en France: Theocrenus (1480–1536)', Revue du seizième siècle xvi (1929), 40–57, and for his friendship with Cortese and Sauli see Gregorii Cortesii, i. 20; ii, letters nos 13, 21–4, 32, 45, 92 at pp. 36–8, 50–6, 67, 80–1 respectively. See also P. Bembo to F. Fregoso, 20 July 1522; Bembo to G. M. Giberti, 6 Oct. 1522; and Bembo to F. Fregoso, 14 Oct. 1522, in Lettere: Pietro Bembo, ed. E. Travi, Bologna 1987–93, ii, nos 428, 430, 431 at pp. 170–2, 173–5.

also met the cardinal's cousin and former *famigliare*, Agostino Giustiniani and his friend Battista Fieschi, a man closely linked to the *divino amore*.[28]

Thus at Genoa Cortese found himself amongst men, some of whom had previously been associated with Cardinal Sauli, who supported the reforms of the Benedictine-Cassinese congregation and the spirituality of the *divino amore*, and like Cortese (the author in 1522 of the *Tractatus adversus negantem Petrum apostolum Romae fuisse* in defence of the pope) looked to reform within the Church.[29] In July 1521 he was transferred again, to Santa Giustina di Padova, where he renewed his contacts with Christophe de Longueil and met Reginald Pole.[30] The rest of his career was illustrious: he was called upon by Paul III to join the *Consilium de emendanda ecclesia* which was investigating the possibilities of reform and became a cardinal in 1542.[31]

And what of the association between the Sauli and Cortese? It seems to have been a meeting of minds: the Sauli were already inclined towards the new spirituality through their contacts with Vernazza, and were developing a devotion to humanism, while Cortese was already established as a leading figure in monastic reform.

Stefano Sauli: piety and learning

Although the efficacy of Stefano's *commenda* of San Simpliciano in Milan may perhaps be questioned, there can be little doubt of his pious inclinations and interest in reform. Evidence is to be found in his own literary output, his patronage of reform-inclined humanists and his financial endowments benefiting the poor. Born in about 1492, by 1511 he was already part of his brother's *famiglia*, receiving the office of *abbreviator de parco minori* on Bendinello's resignation of 25 March.[32] On 28 July 1513 he took clerical orders in Genoa and on 3 October was made a *protonotario apostolico*.[33] On that same day Cardinal Sauli resigned the *commenda* of San Simpliciano to him, which he retained until the abbey joined the Benedictine-Cassinese congregation in 1517. His only other known benefice during his brother's lifetime was his appointment to the *commenda* of the abbey of San Silvestro in the diocese of Benevento on 16 January of that year.[34]

Stefano was a student at Bologna from at least 1513, but his studies there had probably ended by 1516 when he is regularly recorded in Rome until

---

[28] Fragnito, 'Cortese', 734; Giustiniani, *Castigatissimi annali*, c. 224v.
[29] Fragnito, 'Il cardinale', 154 n. 86; Cesareo, *Humanism and Catholic Reform*, 83.
[30] Cesareo, *Humanism and Catholic Reform*, 78.
[31] Fragnito, 'Cortese' 734–9.
[32] See Reg. Vat. 997, fo. 243r and his will in Notai Antichi, 2049, 25 Aug. 1548; Reg. Vat. 990, fos 81, 172v; Cam. Ap., Resignationes, 13, fo. 50v.
[33] Notai Antichi, 1162, no. 139; Reg. Vat. 997, fos 243r–244r.
[34] Reg. Vat. 1070, fos 311v–313r.

late 1517.[35] He then resumed his studies, but at Padua, returning to Genoa in May 1521 when Giovanni Sauli, his elder brother, lay dying.[36] The documents are far from complete, but, with the exception of brief visits to Rome, it appears that Stefano spent the remaining forty-nine years of his life in Genoa, until his death in 1570. He featured briefly in Genoese political life, serving as an *anziano* and a *consigliere di San Giorgio* in 1526 and as a member of the *ufficio monialium* in 1528.[37] Little of great note is known to have occurred: after the death of Sebastiano Sauli in May 1536 he was appointed joint guardian to those of Sebastiano's children who were still minors. In 1546 he was appointed (or rather purchased the title of) a *cavaliere del giglio* by Paul III.[38] A friend of the architect Galeazzo Alessi, he later strove to consolidate the family image through taking a lively interest in the building of Santa Maria di Carignano, adding to the original *luoghi* and providing for the construction of a bridge between Carignano and the town.[39]

Stefano's time in Genoa was dedicated to running the family business and pursuing his deep love of learning; his choice of intellectual companions is of some interest.[40] At some point (probably at Padua, if not earlier) Stefano had met and become the patron of the poet Marcantonio Flaminio (1498–1550), a man who was to remain important to Stefano throughout much of his life. Stefano's circle in Padua eventually included Flaminio, de Longueil and Lazzaro Buonamico (1477/8–1552), a friend of Filippo Sauli, who acted as their tutor in Latin and Greek literature until early 1521.[41]

---

[35] Reg. Vat. 1000, fo. 248v, 3 Oct. 1513; G. M. Cataneo, *Genua*, Rome 1514, p. ii, dedication of 1 Feb. 1514 to Stefano Sauli at Bologna; Archivio Sauli, no. 730, fos 27r, 40r, 209r; no. 731, fos 46r, 59r; BAV, MS Ferrajoli, 424, fos 161r–162r; Cam. Ap., Div. Cam. 67, fos 121v–122r.

[36] Notai Antichi, 1287, no. 583, 21 May 1521; C. Maddison, *Marcantonio Flaminio: poet, humanist and reformer*, London 1965, 28.

[37] Biblioteca Civica Berio, sezione conservazione, raccolta locale, MS m. r. XV. 3.1 (1–5), v, fo. 197r; MS. 10, fo. 228.

[38] See Collegio dei Notai Capitolini 92, fos 310r–312v, 16 Dec. 1536, and undated document 116, fo. 61r–v; Notai Antichi, 2049, 11 Aug. 1548, 2 Mar. 1561.

[39] Notai Antichi, 2049, 31 Jan. 1567.

[40] Archivio Sauli, no. 712, fo. 15v; nos 719–23 passim; no. 1568, fos 9v, 16r; Notai del Tribunale, AC 7151, fo. 171r–v; Bologna, 'L'archivio della famiglia Sauli', 15–16; Notai Antichi, 1830, 21 Aug. 1529.

[41] C. de Longueil to Bembo, n.d., and to L. Massimo, n.d., in *Christophorii Longolii orationes duae pro defensione sua in crimen lesae maiestatis, longe ex actiori quam ante iudicio perscriptae, ac nunc primum ex ipsius authoris sententia in lucem editae*, Florence 1524, cc. 85r–v, cc. 92r–94r; G. Tiraboschi, *Storia della letteratura italiana di Girolamo Tiraboschi*, Milan 1833, iii. 381. For Buonamico's earlier career see also G. Marangoni, 'Lazzaro Buonamico e lo studio paduano nella prima metà del cinquecento', *Nuovo Archivio Veneto* n.s. i (1901), 118–51, 301–18 at pp. 311–12, and R. Avesani, 'Buonamico, Lazzaro', *DBI* xi (1969), 533–40 at p. 534. The Filippo Sauli manuscripts, annotated by Buonamico, are examined in A. Cataldi Palau, 'Un gruppo di manoscritti greci del primo quarto del XVI secolo appartenenti alla collezione di Filippo Sauli', *Codices manuscripti* xii (1986), 93–124, especially pp. 94, 104, and 'Catalogo', 23.

All the members of Stefano's household at Padua were ardent Cicero-nians.[42] Perhaps most significantly, Ciceronianism drew them to two other humanists who were to be important in later attempts at religious reform within the Church in the *cinquecento*: Pietro Bembo and Reginald Pole (1500–58), both friends of de Longueil.[43] Bembo's friendship with Stefano continued, if in a somewhat desultory fashion, throughout the latter's life whilst Buonamico was later one of Pole's tutors and it seems likely, although unproven, that both Flaminio and Stefano met Pole during their time at Padua.[44] At this time Pole's interests were apparently far removed from religion and religious reform: he planned to publish a complete edition of Cicero.[45] Yet he was to play an important part in the later lives of members of the group: Buonamico accompanied him to Rome in 1525 and was in Pole's household during the 1530s; de Longueil became part of Pole's household after the summer of 1521 and died in his house at Padua on 11 September 1522, leading Pole to write a biography of him to preface the 1524 edition of his letters; Flaminio joined Pole's household at Viterbo in 1541 and died in Pole's house in Rome on 17 February 1550; and Stefano and Pole were in contact in the 1550s.[46]

On the return of Stefano and Flaminio to Genoa in May 1521 de Longueil remained in Padua and became close to Pole.[47] But Stefano's humanist friend-ships were not limited to the Paduan circle. Flaminio and Stefano spent the summer of 1521 in quiet study at a villa, probably that at Carignano, just outside the city of Genoa, with Sebastiano Delio (c.1488–1544), a learned, albeit mysterious, Greek scholar, and Giulio Camillo (Delminio) (c.1480–1544).[48] The group was far from inactive: Flaminio wrote eleven *lusus pasto-rales* and in the winter of 1522 was ill from overwork.[49] Giulio Camillo was a scholar of wide-ranging interests who had by this period formulated the

[42] W. Schenck, *Reginald Pole: cardinal of England*, London 1950, 11; M.-M. De La Garand-erie, 'Christophe de Longueil', and T. B. Deutscher, 'Lazzaro Bonamico', in T. Bietenholtz (ed.), *Contemporaries of Erasmus: a biographical register of the Renaissance and Reformation*, Toronto 1985–7, ii. 342–5 at p. 343, and i. 166.

[43] Bembo to de Longueil, 29 May, 20 Aug. 1520, 17 Mar. 1521, *Lettere: Bembo*, ii, nos 399, 403, 415 at pp. 144–5, 147–50, 158–60; Simar, *Christophe de Longueil*, 75, 80.

[44] Bembo to S. Sauli, 31 Nov. 1543, *Lettere: Bembo*, iv, no. 2393 at p. 466. M. Haile, *Life of Reginald Pole*, 2nd edn, London 1911, 21, gives Pole's arrival as 1519. T. F. Mayer, *Reginald Pole prince and prophet*, Cambridge 2000, 48 believes that Pole may have visited Padua in 1519 but was certainly there in 1521. See A. Pastore, 'Flaminio, Marcantonio', *DBI* xlviii (1997), 282–8 at p. 282.

[45] Haile, *Life*, 25.

[46] Schenck, *Reginald Pole*, 34; Haile, *Life*, 21, 27; A. Pastore, *Marcantonio Flaminio: fortune e sfortune di un chierico nell'Italia del cinquecento*, Milan 1981, 38, 117.

[47] Simar, *Christophe de Longueil*, 86.

[48] L. Gualdo Rosa, 'Delio, Sebastiano', *DBI* xxxvi (1988), 650.

[49] Maddison, *Marcantonio Flaminio*, 29, 35.

project of a small-scale wooden theatre with images: what Frances Yates describes as a 'memory theatre'.[50] According to Stefano's contemporary, Sebastiano da Fausto da Longiano (c.1502–c.1560), Sauli contributed to the project during Camillo's stay in Genoa and beyond, and indeed they remained friends.[51] The group disbanded when Adrian VI was elected pope, if not before: Stefano and Flaminio travelled to Rome in January 1522 to try to gain a review of the judgement on Cardinal Sauli for his role in the plot against Leo X.

Equally important were friendships with supporters of the reform ethos of the early decades of the cinquecento. Stefano knew Tagliacarne and was a close friend of Gregorio Cortese. In July 1521 when Cortese was transferred to S. Giustina di Padova he in turn became friends with Reginald Pole: another friendship which linked the two men.[52] He also maintained the family's good relations with Vernazza: de Longueil, in his letters to Stefano, often sent his best wishes to, amongst others, 'our Hector', and as Arturo Bianconi notes, 'Now, who else could this Hector be, if not Vernazza?'[53]

There is, however, no concrete documentary evidence to link Stefano to the Compagnia del divino amore and the spirituality believed to be prevalent in Genoa in this period. However, that Vernazza and Stefano were on friendly terms, Stefano's relationship with Cortese and the fact that Cardinal Sauli and his cousin Filippo lent their support to the compagnia, encourage the belief that, at the very least, Stefano did not disapprove of reformist tendencies. Furthermore, Flaminio, who had remained with Stefano until 1524 when he joined the household of the influential and religious Gian Matteo Giberti (1495–1543), a friend of Filippo Sauli, is listed as a member of the divino amore in Rome in that year.[54] It is thus probable that Flaminio came into contact with the reforming ethos of Genoa in this period, and it seems improbable that Giberti would have taken him into his household if he felt that Flaminio was lacking in religious conviction, given the religious orthodoxy he demanded of his famigliari.[55] Flaminio remained with Giberti, for the most part in his bishopric of Verona, for much of the following fourteen years. In 1538 he then went to Naples and became close to the ideas of Juan de Valdes, before eventually joining Pole at Viterbo in 1541.[56] In addition to his poetry he wrote religious works, including a contribution to the Beneficio di Cristo and these, with many of his letters, bear witness to a deep religious feeling. A letter from Flaminio to Ulisse Bassiano of May 1549

---

[50] F. A. Yates, The art of memory, 2nd edn, London 1992, 51, 136–7, 139.
[51] S. Fausto da Longiano, Orationi di M.T. Cicerone di latine fatte italiane, Venice 1556, ii, pp. iiir–v; G. Stabile, 'Camillo, Giulio', DBI xvii (1974), 218–30 at p. 220.
[52] Jourda, 'Umaniste italien', 40; Musso, La cultura genovese, 16; Gregorii Cortesii, ii, nos 13, 21, 22, 24 at pp. 36–8, 50–2, 54–6; Cesareo, Humanism and Catholic Reform, 78.
[53] Bianconi, L'opera, 35–6.
[54] Pastore, Flaminio, 45.
[55] Idem, 'Flaminio', 284.
[56] Ibid. 282–4.

states that 'I kiss the hand of the reverend Signor Stephano' and there is also testimony of Stefano's depth of feeling towards Flaminio (and indeed Giulio Camillo) when, worried that he had not heard from either of them, he wrote in mid-1528 to Nicolò Giustiniani that if Fortune 'had deprived me of their company, which fully compensated all the other injuries done to me, she would have plunged me into deepest misery'.[57] It seems unlikely that Stefano would have remained in contact with Flaminio throughout his life if he had not shared some of these reforming sentiments. Yet it is only in a document drawn up in the last decade of Stefano's life that there is concrete evidence of Stefano's support for this religious ethos: he stipulated that the *Ospedale degli incurabili* was to receive the generous sum of 1,500 *scudi*.[58]

In later years Stefano was also friendly with Benedetto Ramberto (1503–45), librarian of St Mark's, Venice, and, most important, the man who had earlier befriended de Longueil, Reginald Pole. Both were now promoters of Catholic Reform and Pole had been made a cardinal in 1536.[59] In 1553 Stefano 'spent a great part of the day with that remarkable man, Cardinal Pole, in most serious and holy conversation' and in the same year Stefano completed a religious work entitled *De homine christiano* (now lost) which Pole praised highly.[60]

There is thus some evidence to support the hypothesis that Stefano shared the reforming instincts of 'Christian humanism'. His wills also confirm his piety: he was to be buried without ostentatious display, the money saved from the burial was to be given to the poor, while his body was to be buried in the ground 'at the tabernacle of the *corpus Domini*' with a white marble tombstone on which was to read the words 'the bones of Stefano Sauli which await the Resurrection'.[61] In his will of 1563 the income of forty *luoghi* in the *Casa di San Giorgio* was to be given to good causes and in a document of 14 March 1567 500 Genoese *lire* were to be invested in a *monte di pietà* for loans to the poor at a fixed low annual interest rate.[62]

[57] Flaminio to U. Bassiano, May 1549, in *Marcantonio Flaminio: lettere*, ed. A. Pastore, Rome 1978, no. 60 at p.175; '[M]i harebe in extrema miseria condotto, privandomi di quella compagnia, co' la quale ogni altra injuria factami pienamente compensava': S. Sauli to N. Giustiniani, mid-1528, Archivio Sauli, no. 1568, fo. 68r.

[58] Notai Antichi, 2049, 2 Mar. 1561.

[59] S. Seidel Menchi, 'Passione civile e aneliti Erasmiani di riforma nel patriziato genovese del primo cinquecento: Ludovico Spinola', *Rinascimento* xviii (1978), 87–131 at p. 115; M. E. Cosenza, *Biographical and bibliographical dictionary of the Italian humanists and of the world of classical scholarship in Italy, 1300–1800*, Boston, MA 1962, iv. 2995.

[60] *Epistolarum Pauli Manutii libri XII uno nuper addito: eiusdem quae praefationes appellantur*, Venice 1590, 5, 14.

[61] 'Ossa Stephani Sauli expectantia resurectionem': Notai Antichi, 2049, 25 Aug. 1548; 2870, 22 Mar. 1563.

[62] Ibid; 2049, 25 Aug. 1548.

Filippo Sauli: a reforming bishop

The piety and scholarship which were part of Stefano's life until his death in 1570 are two themes which also run through the life of Filippo Sauli. The reports of contemporaries, the documentary evidence of the running of his benefices and his own little known work, the *Opus noviter editum pro sacerdotibus animarum curarum habentibus* (Milan 1521) all demonstrate that he was an energetic, albeit now little-known, reformer of the episcopate and clergy. He was born in c. 1492 to Antonio Sauli and Geronima Salvago and his rise followed that of Bendinello: on 18 February 1507 he was called as *famigliare* and *continuus commensalis* to Julius II. On 14 June 1512 he was appointed bishop of Brugnato, a small diocese in the mountains of Liguria.[63]

If in this period bishops were generally 'strangers in their own diocese' or only visited in order to take possession of the benefice, this was not the case with Filippo.[64] As Umberto Foglietta noted 'this man was outstanding in that corrupt generation and was one who, along with a few others, was worthy of the dignity and name of bishop'.[65] There had been other good bishops: Leonardo Marchese had been an outstanding bishop of Albenga (1476–1513) and Pietro Barozzi, bishop of Belluno (1471–87) and Padua (1487–1507), was the model for Gaspare Contarini's *De officio viri boni ac probi episcopi* (written in 1517, but not published until 1571).[66] Yet Filippo was an (influential) Italian exception rather than the rule, a bishop whose predominant concern was the welfare of his bishopric and his clergy.

Filippo had still not officially taken possession of the bishopric of Brugnato when, in Genoa, on 2 July 1512, he appointed as proctor on a minor matter a man who was to become one of his mainstays, Pasqualino de Oppicinis.[67] On 11 August Filippo's oath of obedience was taken in Genoa and he appointed Jacobo Filippo de Levanto, described as his *famigliare*, to go to Brugnato and inform the canons, the chapter and clergy and the citizens and vassals of his appointment and to extract the necessary oaths of obedience.[68] He was already well-informed about the affairs of Brugnato: three days later,

---

[63] Despite the different dates of birth given by various authors, Filippo's tombstone in Santa Maria Assunta di Carignano records his premature death in 1528, 'qui vixit annos XXXV' and should be regarded as reliable. Arm. XXXIX, 25, fo. 158r; Vat. Lat. 5664, fos 136v–137r.

[64] A. Prosperi, 'La figura del vescovo fra quattrocento e cinquecento: persistenze, disagi e novità', in G. Chittolini and G. Miccoli (eds), *La Chiesa e il potere politico dal medioevo all'età contemporanea* (Storia d'Italia ix, 1986), 217–62 at p. 220.

[65] U. Folietae, *Clarorum ligurum elogia*, Rome 1574, 197.

[66] Hay, *The Church in Italy*, 100, and 'Renaissance cardinals', 40; G. Fragnito, 'Cultura umanistica e riforma religiosa: il "De officio viri boni ac probi episcopi" di Gaspare Contarini', *Studi Veneziani* xi (1969), 1–115 at pp. 3, 6; F. Gaeta, 'Barozzi, Pietro', *DBI* vi (1964), 510–12. For examples outside Italy see Mullett, *Catholic Reformation*, 19–21.

[67] Notai Antichi, 1162, no. 290.

[68] Ibid. nos 327–9.

on 14 August, he appointed Hieronimo de Vernatia to deal with any quarrels pertaining to the bishopric and on 16 September, wanting to provide a suitable *vicario* so that the affairs of the see did not suffer while he was in Rome, Filippo appointed Hieronimo as his *vicario generale*, a position he held until mid-1519.[69] Hieronimo was to officiate in Filippo's name, dealing with all disputes and conferring minor benefices. Special emphasis was given to de Vernatia's powers over the clergy: he was to ensure that all candidates for the priesthood were of good morals and literate – themes close to Filippo's heart – and had the authority to dismiss errant clerics.[70] Examination of the suitability of the clergy anticipated part of the bull *Supernae maiestatis praesidio* of the eleventh session of the Fifth Lateran Council (19 December 1516) which Filippo attended.[71] It is clear that, although Filippo did not reside in his bishopric, he took pains to ensure that it was in good hands.

Like Cardinal Sauli, Filippo leased the incomes of his bishopric. On 17 March 1513 de Vernatia formalised the leasing of its fruits, taxes and pensions, with three minor exceptions, to Pasqualino de Oppicinis. The agreement was for three years (and was obviously already in place as the term ran from 25 December 1512 until 25 December 1515) with a rental *per annum* of a quantity of grain and fifty-five Genoese *scuti*.[72] When the agreement was eventually renewed it had a different emphasis. The document drawn up in Genoa on 18 January 1518, with Filippo present, leased the incomes to Pasqualino de Oppicinis, Baptista *quondam* Jacobi de Cattaneis, and Baptista de Porta for three years. The price was the same as in the agreement of 1513 (this was unusual in itself considering the rental increases Cardinal Sauli demanded for the abbey of San Simpliciano and bishopric of Gerace) but, as Filippo wished, the payment method was varied to ease the burden on the lessees.[73] De Oppicinis and de Porta were both canons of the cathedral and, unusually, Filippo was determined that the rental should carry religious overtones: all three were obliged to supply oil for the lamp on the main altar of the cathedral at their own expense.[74]

Filippo was a far from uninterested bishop and often intervened personally in the affairs of Brugnato. In 1513 he visited the bishopric and, on finding such a state of neglect that, among other things, the divine office was not heard in the cathedral, he re-endowed the existing three canonries and founded and endowed three more with money from the income of the diocese, thus forming a chapter. The canonries were instituted on 6 October

---

[69] Ibid. no. 24. As far as can be ascertained Hieronimo was not a relation of Ettore Vernazza: his name derives from his place of birth: ibid. 1162, no. 81; 1165, no. 60, 6 Mar. 1517; 1166, no. 130, 21 May 1519.

[70] Ibid. 1162, no. 81.

[71] Mansi, *Sacrorum consiliorum*, xxxii. 945–6.

[72] Notai Antichi, 1162, no. 62.

[73] For the interim arrangements see ibid. 1164, no. 60. See also 1165, no. 15; 1162, no. 72.

[74] Ibid. 1162, no. 72.

1513, one of the canons being the ubiquitous Pasqualino.[75] The canons were to be resident in the cathedral and to celebrate at least two masses every weekday and three on Sundays and religious holidays. In turn they looked after the cathedral from this date.[76] Pastoral visits were not totally unknown in this period: Cardinal Sauli's predecessor at Albenga, Leonardo Marchese, had undertaken one, but Filippo was not satisfied with just one visit.[77] By 23 August 1518 he had already embarked on a second, accompanied by his chaplain Ippolito de' Merli, which ended on 10 October of that year. On the following day he opened a diocesan synod, with a penalty of twenty-five ducats to be paid if the priests of the various churches failed to attend.[78] Again, this was a rare, but not unknown, event: Pietro Barozzi had held a diocesan synod in 1488 and later published its findings and in 1497 and 1498 Cardinal Ximenes de Cisneros had held synods at Alcala and Talavera in Spain.[79] A third pastoral visit probably occurred in 1524. Filippo retained the see until the end of his life.[80]

Detailed reports of Filippo's visit of 1518 show that he paid close attention to the behaviour of the clergy 'recalling his orders of the previous visit, recommending that parish priests reside in the parish ... [and] the conservation of the Holy Eucharist'.[81] His recommendations to the clergy of each individual church were detailed and demanding: the correct priestly vestments were to be provided; the sanctity of church buildings was to be preserved; and the populace was to be reprimanded for not gathering to greet their bishop.[82] His visit ended with an inspection of the cathedral of Brugnato on 10 October 1518 where he stipulated that in order for mass to be celebrated in a decent manner, two suitably attired clerics were to be always present in the cathedral and the canon, Guglielmo Cattaneo, was to supervise their morals and education. Further instructions were given to the existing canons and Sauli also donated clerical vestments and lamps, candelabra and other liturgical objects to the cathedral.[83] The roof and floor of the cathedral were to be repaired and the necessary provisions were made. Further financial provision for the canonries, cathedral and diocese was made in his will of 1528 and Brugnato was also to receive his books on canon and civil law,

---

[75] P. Tomaini, *Attività pastorale di Filippo Sauli vescovo di Brugnato (1512–1528)*, Città di Castello 1964, 9, 71.

[76] Idem, *Brugnato città abbaziale e vescovile: documenti e notizie*, Città di Castello 1961, 268–9, and *Attività pastorale*, 71–3.

[77] A. Granero, *Albenga sacra*, Albenga 1997, 153.

[78] Tomaini, *Attività pastorale*, 10, 15, 33, 35–6; Archivio Sauli, no. 730, fo. 21r.

[79] Gaeta, 'Barozzi', 511; M. Bataillon, *Erasme et l'Espagne*, 2nd edn, Geneva 1991, i. 3.

[80] Tomaini, *Attività pastorale*, 10. The last known notarial act in which he deals with the bishopric is Notai Antichi, 1488, 26 Apr. 1528.

[81] Tomaini, *Attività pastorale*, 10.

[82] Ibid. 20, 22–3.

[83] Ibid. 71–3, 77.

those on church matters and his Latin printed books, together with his vestments, for the use of the canons and his successors.[84]

As a result of his activities at Brugnato, and of his cousin's support, Filippo received further preferment. In August 1514 he was awarded *in commenda* the *archipresbyteratus* of the church of Santo Stefano de Lavania, also in the diocese of Genoa, which carried an income of 100 ducats. In the same year the administration of the incomes was linked to the personal residence of their newly appointed holder, a priest named Theramo de Alfanetis, to the saying of the mass and to the well-being of the souls of his parishioners.[85] Filippo received further benefices in the following years: in August 1515 he was granted a canonry and prebend in the cathedral of Ventimiglia and a chaplaincy at the altar of St Sebastian in the same church.[86] In May 1516 he was awarded benefices in Otranto.[87] He divided his time between Rome, Bologna and Genoa. He was in Rome in 1512 and 1515 and in 1516–17 was present at the Fifth Lateran Council, attending sessions 10–12, and was then often at his cousin's side following the cardinal's disgrace.[88] It seems likely that he lodged in his cousin's palace when in Rome; indeed Cardinal Sauli and his cousin seemed to be close: Filippo followed the cardinal to Genoa for his visit of early 1516 and Bendinello resigned some benefices in Spain in Filippo's favour in 1513.[89] Filipppo's reputation was such that on the death of Lorenzo Fieschi in 1519 he was appointed *vicario generale* of the archbishopric of Genoa, but he in turn appointed a second *vicario* to act for him and had certainly been replaced by 1523 if not earlier.[90]

The *Opus noviter editum* and its influence

From his administration of Brugnato it is clear that Filippo's aim was not only to run his benefices profitably, but also to do his best for the churches and the souls that were in his charge. He never forgot that the holding

---

[84] Ibid. 73; Notai Antichi, 1488, 20 May 1528. See 1947, 1 Jan. 1531, for the inventory of the vestments and books, cited also by, amongst others, A. Petrucciani, 'Il catalogo di una biblioteca genovese del '700', *Accademie e biblioteche d'Italia* liv/ii (1986), 32–43 at pp. 36–7, where some of the books which made up his library are examined.

[85] Reg. Vat. 1003, fos 252v–254v; Notai Antichi, 1163, nos 212–13, 223, 263, 265; 1164, no. 58.

[86] Reg. Vat. 1051, fos 138v–140r; Notai Antichi, 1164, no. 67, 16 Feb. 1516.

[87] Reg. Vat. 1051, fos 136v–138v.

[88] Mansi, *Sacrorum conciliorum*, xxxii. 937, 977; Tomaini, *Brugnato città*, 259; Archivio Urbano, sezione 66, protocollo 14, fos 167r, 166v, 3 Sept., 3 Nov. 1515; Cam. Ap., Resignationes 17, fo. 253v, 1, 6 Aug. 1517.

[89] Notai Antichi, 1164, no. 58, 11 Feb. 1516; 1162, no. 121, 1 July 1513.

[90] D. Cambiaso, 'I vicari generali degli arcivescovi di Genova', *ASLSP* n.s. xii (1972), 11–70 at p. 40; cf. D. Puncuh (ed.), *I manoscritti della raccolta Durazzo*, Genoa 1979, 30, 161 n. 20. He is recorded as *vicario generale* of the archbishop of Genoa on 4 Apr. and 27 June 1519: Notai Antichi, 1166, no. 98; 1483, 18 Oct. 1523.

of a benefice also involved the 'care of souls'. His concerns for the holy office, the learning, morals and lifestyle of his clergy and for the fabric of his churches were echoed in the book he wrote at the request of his clergy following the diocesan synod of 1518: the *Opus noviter editum*. Now mostly forgotten, it was influential not only in his own diocese but also with later reformers. The book falls into three parts: an introduction; forty-seven pages that cover his recommendations to his clergy as given at the synod which include instructions as to the clergy's behaviour, their dress, their required degree of learning, and instructions regarding the holy mass, the care of souls, the seven sacraments, the custody of their churches and of the sacraments. The remaining eighty-seven pages are devoted to penances for sins and a lengthy explanation of the different types of ecclesiastical censures.

The second section of the book was the most influential. In writing it, Filippo may have been influenced by the synodal recommendations of Cardinal Ximenes de Cisneros with which there are some similarities, for example on the necessity of residence in the benefice and the explanation of the Gospel after mass every Sunday, but more likely sources seem to be either sound common sense and his own experience and/or some of the promulgations of the Council of Florence and of the Fifth Lateran Council. The purpose of the Council of Florence, instigated by Cardinal de' Medici in 1516–17 as archbishop of Florence, was to implement the decrees of the Lateran Council. The order that the council's findings should be observed was promulgated on 8 March 1518.[91] Its decrees, although of course far more extensive than Filippo's recommendations, also included directives on dress and tonsure, the need to avoid taverns, games and secular business, strictures on the right utensils for the mass and the necessary level of learning for the clergy.[92] Filippo echoed these but particularly emphasised the need for purity in behaviour and speech, modesty, awareness of the priest's position and of all the necessary rules regarding the saying of the mass and the giving of the sacraments, and the attention to be given to the upkeep of churches and their contents.[93] The decrees of the Fifth Lateran which most interested Filippo were those of the eleventh session, at which he is known to have been present. They were, in essence, the examination of clergy as to their moral integrity and knowledge and the importance of preaching the Gospel.[94] Perhaps most important, his book reflected the criticisms that he had levelled at the clergy of Brugnato during his visit of 1518, and it was

[91] N. Minnich, 'Raphael's portrait *Leo X with Cardinals Giulio de' Medici and Luigi de'Rossi*: a religious interpretation', *Renaissance Quarterly* lvi (2003), 1005–52 at pp. 1017–18.
[92] Mansi, *Sacrorum conciliorum*, xxxv. 215–303, especially pp. 217–20, 223–5, 241, 256.
[93] P. Sauli, *Opus noviter editum*, Milan 1521, 2, 4, 5, 7, 10, 43–4.
[94] Mansi, *Sacrorum consiliorum*, xxxii. 945–6.

designed to be a handbook for practical use, albeit in Latin, and in that lay its importance.[95]

The book's influence was felt most of all by the important reformer Gian Matteo Giberti, who became bishop of Verona in 1524. Later, Giberti also became involved in the administration of the *Arcispedale di San Giacomo* in Rome, and was at one time linked to the *Compagnia del divino amore*.[96] He was a close friend of Filippo's elder brother, Domenico Sauli: when speaking of the year 1524 Domenico notes in his autobiography that 'between the said Giberti and myself there had been great friendship and good feeling for many years'.[97] Filippo and Giberti would almost certainly have met in Rome where Giberti was living from 1513, but this was not the first time that the paths of the Sauli and Giberti families had crossed: Giberti's father, Franco, had worked for the Sauli in the early *cinquecento* and the Sauli intimate Marcantonio Flaminio would later join Giberti's household after his time with Stefano Sauli, so the families were obviously close.[98] Indeed, in 1517, after the implication of Cardinal Sauli in the plot to murder Leo X, Franco Giberti lent Stefano and Giovanni Sauli 1,000 ducats to help release the cardinal from prison. This was double the average sum lent by others.[99]

In Rome, as secretary to Cardinal de' Medici from 1514, and later as datary on the election to the papacy of Clement VII, Giberti would have been aware of the resolutions of the Council of Florence and of the Lateran Council. He was also instrumental in Clement VII's own attempts at reform in 1525. There is no doubt, however, that he placed considerable stress on the example set by Filippo Sauli.[100] He was influenced by Sauli's episcopal diligence at Brugnato – especially his pastoral visits and his exhortations to the priests – and undertook the moral and spiritual renewal of the clergy of his own Veronese diocese. This was to be achieved through, amongst other things, the example of Giberti's own conduct and that of his followers, and detailed pastoral visits either by himself or his *vicarii*. In 1530, on one of his visits, he gave to every priest a copy of the *Breve ricordo*, a 'booklet of instructions in Italian' published at Giberti's expense and written by Tullio

---

[95] For Filippo's complaints of 1518 see Tomaini, *Attività pastorale*, 20–2, 29, 30, 33, 37, 47.

[96] Cataldi Palau, 'Catalogo', 30–1; Paschini, *La beneficenza*, 49.

[97] 'Fra 'l ditto Giberto et me era molt'anni inanti grand'amicitia et benevolentia': Biblioteca Angelica, Rome, MS 1826, fos 3–4.

[98] Cam. Ap., Div. Cam. 62, 55r–70r.

[99] MS Ferr. 424, fo. 161v.

[100] Sauli's influence on Giberti is acknowledged on a general level by A. Prosperi, 'Le visite pastorali del Giberti tra documento e monumento', in A. Fasani (ed.), *Riforma pretridentina della diocesi di Verona: visite pastorali del vescovo G. M. Giberti, 1525–1542*, Vincenza 1989, i, pp. xxxiii–lx at pp. xlvi–xlvii. It is difficult to agree with Prosperi's conclusion (p. li) that Giberti did more than Filippo for the clergy of his diocese given that Prosperi seems unaware of the aim and content of Filippo's work. A. Turchini, 'Giberti, Gian Matteo', *DBI* liv (2000), 623–9 at p. 626 also emphasises Filippo's influence, as well as that of Contarini.

Crispolti (1510–73) who accompanied Giberti on his visits in the role of preacher. The model for his booklet has been identified as Filippo's *Opus noviter editum*.[101]

Angelo Turchini describes the *Opus* as having a 'more generic tone' and underlines the innovatory nature of Crispolti's work, yet although Filippo's work is much longer than the *Breve ricordo*, there are, in addition to resonances with the Council of Florence, striking similarities between the two works.[102] Both begin with exhortations as to the appropriate behaviour of priests, then deal with the sacraments (and in Filippo's case, the censures). Both underline the importance of the tonsure; priests are to set good examples; they are to have a Bible and some commentaries on it, including in both cases some *Summae* and the *Defecerunt* of the Beato Antonino.[103] Both authors detail how priests are to declaim the Gospel every Sunday, avoid taverns and follow the rules on the necessary qualities of the altar for the celebration of mass.[104] No acknowledgement was made of Crispolti's debt to Filippo, but, although unacknowledged, Sauli's influence continued through the success of the *Breve ricordo* even outside the diocese of Verona in Bologna, Belluno and Mantua.[105] Such was Giberti's respect for Filippo that he sponsored the posthumous publication of Filippo's translation of the *Commentationes in omnes psalmos* of Eutimius Zigabenus with a laudatory preface written by Paolo Turchio, a Giberti intimate.[106]

Filippo and humanist studies

Filippo's religious zeal was combined with deep scholarship. He studied civic and canon law at Bologna and by 1515 was a *referendarius* in the curial *signatura*.[107] Musso places him alongside Agostino Giustiniani as amongst those Genoese scholars who were most attracted by religious humanism and

101 Turchini, 'Giberti', 626. The *Breve ricordo* was until recently believed to have been written by Giberti himself: P. Simoni, 'Appunti sulle opere a stampa del vescovo veronese G. M. Giberti', *Studi storici Luigi Simoni* xliii (1993), 147–67. Only one copy of it is known to have survived. It is reproduced by A. Prosperi, 'Note in margine ad un opuscolo di Gian Matteo Ghiberti', *Critica Storica* iii (1965), 367–402. The importance of Contarini is underlined at p. 370, while that of Sauli is ignored.
102 Turchini, 'Giberti', 626; Prosperi, 'Note', 375.
103 Prosperi, 'Note', 393–4; Sauli, *Opus noviter*, 2, 3, 43.
104 Prosperi, 'Note', 394, 398; Sauli, *Opus noviter*, 3, 7, 43.
105 A. Prosperi, 'Le costituzioni tra evangelismo e controriforma', in R. Pasquali (ed.), *Le costituzioni per il clero (1542) di Gian Matteo Giberti, vescovo di Verona*, Vicenza 2000, pp. xix–xxvi at p.xix.
106 *Euthymii Monachi Zigaboni commentationes in omnes psalmos de greco in latinum conversae per R. D. Philippum Saulum episcopum brugnatenem*, Verona 1530, i; Cataldi Palau, 'Catalogo', 32.
107 R. Abbondanza, 'Alciato, Andrea', *DBI* ii (1960), 69–77 at p. 69; Reg. Vat. 1051, fos 138v–140r; Frenz, *Die Kanzlei*, 435.

sees him as a scholar whose real talent lay in the 'exegesis of sacred works'.[108] Although he collaborated with Andrea Alciato (1492–1550) on his *Annotationes in tres posteriores libros codicis Iustiniani* (and was duly honoured with a dedication), his chief interest lay in the Greek language, and his only surviving work in this field, the *Commentationes*, is a translation from Greek into Latin. He also accumulated a large library of more than 300 Greek manuscripts, in addition to sacred texts (and perhaps works on medicine), which were collected from far afield.[109]

Filippo's reformist inclinations and scholarly interests meant that he and Gregorio Cortese had much in common when they met in Genoa in 1519. Two of Filippo's manuscripts were probably copied at Lérins under Cortese's direction and there was an exchange of texts between the two.[110] Cortese also helped with and later read Filippo's translation of Zigabenus and praised it as 'an elegant, clever and erudite work'.[111] In the autumn of 1522 Filippo visited Cortese at Lérins, returning to Genoa in 1523, possibly remaining there for the rest of his life.[112]

Although there is no surviving evidence that Filippo was a member of the *Compagnia del divino amore*, he did continue his family's support for Vernazza. In his will of 1528 he left all his Greek books, printed and in manuscript, all Latin manuscripts including three manuscript volumes on the councils, copied by his secretary Antonio de' Merli, and the Toledan Bible to the *Ospedale degli incurabili*, where they were to be kept under lock and key but could be borrowed on payment of a healthy deposit of between fifty and one hundred ducats for each book, depending on its 'quality'. In addition he left a bequest of 200 Genoese *lire* and all pensions owed to him on benefices in the dioceses of Toledo and Seville.[113] His will also carried a separate bequest of 3,000 *lire* to be spent on the poor within the following five years. He died from the plague in 1528 and was originally buried, if his instructions were

---

108 Musso, 'La cultura genovese' 166, 168.
109 N. Calvini, 'Biblioteche rinascimentali in Liguria', *Atti e Memorie della Società Savonese di Storia Patria* x (1976), 97–107 at p. 100; *Gregorii Cortesii*, ii, no. 41 at pp. 76–7; Cataldi Palau, 'Catalogo', 10 n. 2, 11, 27. For the question of whether Sauli owned manuscripts on medicine see A. Petrucciani, 'Le biblioteche', in D. Puncuh (ed.), 'Storia della cultura ligure', *ASLSP* xlv/1 (2005) iii. 233–345 at p. 250
110 Cataldi Palau, 'Un gruppo', 103–4, and 'Catalogo', 26.
111 See *Gregorii Cortesii*, ii, nos 41, 79 at pp. 76–7, 126–8, and two in Greek written to Filippo Sauli and which can be dated to 1523–4: Cataldi Palau, 'Catalogo', 18 n. 53.
112 Cataldi Palau, 'Catalogo', 25–6, 28. For Filippo's presence in Genoa see Notai Antichi, 1288, no. 539, 6 June 1523.
113 Notai Antichi, 1488, 20 May 1528. The provisions of this part of his will are cited by, amongst others, A. Oldoinus, *Athenaeum ligusticum seu syllabus scriptorum ligurum nec non sarzanensium, ac cyrnensium reipublicae genuensis subditorum*, Perugia 1680, 473; G. Bertolotto, 'Il codice greco Sauliano di S Anastasio scoperto ed illustrato', *ASLSP* o.s. xxxv (1892), 7–48 at p. 13; and Langasco, *Gli ospedali*, 261–2. For the benefices in Toledo see Notai Antichi, 1488, no. 80, 29 Jan. 1528; 1532, no. 182, 20 June. 1528. For his codicil of 7 Aug. 1528 see 1532, no. 88.

followed, without pomp in San Domenico. His bones were later transferred to Santa Maria Assunta di Carignano, where they now lie.[114]

In his own lifetime Filippo's reputation as a man of great character was widely recognised. Paolo Giovio, who must have known Filippo when he was in Rome, described him as next only to Gian Pietro Carafa 'in doctrine and piety ... but in temperament humane and clement and far from the grim severity of the more religious life'.[115] This view is confirmed by Matteo Bandello who dedicated a *novella* to him, describing his generosity towards others, especially the poor, and posthumously praising his 'singular virtues and rare gifts'.[116] Of all the family, he is the clearest and best documented example of a strong proponent of reform within the Church. There are practical reasons for this: more documents have survived for Filippo's administration of his benefices than for those of Bendinello or Stefano; he was an active churchman (1512–28) for longer than his cousins: as a cardinal Bendinello Sauli was almost automatically removed from close contact with his benefices and Stefano had little ecclesiastical influence after Bendinello's death. Furthermore, Filippo was not tainted by disgrace – indeed his reputation in his own lifetime was high – and thus documents and opinions about him are more likely to have survived.

Cardinal Sauli, unlike Cardinal Fregoso with whom he is linked by John Symonds, lived a short life and showed an interest in reform when this was far from being the Church's main interest. During his lifetime there was no real close-knit circle of reformers such as that of Giberti, Pole, Cortese and others some few years later. Hence what evidence has survived has done so in isolation. However, there is clear evidence of the friendship between the cardinal, Stefano and Filippo and reformers such as Ettore Vernazza and Gregorio Cortese which tends to indicate that the Sauli were, in varying degrees, sympathetic to the movement towards Catholic Reform.

---

[114] For instructions for his burial see Notai Antichi, 1488, 15 Sept. 1528, attached to his will, and the will itself. See also Petrucciani, 'Il catalogo', 35 n. 19.

[115] P. Giovio, 'Dialogus de viris et foeminis aetate nostra florentibus', in *Pauli Iovii opera*, ed. E. Travi and M. Penco, Rome 1984, ix. 253. The Dialogus was probably written in the late 1520s: ibid. ix. 157.

[116] *Tutte le opere di Matteo Bandello*, ed. F. Flora, Milan 1934, liii. 662, 701.

PART II

THE PATRONAGE OF CARDINAL SAULI

4

'He Surpassed All in Splendour and Pomp'?

An apparently profligate lifestyle may seem surprising in one who expressed an interest in ecclesiastical affairs and reform, but the role of cardinal was multifaceted. If the degree of spiritual concern with which he ran his benefices was left in practice to his own conscience, the promotion of a cardinal's reputation and that of the Church was not. Image was important both to those cardinals resident in Rome and to the pope as the head of the Church. *Dignitas*, as outlined by Paolo Cortesi in his handbook on the cardinalate, *De cardinalatu* (1510) and in the Lateran Council bull *Reformationis curiae* of 5 May 1514, was vital.[1] It was sustained by maintaining a large staff – both to run the cardinal's household and to accompany him on his official outings – and by suitably palatial accommodation in which to house his *famiglia* and to offer entertainment. Whether Paris de' Grassis was correct in maintaining that Sauli was at the forefront in ostentatious display will become clear through an examination of his residences in Rome, his household and his expenses.[2]

From the Vatican Palace to Santa Maria in Via Lata

Documents concerning Sauli's resignation of benefices, drawn up 'in the apostolic palace in the room of the usual residence of the aforesaid Bendinello', show that from at least 1506 until 1510 Sauli, as a *cubicularius summi pontificis* (chamberlain), was resident in the Vatican Palace.[3] He is not mentioned at all in any surviving documents of this nature from the period 1510–13 and when the documents in the *resignationes* series resume they are simply drawn up either 'in the apostolic chamber' or 'at St Peter's'. It can thus be assumed that, presumably shortly after his elevation to the

---

[1]   D. S. Chambers, 'The economic predicament of Renaissance cardinals', in W. M. Bowsky (ed.), *Studies in medieval and Renaissance history*, ii, Lincoln, Nebraska 1966, 289–313 at pp. 291, 294; Mansi, *Sacrorum conciliorum*, xxxii. 874–85; Olin, *Catholic Reformation*, 59–60.

[2]   'non cedebat alicui in fastu et pompa': Barb. Lat. 2683, fo. 269r. This is de' Grassis's posthumous (1518) description of Sauli.

[3]   'in palatio apostolico in camera solite residentie prefati Bendinelli': Cam. Ap., Resignationes 10, fo. 174v, 27 Apr. 1506; 11, fo. 33v, 22 Apr. 1507; 12, fo. 204r, 19 Mar. 1510; fo. 287r, 5 July 1510: all with only slight variations on this wording. For the different types of *cubicularii* see Moroni, *Dizionario*, vii. 20.

cardinalate in 1511, he moved out of the apostolic palace and was there only to pursue family or church business.[4]

This is confirmed by other sources. As Kate Lowe notes, for non-palatine cardinals, that majority who were not resident in the Vatican Palace, there were three options: to rent or buy a palace; to buy a property and alter it; or to build a new palace.[5] Sauli seems to have favoured the first, and not necessarily the most economically sound, option. On 15 December 1512 he ratified the rental of the income of San Simpliciano in a document drawn up in Rome 'in his palace'.[6] On 28 June 1513 a document regarding Sebastiano Sauli was drawn up 'in the house or palace of the most Reverend Cardinal de Saulis'.[7] From January 1514 to April 1515 copies of other notarial documents provide more details. With two anomalies, all the original documents were drawn up 'in the house of the aforesaid Reverend Cardinal sited at Sant'Agostino', namely near the church of Sant' Agostino in Rome.[8] The exceptions to this formula also lend support to a stay by Sauli in this area: the first is a document dated 3 March 1514 and drawn up in 'the house of the most Reverend Bindinello [sic] de Saulis cardinal priest of Santa Sabina near the church of San Salvatore delle Cupelle [sic]'.[9] The words 'Sant'Agostino' have been crossed out and replaced by 'San Salvatore delle Cupelle'. The second exception is the final notarial act which places him in this area, and which was drawn up on 17 April 1515 'in the house of the aforesaid most Reverend Cardinal sited at Torre Sanguigna'.[10] The church of Sant' Agostino, the Torre Sanguigna and the church of San Salvatore delle Coppelle, however, are all relatively close to each other and indeed the whole area was also known as Torre Sanguigna, described by Carol Maddison as the heart of literary Rome.[11] It is unlikely that Sauli and his household moved three times in little over a year and it thus seems reasonable to conclude that the area, but not the building, in which he spent at least one year of his cardinalate, can be identified. Given what is

---

4 'in camera apostolica': Cam. Ap., Resignationes 15, fo. 26r, 1 June 1513; 'apud Sanctum Petrum': fo. 57v, 16 Aug. 1513.
5 K. J. P. Lowe, 'A Florentine prelate's real estate in Rome between 1480 and 1524: the residential and speculative property of Cardinal Francesco Soderini', *Papers of the British School at Rome* lix (1991), 259–82 at p. 259.
6 'in eius palatio': Notai del Tribunale, AC 7151, fo. 233r.
7 'in domo seu palatio Reverendissimi domini Cardinalis de Saulis': MS Ferr. 424, fo. 53r.
8 'in edibus prefati domini Reverendissimi Cardinalis sitis apud sanctum augustinum': Archivio Urbano, sezione 66, protocollo 13, fos 106r–v, 108r–v, 109r–110r; 21, fo. 113r; 25, fos 114r–v, 116r–v. They are dated between 11 Dec. 1513 and 17 Apr. 1515 with variations on the above wording.
9 'in edibus Reverendissimi domini Bindinelli tituli Sancte Sabine presbiter Cardinalis de Saulis prope ecclesiam sancti Salvatoris delle cupelle': ibid. 21, fo. 114v.
10 'in edibus prefati Reverendissimi domini Cardinalis sitis apud turrem Sanguineam': ibid. 25, fo. 116r–v.
11 Lowe, *Church and politics*, 215; Maddison, *Marcantonio Flaminio*, 26.

known of his later movements, it seems improbable that Sauli purchased this unidentified palace or had it built especially for him and more probable that he rented it, settling temporarily in the area while he waited for another, more sumptuous, palace to fall vacant.

Since late 1513, if not earlier, Sauli had had his eyes trained on a luxurious residence, more than worthy of a cardinal and one which had indeed previously caught the eye of a pope. This was the Palazzo Doria Pamphilij, attached to the church of Santa Maria in Via Lata. The first palace on the site was built by Cardinal Niccolò d'Acciapacci (1439–47) and was probably begun in 1440.[12] Passing through various hands, it was finally purchased by Cardinal Fazio Santoro (1503–10), a former chamberlain and intimate of Julius II, who had it rebuilt between December 1505 and September 1507 by a pupil of Bramante.[13] Santoro has been described as 'the first [cardinal] to build a palace of a certain size' and such was its success that on 21 September 1507, or earlier, whilst visiting the palace Julius II decided to 'ask' Santoro to donate it to his nephew Francesco Maria della Rovere, shortly to become the duke of Urbino.[14]

What was it about the palace that had so captured Julius' imagination? In 1510 Albertini described how Santoro had enlarged and embellished the palace in a sumptuous fashion.[15] But Francesco Maria della Rovere was rarely in Rome and was seemingly little interested in his Roman residence: indeed, there is still debate as to the extent, if any, to which della Rovere altered the palace in this, and later, periods and, given that Santoro's coat of arms and inscriptions with his name were still visible in much of the palace at the end of the sixteenth century, it seems likely that Sauli's tenancy began in a palace which was still pretty much as Santoro had built it.[16] The first rental agreement between della Rovere's proctors, Giovanni Battista Bonaventura and Orazio Florio, and Cardinal Sauli was drawn up on 11 December 1513. It states that the cardinal was to pay 400 ducats per year, a high figure, reflecting the size and prestige of the palace.[17] Presumably something then

---

[12] C. L. Frommel, *Der romische Palastbau der Hochrenaissance*, Tübingen 1973, i. 94.

[13] G. Carandente, *Il Palazzo Doria Pamphilij*, Milan 1975, 22; Frommel, *Der romische Plasthaus*, i.95.

[14] F. Cappelletti, 'Le origini cinquecentesche: dal Palazzo Fazio Santoro al Palazzo Aldobrandini al Corso', in A. G. De Marchi (ed.), *Il Palazzo Doria Pamphilij al Corso e le sue collezioni*, Florence 1999, 13–29 at p. 14; Carandente, *Il palazzo*, 309 n. 47.

[15] 'sumptuosissimis aedificiis ampliata, cum atrio et porticu et capellis et aula pulcherrima depicta. Omitto viridaria, in quibus sunt vasa marmorea sculpta cum sacrificiis et raptu Sabinarum. Omitto aquarum conservationem subterraneam, et cameras variis picturis et status exornatas, ut eius insignia palmae indicant': cited in Frommel, *Der romische Palastbau*, i. 89.

[16] Ibid. i. 94, 96; Carandente, *Il palazzo*, 55–6; R. Lanciani, 'Il codice Barberiniano XXX, 89 contenente frammenti di una descrizione di Roma del secolo XVI', *ASRSP* vi (1883), 223–40, 445–96 at p. 459.

[17] Archivio Urbano, sezione 66, protocollo 21, fo.114r–v. The average rent for a 'palace of moderate size' was between 200 and 400 ducats: Partner, *Renaissance Rome*, 138.

occurred which led the cardinal to remain in his residence near Sant'
Agostino and a second agreement was not drawn up until 17 April 1515
when Giovanni Battista Carosino, the della Rovere proctor in Rome, and
Sebastiano de Bonaventura, the head of the duke's household, rented the
palace and its holdings (with the exception of a *carcoaria* and a *domus feni*
which were rented to Cardinal Fieschi) to Sauli for the same annual sum.[18]
The delay may have been occasioned by an existing, unidentified tenant
who wished to extend his lease or perhaps Sauli had lacked the necessary
income to pay such a high rent: it is worth noting that in the period between
the two contracts – more precisely in July 1514 – Sauli had been granted
the lucrative abbey of San Dionigi in Milan with a reported annual income
of 1,200 ducats. Tenancy of the palace was to begin on acceptance of the
keys and a document of 23 May 1515 was in fact drawn up 'at Santa Maria
in ViaLata'; Sauli lived there until his disgrace in May 1517.[19] There is no
surviving evidence of any major building work undertaken during his short
tenancy, although entries in the Sauli bank books for 1516 note a payment
on 28 May of twenty-five ducats 'for the price of a doorway' and thirty ducats
on 26 October to his *maestro di casa* 'for expenses being carried out in the
house'.[20]

Sauli now had a luxurious residence for himself and his *famiglia*, and when
his kin visited Rome they stayed with him: the series of documents witnessed
by Filippo Sauli in 1515 were all drawn up in the palace at Santa Maria in
Via Lata. Other members of the family already resident in Rome frequently
visited. But this was not the only Roman residence of the Sauli family.
Under Leo x the main Sauli banking firm in Rome was that of Sebastiano,
Giovanni and Agostino Sauli. As Peter Partner notes, Genoese bankers were
to be found in the Ponte quarter of Rome, and the Sauli were no exception.[21]
Documents drawn up by Ettore Vernazza in his role of notary during his stay
with Sebastiano are 'at Rome in the house or usual residence of Sebastiano,
Giovanni and Agostino de Saulis in the region of the Castel Sant'Angelo
bridge'.[22] This house remains unidentified but further information can be
gleaned from a letter of 11 April 1513 from Federico Gonzaga to his father
recounting the *posesso* of Leo x. Whilst describing the pope's return from the
Lateran he notes a triumphal arch, one of the many erected to celebrate the
new pontificate, 'at the fork which goes to Monte Giordano and the *cancelleria*' (the palace of Cardinal Raffaele Riario, now on the Corso Vittorio

---

[18] Archivio Urbano, sezione 66, protocollo 25, fo.116r–v.

[19] Ibid. 14, fo. 166v. For some of the rental payments in early 1516 see Archivio Sauli,
no. 730, fo. 40r.

[20] 'pro pretio unius portalis': Archivio Sauli, no. 730, fo. 40r; 'pro expensis faciendis pro
domo': fo. 209r.

[21] Partner, *Renaissance Rome*, 78.

[22] 'Actum Rome in domo solite habitationis dominorum Sebastiani Johannis et Augus-
tini de Saulis sita in regione ponti sancti angeli': Notai Antichi,1522bis, nos 125–6, 16,
24 Aug. 1516.

Emanuele) and 'next to this' he then describes an arch which can be identified through its inscription as that of the Sauli.[23] Further details are provided by Gian Giacomo Penni's description of how 'having already passed the *cancelleria* to the house of the Sauli ... there was an arch of great ingenuity' and he then goes on to describe inscriptions and the figures 'on the facade [of the arch] facing the *cancelleria* ... and on the side facing the *banchi*'. Thus one side of the arch, and presumably the palace, faced the *cancelleria* and one faced the *banchi*, and, given the itinerary he follows, the house was thus between the *cancelleria* and the Mint.[24]

The banking records of Sebastiano, Giovanni and Agostino Sauli for April 1516 detail building work undertaken on the property 'in which we live'. This, like the cardinal's palace, was rented but at a much lower cost: 120 cameral ducats per year.[25] The building work cost 100 ducats which included the rebuilding of one or more bedrooms, walls in the garden and courtyard and the provision of glass windows throughout. One of the bedrooms was frescoed the following year by a painter who was regularly employed by the Sauli (and who had perhaps worked on the triumphal arch), the unidentifiable 'Andrea the painter'.[26] Although the Sauli banking operations in Rome were scaled down following the loss of the posts of *depositarii generali* and the later disgrace of Cardinal Sauli, the house seems to have been of a reasonable size. Assuming the house in question to be the same, in the census of late 1526 there were seventeen houses which can be identified as belonging to bankers, with the number of *bocche* (mouths) ranging from nine to twenty-five; that of 'Sebastiano de Saulis' numbered fourteen mouths, just slightly below the average of fifteen.[27]

The cardinal's *famiglia* and *famigliari*

Cardinal Sauli would certainly have been expected to feed more than fourteen mouths. Writing in 1510 in *De cardinalatu*, Paolo Cortesi prescribed 'sixty upper servants and eighty lower servants'.[28] In the census of late 1526

---

[23] A. Luzio, *Isabella d'Este ne' primordi del papato di Leone X e il suo viaggio a Roma nel 1514–15*, Milan 1907, 93.

[24] G. Giacomo Penni, *Croniche delle magnifiche e honorate pompe fatte in Roma per la creatione et incoronatione di Papa Leone X. pont. ot. mx.*, Florence 1513, cc. 234r, 235r. For the inscriptions on the arch and on their house for the occasion see Barb. Lat. 2273, fos 7r–v.

[25] Archivio Sauli, no. 730, fo. 121r.

[26] Ibid. no. 731, fo. 9r.

[27] D. Gnoli, 'Descriptio urbis o censimento della popolazione di Roma avanti il sacco Borbonico', *ASRSP* xvii (1898), 375–520 at pp. 427–30; *Descriptio urbis: the Roman census of 1527*, ed. E. Lee, Rome 1985, 17, 59–61.

[28] P. Cortesi, *De cardinalatu*, Rome 1510, fos 56v–57r, cited in Chambers, 'Economic predicament', 293.

the average size of a cardinal's *famiglia* was 134 members, although this figure takes no account of cardinals not resident in Rome at the time and the members of those cardinals' families and their own *famiglie* who took advantage of the cardinals' hospitality when in Rome. However, the average given was thus reasonably similar to the figure of 154 recorded in a document of 28 December 1509.[29] A *famiglia* of fewer than 100 members was to be considered 'small' and, according to Partner, only four out of twenty-one cardinalitial *famiglie* fell into this category at that time.[30] As Mary Hollingsworth rightly notes, the 'size of one's household ... was the indicator of rank, and for the most prosaic of reasons – a large household was very expensive to maintain. In addition to salaries, there was food and accommodation'.[31] It was also an opportunity for the cardinal to display liberality through his treatment of his *famigliari*, and indeed some cardinals, such as Antoniotto Pallavicino (1489–1507) were remembered by later commentators for this.[32] Yet a *famiglia* was also 'one of the great ceremonial expressions of pontifical society': when attending the funerals of cardinals and the official entries of visiting ambassadors the greater the number of *famigliari* present, the greater the respect shown.[33] When the Genoese ambassadors went to pay homage to the pope in consistory, they were 'greatly honoured' by, amongst other things, 'the *famiglie* of our most reverend cardinals and other bishops and priests of our nation'.[34]

The same divisions as those in the *famiglia* of the pope and in the court of a secular lord applied: namely the division into upper and lower offices, as noted by Cortesi. Within the household the *familiares continui commensales* had their own status, were generally resident in the cardinal's palace and held the more important positions in the household.[35] Although in Sauli's case no specific household accounts survive, as they do for a very small number of other cardinals, notarial documents throughout the period and the accounts of the Sauli bank of Sebastiano, Giovanni and Agostino Sauli for 1516–17 allow the identity and roles of some of the members of his household to be reconstructed.

[29] J. F. D'Amico, *Renaissance humanism in Rome*, Baltimore–London 1983, 47; Chambers, 'Economic predicament', 293. For the numbers in each cardinal's household see Gnoli, *Descriptio urbis*, 387.

[30] P. Partner, 'Il mondo della curia e i suoi rapporti con la città', in *Roma, città dei papi* (*Storia d'Italia* xvi, 2000), 203–34 at p. 221.

[31] M. Hollingsworth, *The cardinal's hat: money, ambition and housekeeping in a Renaissance court*, London 2004, 188.

[32] G. Garimberto, *La prima parte delle vite, overo fatti memorabili d'alcuni papi, et di tutti i cardinali passati*, Venice 1567, 137–8.

[33] Partner, 'Il mondo della curia', 221.

[34] 'summamenti honorati ... da le famiglie de nostri Reverendissimi Cardinali et altri episcopi e prelati de la nation nostra': Lasagna to Genoese government, 2 June 1514, Archivio Segreto 2342.

[35] McClung Hallman, *Italian cardinals*, 100.

The *maestro di casa*, or major-domo, was the most important person in a cardinal's *famiglia*. He selected and supervised some of the lower-rank servants and had a judicial role within the household.[36] In accordance with his position he was, as Francesco Priscianese wrote in 1543, to be 'a very excellent and wise person, practical and discreet'.[37] Two people are known to have held this position in Sauli's household. On 19 March 1510 one of the witnesses to the resignation of benefices by Agostino Sauli 'in the Apostolic Palace in the room of the aforesaid Bendinelli' was 'Sebastiano Viscardi cleric of Turin'.[38] Viscardi, also cited as Gui(s)chardi), was a trusted *famigliare* of the pope: on 4 May 1507 Julius had sent him to Spain, under the aegis of Sebastiano Sauli, to recover money owing to the papacy.[39] By 1513, if not earlier, he was 'Sebastiano Guischardi major-domo of the most Reverend B Cardinal de Saulis'.[40] By 2 January 1516 at the latest he had been replaced by a person who was already intimate with Sauli: Giovanni Angelo Gometius, a notary who had drawn up many of his notarial documents.[41] Gometius stayed with Sauli until 3 March 1517 when he is recorded by name in the Sauli bank books for the last time. Had he left Rome on other business, or had he had warning of the trouble which was to come in future months and fled, as later so many of Sauli's *famigliari* did after the cardinal's arrest in May of that year? Gometius had returned to Sauli's service by 11 December 1517 when the cardinal lay ill after his release from prison, but only in his role as notary and there is no further news of him in either of his roles after that date.[42]

The identities of the other servants who came under the jurisdiction of the *maestro di casa* are not known in great detail, but several figures stand out. The personal qualities required of the *camerieri* (chamberlains) in a household were many and included politeness, good looks, honesty and discretion. Their duties were to maintain the bedroom, rooms and clothes of the cardinal, to make sure everything smelled sweet, to keep an eye on the household and to accompany the cardinal on his travels.[43] The most trusted in Sauli's household was seemingly Domenico de' Caffis, a *continuus commensalis*. He was associated with Sauli as early as July 1507 when he was awarded a benefice through the cardinal's advocacy.[44] Smaller benefices were

---

[36] D. S. Chambers, *A Renaissance cardinal and his worldly goods: the will and inventory of Francesco Gonzaga (1444–1483)*, London 1992, 14; D'Amico, *Renaissance humanism*, 52.
[37] F. Priscianese, *Del governo della corte d'un signore in Roma dove si ragiona di tutto quello che al signore e a' suoi cortigiani si appartiene di fare, opera non manco bella, che utile e necessario*, 2nd edn, Città di Castello 1883, 45.
[38] Cam. Ap., Resignationes 12, fo. 240r.
[39] Arm. XXXIX, 25, fos 225r–237v, 4 May 1507.
[40] Notai Antichi 1162, no. 189, 23 Sept. 1513.
[41] For copies of these documents see Archivio Urbano, sezione 66, protocollo 13, 14, 19, 20, 21, 25, 28 passim; Archivio Sauli, no. 730, fo. 27r.
[42] Archivio Sauli, no. 731, fo. 91r; Collegio de' Notai Capitolini 1914, fo. 370r.
[43] Priscianese, *Del governo della corte*, 72–3.
[44] Reg. Lat. 1283, fo. 154v; 1200, fos 139r–140v.

part of the patronage network, used by cardinals to reward servants, and it seems reasonable to assume that the five other benefices he received during the cardinal's lifetime were also due to Sauli's influence; their value indicates that de' Caffis enjoyed particular favour.[45] He also received some of the privileges accorded to Sebastiano Sauli who had acted as Sauli's aide in the conclave of 1513, accompanied the cardinal on his travels and seems to have been one of the few who remained with him after his disgrace.[46] Another *cameriere*, but on less intimate terms, was Claudio Campana. He features as a witness in documents from June 1513 until August 1516, and, like de' Caffis, travelled with the cardinal and also received a benefice.[47]

Another important, and intimate, *famigliare* was the Genoese *popolare* Paulo Hieronimo de' Franchi. His involvement with the Sauli family is known to have begun in Genoa in 1509 when he replaced Vincenzo Sauli as proctor for Cardinal Riario in order to take possession of a benefice.[48] By June 1513 he was in the service of Cardinal Sauli in Rome, remaining at least until May 1517, but probably later given that he lent Stefano and Giovanni Sauli money to help pay the fine to release the cardinal from prison in 1517.[49] He was Cardinal Sauli's 'secretary and *continuus commensalis*'. In November 1513 Sauli resigned 125 ducats of a pension on a benefice in Toledo to him, giving the remaining 100 ducats to his other secretary, Giovanni Maria Cattaneo.[50] De' Franchi would seem to have received other benefices: he is cited in June 1513 as a 'Genoese cleric' and had previously held benefices in Otranto which then passed to Filippo Sauli on 14 May 1516.[51] Although by 1525 he had become the *maestro di casa* of Cardinal Alessandro Farnese (1493–1534), he seems to have remained within the Sauli family ambit after the cardinal's death: two letters of Stefano Sauli of 1527 describe him as 'our Pauli Ieronimo de Franchi our proctor'.[52]

Other figures are recorded as close to Sauli for varying periods. These include Antonio Cocchio, *protonotario apostolico*, a *famigliare* of Alexander VI and an intimate and proctor of the Cibo family. Sauli resigned a benefice to him in 1505 and from that year onwards he appears to be linked to the

[45] Cam. Ap., Resignationes 15, fos 26r, 288r; 8, fo. 86v; Reg. Lat. 1283, fos 153v–155r (ninety ducats); Reg. Vat. 1214, fos 66r–69v (120 ducats in an *expectativa*).

[46] Reg. Vat. 1214, fos 66r–69v; Notai Antichi, 1285, no. 72, 9 Mar. 1516; Cam. Ap., Resignationes 16, fo. 71v.

[47] Archivio Urbano, sezione 66, protocollo 20, fos 49v–56v; 13, fo. 106r–v; 25, fo. 116r; 28, fos 73r–74v; Notai Antichi, 1285, no. 72, 9 Mar. 1516.

[48] Notai Antichi, 1160, no. 96, 1 Apr. 1509.

[49] MS Ferr. 424, fo. 54r, 29 June. 1513; fo. 161r; Archivio Urbano, sezione 66, protocollo 20, fos 129v–130r; 21, fo. 114r–v; 13, fo. 106r; 14, fo. 166v; 28, fos 73r–75r; Archivio Sauli, no. 707, unfoliated.

[50] Notarile Ante-Cosimiano, 1002, 17 Nov. 1513. I am grateful to Philippa Jackson for bringing this document to my attention.

[51] MS Ferr. 424, fo. 161r; Reg. Vat. 1051, fos 136v–140r.

[52] Vat. Lat. 11172, fos 52r–53v, 8 Aug. 1525; Archivio Sauli, no. 1568, fos 45v, 47v.

cardinal and his family.[53] His will of 15 September 1514 was drawn up 'in the house of the Sauli' and was witnessed by some of the Sauli family's *famigliari*. Cocchio survived and he and Cardinal Sauli resigned the *regressus* on San Giorgio in Genoa on 8 April 1515.[54] A Didaco de Pace was witness to documents on four occasions between 1506 and 1510, and Sauli resigned a benefice to an Andrea de Pace in March 1508 and to a Sebastiano de Pace in 1510.[55] A Cristoforo Mariano was a witness to documents between 1508 and 1515 and in that year Sauli received benefices previously held by him.[56]

Two brothers, Aloysio and Benedicto (Benedetto) Tagliacarne, also had close contact with the cardinal and his family throughout the early *cinquecento*. Given Benedetto's humanist inclinations, his position may have been that of an educated young man who (in this case briefly) lived with the then *protonotario* Sauli, to provide illuminating conversation. This was not an uncommon practice in this period; similar examples survive for Cardinal Soderini and Cardinal Bainbridge.[57] Aloysio was witness to various Sauli documents regarding the cardinal and Sebastiano Sauli from 1506 to 1516 and had business dealings with Vincenzo Sauli. He seems to have been a 'floating' *famigliare*: a family intimate who moved from household to household as need arose.[58]

There is also a series of names, many of which feature only once or twice and for whom no further biographical information survives. Yet some can be identified as having been close to Sauli: Petrus Francus Cathaneis was a *continuus commensalis* of the cardinal, but then 'had withdrawn from this role'. He had previously held benefices in the diocese of Milan, including the canonry of San Lorenzo de Arsago which later passed to Domenico de' Caffis, and he had died by December 1516.[59] He can probably be identified with the Petrus Francescus de Capitaneis who was active in Genoa for the most part

---

[53] For his links to the Cibo, which necessitated further contact with the Sauli, see Notai Antichi, 1160, no. 288, 23 Nov. 1509; 1161, no. 168, 20 June 1510; no. 279, 16 Nov. 1510; no. 200, 7 May 1511; Cam. Ap., Resignationes 10, fo. 142v, 4 Dec. 1505. Cocchio (spelled variously) then witnesses the cardinal's resignation of another benefice on 27 Apr. 1506: Resignationes 10, fo. 174v.

[54] For his will see Notai del Tribunale, AC 7153, fos 227r–228v; Cam. Ap., Resignationes 15, fo. 166r.

[55] Cam. Ap., Resignationes 10, fo. 174v; 11, fos 33v, 121v; 12, fo. 287r.

[56] Ibid. 11, fo. 166v, 24 Mar. 1508; 12, fo. 287r, 4 July 1510; Archivio Urbano, sezione 66, protocollo 13, fo. 106r; 21, fo. 113r; Reg. Vat. 1070, fos 251r–253r.

[57] Lowe, *Church and politics*, 243–4, and 'Un episcopato', 117; Chambers, *Cardinal Bainbridge*, 116.

[58] Notai Antichi, 1159, no. 259, 7 Oct. 1506. By 20 Nov. 1507 he was in Rome and witnessed the resignation of a benefice by Bendinello: Cam. Ap., Resignationes 11, fo. 121v. He was in Genoa again in 1516 when he was witness to a document for Sebastiano Sauli: Notai Antichi, 1285, 12 Feb. 1516.

[59] 'ab ipsa familiaritate recesserat': Reg. Lat. 1363, fos 370v–372r.

and was also described as in the employ of Sebastiano Sauli.[60] Indeed, a 'Petro de Cathaneo' was witness to the will of Antonio Cocchio in the Sauli family home on 15 September 1514. If they are one and the same then he was also appointed by Cardinal Sauli as proctor to take possession of a *prepositura* in the diocese of Monreale.[61] The Ligurian Secondino Celexie was described as a *famigliare* and *continuus commensalis* of Sauli and was appointed rector of the parish church of San Marcellino (under the jurisdiction of San Siro) in Genoa in 1505.[62] Paulo de Marcati was a member of Sauli's household by mid-1513 at the latest. He was appointed as general proctor in a quarrel over a Spanish benefice and described as a *famigliare*. On 30 May 1517 he features in the Sauli accounts as the cardinal's *auditor*.[63] Francesco de Palastrellis was with Sauli in Genoa in 1516 and in Rome at his side when the cardinal was lying mortally ill.[64] The Ligurian Lorenzo de Gallis de Pontremulo is known to have been a Sauli *famigliare* from 1514 to 1517, holding a position of trust as demonstrated by the fact that he was appointed *vicario* and proctor of Sauli's benefices in Otranto.[65] He also lent money to Sauli's brothers to raise the fine to release Sauli from the Castel Sant'Angelo following his disgrace.[66] Marcantonio de Manarijs repaid a loan to Agostino and Giovanni Sauli on 8 March 1514 and was clearly still close to the cardinal and his family in 1517 when Sauli resigned a benefice to another *famigliare*, Giorgio Torniello, and awarded Marcantonio a pension on the same.[67] Domenico Andrea de Ancona was a witness to the rental document of the palace of Santa Maria in Via Lata in 1515, replaced Giovanni Sauli as Sebastiano Sauli's proctor on 6 September of that year and was still with the cardinal in the months leading up to his death.[68] His early role in Sauli's household is unrecorded but in 1517 he was described as 'secretary' and clearly occupied a position of trust given that he was in Bologna on unidentified business for Sauli in January of that year and in July was paid for the delivery of letters to the French court which pleaded Sauli's case following his arrest.[69] He is also described as a *penitentiarius* in 1517 but it is not known whether Sauli helped

---

60 Notai Antichi 1163, no. 89, 22 Apr. 1514.
61 Archivio Urbano, sezione 66, protocollo 13, fo. 109r, 9 Feb. 1514.
62 Notai Antichi 1158, no. 213, 22 July 1505.
63 Reg. Vat. 1037, fos 272r–275r, 17 May 1513; Archivio Urbano, sezione 66, protocollo 20, fos 129v–130r, 2 Dec. 1513; Archivio Sauli, no. 731, fo. 46r; no. 707 unfoliated.
64 Notai Antichi 1164, no. 47, 7 Feb. 1516; Cam. Ap., Resignationes 20, fo. 86v, 9 Feb. 1518.
65 Archivio Urbano, sezione 66, protocollo 13, fo. 106r; 14, fo. 167r.
66 MS Ferr. 424, fo. 162r.
67 Archivio Urbano, sezione 66, protocollo 21, fo. 171v; Cam. Ap., Resignationes 18, fo. 202v, 17 Apr. 1517.
68 Archivio Urbano, sezione 66, protocollo 25, fo. 16r–v, 17 Apr. 1515; 14, fo. 167v; Cam. Ap., Resignationes 17, fo. 253v, 6 Aug. 1517; Archivio Sauli, no. 707, unfoliated.
69 Archivio Sauli, no. 731, fos 19, 46r.

in obtaining that office for him. At some point after Sauli's death he entered Cardinal Soderini's household.[70]

Others appear only once in the accounts as *famigliari* and their roles are never identified: Perico, Thomaso Capriola Bresano, Franco de' Franchi (presumably a relative of Paulo Hieronimo de' Franchi), Hieronimo de' Fornari (a Ligurian) and Michaele Brege.[71] Sauli was an enthusiastic horseman who accompanied Leo on hunting trips and in 1513 the cardinal's head of stables was a certain Petro de Aladio. Various account entries survive for payments to grooms (*palafrenieri*) called Ermano, Andrea, Marioto and Ambrozio and on 20 September 1516 the sum of fifty ducats was paid to Sebastiano Giustiniani for the price of a horse purchased for the cardinal's use, but it is impossible to establish the size of his stable.[72]

Although the nationalities of some members of his *famiglia* are not clear, Sauli, and his brothers, were the patrons of Ligurians – the Tagliacarne brothers were from Levanto, Lorenzo de Gallis was from Pontremoli and Cathaneo was Genoese. The proctors appointed to deal with ecclesiastical or business affairs in Genoa and Albenga (Giacomo Anselmo, Hieronimo de Vernazza, Giovanni Battista de Balanchiis, Sebastiano de Pelitia, Secundo Marchesio and Verano Riccio) were all natives of Genoa or surrounding towns. Other members of Genoese *popolari* families were also appointed: Carolo de' Fornari was Sauli's proctor, and then rentor, of the abbey of San Simpliciano at Milan, and Hieronimo de' Fornari, a cleric, was witness to a document on 2 December 1513, but this is the only notice of him.[73] Various members of the Giustiniani, related to Sauli through his mother, Mariola Giustiniani, witnessed documents or seem to have been part of the larger Sauli entourage both in Genoa and in Rome. Of these, the most intimate was seemingly Sebastiano Giustiniani, cleric and chamberlain, who was certainly with the cardinal for six months: he witnessed documents on 30 June 1513 and 11 December 1513.[74] Filippo Maruffo (possibly an early member of the cardinal's entourage) and Luca Maruffo were appointed proctor and rentor of Otranto and Gerace and Oppide respectively.[75] The Genoese *nobile*,

[70] A.A., Arm. I–XVIII, 4770, fo. 2r; Lowe, *Church and politics*, 241 n. 38.

[71] Archivio Sauli, no. 730, fos 40r, 72r, 97r–v, 209v.

[72] MS Ferr. 424, 15r; Archivio Sauli, no. 714, fo. 36v; 730, fos 27r, 97v, 209v; no. 731, fos 19r, 59r; no. 707 unfoliated.

[73] I am grateful to Andrea Lercari for his help in identifying the Ligurian members of Sauli's household. See Archivio Urbano, sezione 66, protocollo 13, fo. 108r, 2 Jan. 1514; 21, fo. 113v, 27 May 1514; 20, fos 129v–130r (Carolo and Hieronimo de' Fornari respectively).

[74] See ibid. 20, fos 49v–56v; 21, fo. 141r. For Benedicto Giustiniani, bishop of Chios, present in Sauli's palace in January 1514, see 13, fos 108r–v. For Bernardo and Jeronimo Giustiniani see Cam. Ap., Resignationes 15, fo. 274, 28 Aug. 1514, and MS Ferr. 424, fo. 54r, 29 June 1513.

[75] For Filippo Maruffo see Cam. Ap., Resignationes 10, fo. 142v, and Archivio Urbano, sezione 66, protocollo 14, fo. 166v, 3 Nov. 1515. For Luca see 13, fo. 109v, 31 Mar. 1514, and 28, fos 73r–75v, 23 Aug. 1516.

Francesco Salvago, was appointed proctor to take possession of a church in Corsica.[76] The support of one's own 'countrymen' was usual in this period: de' Grassis noted in 1514 that many of Cardinal Bainbridge's *famigliari* were English.[77] In return a sense of common interest – the benefit of the *patria* through the success of the cardinal – ensured the loyalty of such servants.

Some members of Sauli's *famiglia* were laymen whilst others were rewarded by benefices and thus became clerics. Only two *frati* are mentioned in the surviving notarial sources: a Frate Valerio from Genoa, an Augustinian, who witnessed a resignation of Agostino Sauli to Bendinello in 1510 and a Frate Carolo de Marchionibus Ceve, a Franciscan, who witnessed two documents drawn up in the palace at Santa Maria in Via Lata in 1515 and who is mentioned in the Sauli accounts in September 1516.[78] We also know that in the autumn of 1517 or later Sauli's confessor was Fra Silvestro de Prierias. Undoubtedly there would have been other members of religious orders whose recorded membership of Sauli's *famiglia* is now lost, but it is unlikely that Sauli's *famiglia* was on the same scale as that of Rome's most lavish cardinal, Raffaele Riario. Garimberto described how the latter had 'a noble, and numerous *famiglia*, which included sixteen bishops as his *famigliari*, and other notable persons'.[79] But just how large was Sauli's *famiglia* and what indications do we have about his lifestyle?

Size and splendour

The change in lifestyle that must inevitably have occurred when Sauli's became a cardinal was reflected in his move at some date from the Vatican Palace to larger and more suitable accommodation. The cardinalate required greater degrees of magnificence, reflected in furnishings, entertainment and the size of the *famiglia*. The accounts of Cardinal Francesco Armellini demonstrate that upon becoming a cardinal in July 1517 his monthly withdrawals from his bankers increased and he incurred considerable additional expense in order to celebrate his elevation and the increase in size of his *famiglia* (for example the purchase of new mattresses, new silverware and the creation of a room in his living quarters for a domestic secretary).[80] In the census of late 1526 Armellini's household is given as 130 mouths, including his stables, although, as Emmanuel Rodocanachi notes, it may have been

---

[76] Ibid. 13 fo. 106r, 10 May 1514.

[77] Barb. Lat. 2683, fo. 109r; cf. Lowe, *Church and politics*, 242.

[78] Cam. Ap., Resignationes 12, fo. 240r; Archivio Urbano, sezione 66, protocollo 14, fos 166v–167r, 23 May, 9 Aug. 1515; Archivio Sauli, no. 730, fo. 97r.

[79] Garimberto, *La prima parte*, 371.

[80] G. De Caro, 'Armellini, Francesco', *DBI* iv (1962), 234–7; ASR, Camerale I, app. 16, fos 6r, 112r–v, 113v–114r, 117v, 124r; Lowe, 'Questions of income', 184–5.

larger at one time.[81] If the Armellini accounts for 1518 are compared with surviving Sauli household records a reasonable estimate of the size of Sauli's household may be made.

The main Armellini bank account for household expenses ('le spese di Casa') from the start of his banking records in March 1517 until 28 April 1523 was held with the bank of Martelli and Capponi. From September 1517 until early 1522 Armellini also authorised monthly sums to be withdrawn from the Gaddi bank, which, given the nature of the withdrawals, were also for the same purpose.[82] In 1518 Armellini received 2,400 ducats from Martelli and Capponi (160 per month, with the exception of May, June and July when he received 320) and 792 ducats (66 ducats per month) from the Gaddi: a total of 3,192 ducats giving an average monthly household expenditure budget of 266 ducats. There is also a one-off payment, on 23 August 1518, from Martelli-Capponi of 320 ducats to cover 'a considerable sum of money we had paid on the Cardinal's orders'.[83] This gives an annual total of 3,512 ducats.

What of Sauli's expenditure? If, as Peter Partner believes, an income of 12,000 ducats (which was also the sum recommended by Cortesi in his *De cardinalatu*) 'made a cardinal rich', then Cardinal Sauli was rich in 1516.[84] It is almost impossible to ascertain the exact nature of a cardinal's income, especially when, as in Sauli's case, much of it was derived from benefices and some difficult to define business interests in Genoa, and not, as in the case of Soderini and Armellini, also from properties held in Rome. Properties and money held in Genoa were for the most part inherited from Pasquale Sauli, and were in the joint names of Bendinello and his brothers and thus his share of the income would have been merely one fifth, increasing to a quarter on the death of Pasquale II in 1515.[85] The situation with reference to his ecclesiastical benefices is equally murky: even when the document in which a benefice is conferred has survived, and this is not always the case, it is more than likely that the document in which the holder resigned it is missing, so that it is impossible to tell how long he held the benefice. These difficulties notwithstanding, it is possible to estimate that in 1516,

---

81 Gnoli, *Descriptio urbis*, 387, 452; E. Rodocanachi, *La Première Renaissance: Rome au temps de Jules II et de Léon X*, Paris 1912, 75.

82 Cf. Rodocanachi, *La Première Renaissance*, 74, and Partner, *Renaissance Rome*, 138. For Martelli and Capponi see Camerale I, app. 15, fo. 5v; 16, fo. 6r–v; 17, fo. 2r; 18, fo. 3r–v; for the Gaddi see app. 16, fo. 8r (1517–18); 15, fo. 4r (1519–20), and 18, fo. 4r (1521–2).

83 'parechi denari havevemo pagati p comissione dil Cardinale': Camerale I, app. 16, fo. 7r.

84 See Partner, *Renaissance Rome*, 137, where he also notes that in 1501 only one in six cardinals possessed this or a higher income. See also D'Amico, *Renaissance humanism*, 49–50.

85 The history of Sauli business interests in Genoa for this and earlier periods is still to be written, as is that of many other Genoese families.

prior to his disgrace, Sauli probably garnered approximately 13,500 ducats *per annum* from his benefices, a figure which was then greatly inflated by the pension of 4,000 ducats that he acquired in April 1517 when San Simpliciano passed to the Benedictine-Cassinese Congregation. He would also, when in Rome, have received a share of the common services which, during the period in question, seem to have averaged about 900 ducats *per annum* for each cardinal.[86]

Did Sauli's lifestyle reflect his wealth? Unlike many cardinals he was never greatly in debt: from January 1516 until the beginning of May 1517 the amount he owed to his bankers varied between 1,649 and 3,850 ducats. At their worst his debts were approximately one quarter of his income, a mere pittance if compared to the debts of Cardinal Federico Sanseverino (1489–1516) who on his death owed 37,000 ducats against an income of *c.* 26,000 ducats or Cardinal de' Medici who in 1521 owed more than his income of 20,000 ducats.[87] However great or small was his private income, it is clear that his benefices were an important source of income to Cardinal Sauli: during and after his imprisonment in the Castel Sant'Angelo nearly all his benefices were redistributed so that on his release his lifestyle changed dramatically.

No evidence survives of Sauli's daily household expenses but there is evidence of the sums paid on the basic monthly household expenses from January 1516 to March 1517. It is clear from surviving details of his withdrawals from, or payments made on his behalf by, the bank of Sebastiano, Giovanni and Agostino Sauli that payments for supplies on contract for his household, for example wine, grain, bread, oil, straw and hay, were for the most part withdrawn separately from the cardinal's account.[88] Payments to cover the rest of the household expenses were, for the most part, made to the *maestro di casa* (Giovanni Angelo Gometius) 'for the expenses of' the month(s) in question. Some small additional payments were made separately, first to a Giovanni Antonio then to an Antonio de Faventia (Faventino) the *spenditori* (purveyors), apparently as and when necessary or when Gometius was absent. The specific reason for the payments to the purveyors is never clear, but their role seems to have been to shop on a daily basis for fresh and seasonal food and for food not supplied on contract.[89] Such separate payments are not listed in Cardinal Armellini's accounts and indeed in the Sauli account books, with the exception of March 1517 when Antonio

---

[86] Lowe, *Church and politics*, 248. The estimate of his income is based on documented sources which I have been able to trace in the ASV.

[87] Archivio Sauli, no. 730, fos 27r, 40r, 72r, 97r, 209r, 227r; no. 731, fos 19r, 41r, 46r; Partner, *Renaissance Rome*, 137; Barb. Lat. 2683, fo. 166r.

[88] For example eighty-six ducats were paid on 13 March 1516 for bread for the period of 1 Nov. 1515 to 28 Feb. 1516: Archivio Sauli, no. 730, fo. 27r. See ibid and fo. 72r for payments for grain; no. 730, fos 40r, 72r, and no. 731, fos 19r, 46r, 91r for payments for other goods.

[89] Hollingsworth, *The cardinal's hat*, 54.

Faventino substituted for Gometius, they represent only six out of twenty-five payments for general household expenses for the period in question (for a total of 329 out of 4,028 ducats). Thus in the cases of Cardinal Sauli and Cardinal Armellini it seems that the *maestro di casa* gave the purveyor whatever money was needed on a daily basis and the payments to Antonio, the Sauli purveyor, were 'extras' to be added to the Sauli household expenses, perhaps reflecting additional expenses for entertainment and hospitality, the details of which have not survived.

The overall Sauli figures (including payments made to the purveyor) naturally reflect the cardinal's movements and those of his *famiglia*. The payments for early 1516 – when it is known that Sauli went to Genoa (and presumably lived there mostly at his brothers' expense) following the meeting of the papal court with Francis I at Bologna in December 1515 – are minimal: approximately 147 ducats for January; a mere 41 ducats for February.[90] By mid-March he had returned to Rome and the figures increase to approximately 213 ducats in March; 206 in April; 331 in May; 259 in June; 180 in July, reflecting the greater numbers of mouths to feed.[91] August, September and October were more expensive: 307, 458 and 433 ducats respectively.[92] There are two possible explanations for this dramatic increase: celebrations were perhaps held for Sauli's permanent transfer to Santa Maria in Trastevere on the death of Cardinal Vigerio in July 1516 and in September Sauli (and some of his household) accompanied Leo and other cardinals to Viterbo for two costly months of hunting, returning to Rome at the latest by 22 October 1516.[93] Expenses for November and December were 317 and 324 ducats respectively: higher, that is, than the period before his transfer to Santa Maria in Trastevere.[94] January 1517 was also an expensive month: 394 ducats, but then there was a swift decrease to 183 ducats in February and 235 in March.[95] In 1516 Sauli's annual expenditure on general household expenses was 3,216 ducats (268 ducats per month), compared to the 3,512 spent by Cardinal Armellini in 1518 (292 ducats per month). Both had additional expenses which are included in these figures: Sauli went on hunting trips and Armellini had the unspecified expenses covered by the 320 ducats provided by Martelli-Capponi in August 1518, but the figures are remarkably similar.

From July 1516 the sum of 150 ducats seems to have been what Gometius

---

[90] Archivio Sauli. no. 730, fo. 27r.

[91] Ibid. fos 27r, 40r, 72r–v.

[92] Ibid. fos 72v, 209r.

[93] For the expense see Hollingsworth, *The cardinal's hat*, 81, and Rodocanachi, *La Première Renaissance*, 76. For the hunting see Cod. Reg. Lat. 387, fo. 184, and Archivio Sauli, no. 730, fo. 97v for the payment of 20 Sept. of 300 ducats to Paulo Hieronimo de' Franchi 'pro viagio sue reverendissime domini cum Sanctitate domini nostri'.

[94] Archivio Sauli, no. 730, fos 209r, 227r.

[95] Ibid. no. 731, fos 19r, 91r. The figures for April and May 1517 are, for some reason, incomplete and are made more difficult to analyse by Sauli's arrest in May. They have thus not been included.

normally had to work with 'for this month' (with the exception of the period in Viterbo) and all other expenses were met later. It should also be remembered that payments for grain, bread, straw, hay, wine and oil were made separately. Overall, what do these figures show? Armellini ran a *famiglia* of approximately 130 people on 292 ducats per month in 1518: Sauli's then was probably of at least the same size and, given the average monthly expenditure from November 1516 to January 1517, he probably entertained on a more lavish scale.

This way of life ended when Sauli was implicated in the plot to murder Leo X. The cardinal was arrested on 19 May 1517 and Stefano Sauli seems to have taken over his household, initially authorising payments to Antonio, the purveyor, to keep it running.[96] Sauli was imprisoned for more than two months and incurred heavy expenses in addition to the fine to be paid for his release. After he was freed he was kept a virtual prisoner in the Vatican, perhaps returning briefly to the palace at Santa Maria in Via Lata, then to be exiled to Monterotondo in October. He was not there long: his health had never been robust and in Monterotondo he seems to have contracted tertiary fever. He had returned to Rome, escorted by Stefano Sauli, by 6 November 1517.[97]

The cardinal did not return to his palace, nor did he live with his brothers. Instead, from 9 November (and probably until his death), he lived in a property provided by the noble Roman Santacroce family in the parish of San Salvatore in Campo, taken on a three-month rental at the price of twenty-five ducats per month (the equivalent of 300 ducats *per annum*).[98] This house was probably the present-day Palazzo Santacroce: a census of late 1517/early 1518 records 'first the palace of those of the Santacroce, where Cardinal Sauli lives at present', although the Sauli bank records describe the rental payments to the Santacroce as only 'for the provision of a home' and not specifically for the Santacroce palace.[99] The survival of the date on which the rental started provides a more secure dating for this census: it was drawn up between 9 November 1517 and Sauli's death on 29 March 1518. The census of late 1526 lists the Santacroce houses as in Regola but, as Anthony Majanlahti notes, their 'contrada crossed the boundaries of three rioni', Regola, Arenula and Santo Martinello. Since the document of 3 February

[96] Ibid. fo. 46r. The last payment to Antonio is on 26 July 1517, after which point he disappears from the banking records.

[97] H. Lippomano to M. Sanuto, 21 Oct. 1517, Sanuto, *Diarii*, xxv. 66; Archivio Sauli, no. 731, fo. 59r; Ferrajoli, *La congiura*, 99 n. 4.

[98] Archivio Sauli, no. 731, fo. 67r, where it is recorded that seventy-five ducats were paid to Antonio Santacroce, Petro Tarquinio and Noffrio Santacroce on 10 December 1517 for the three months beginning on 9 November.

[99] M. Armellini, *Un censimento della città di Roma sotto il pontificato di Leone X: tratto da un codice inedito dell'Archivio Vaticano*, Rome 1882, 9, 95; 'Prima lo pallazo de queli de Sta + habita al presente el Reverendissimo Cardinale de Sauli': Vat. Lat. 11985, fo. 51v; 'pro provisione domus': Archivio Sauli, no. 731, fo. 67r.

1518, written some seven weeks before Sauli's death, was drawn up 'in the district of Santo Martinello, or Arenula in the house of the most Reverend Cardinal Sauli' it seems likely that Sauli was still in the Santacroce house at that time and probably died there.[100] Given that, according to the census of late 1526, the four houses listed as belonging to the Santacroce in this area housed a maximum of twenty-eight mouths, it is clear how far Sauli had fallen, and indeed how the Santacroce profited from a short-term lease to a man in poor health and in desperate need of accommodation.[101]

It is interesting to compare the behaviour of his own family and his *famiglia* following Sauli's disgrace: both were equally affected by his downfall, loss of prestige and subsequent change to their livelihoods. The Sauli had to pay a deposit and a fine to secure his release from the Castel Sant'Angelo and the cardinal's reduced financial circumstances may well have had an impact on the payment of salaries to his staff, but while the Sauli rallied round their sick relative the same cannot be said of his *famigliari*. Blood ties were obviously stronger than patronal ties and in a Rome where reputation and profile were so important, the contagion of disgrace overcame any sense of loyalty. Thus the names which had so regularly featured in earlier account book entries disappear. Gometius had, for whatever reason, left the cardinal's service; Antonio the *spenditore* is replaced by a Giovanni Birtono and all payments to him are authorised by Domenico de' Caffis who was clearly running the household by this date. In November and December 1517 a mere 125 ducats and 190 ducats were paid to Birtono. Since no separate payments are recorded for bread, oil, wine and grain, as was the case before his arrest, it is likely that these expenses were also met from these sums. It can thus be assumed that his household was considerably less than half its previous size and, whichever of the Santacroce properties Sauli was residing in, it was in cramped conditions.[102]

So what of de' Grassis's remark that Sauli surpassed all in splendour and pomp? Whether he surpassed all other cardinals is very much open to debate: little is known about the lifestyles of other members of the college and Sauli's debts were never excessive. But he certainly lived on a par with Cardinal Armellini. It can be deduced from the amount spent on running his household, and its probable size, that Sauli maintained a level of splendour and pomp proper to the dignity of the cardinalate, but not on the same scale as, for example, the debt-ridden San Severino or de' Medici. Within this context Giovio's later comment on the 'goodness of his habits, and the

---

[100] Gnoli, 'Descriptio urbis', 480; A. Majanlahti, *The families who made Rome: a history and a guide*, London 2005, 16; Notai Antichi, 1522bis, no. 135.

[101] Gnoli, 'Descriptio urbis', 477, 480; *Descriptio urbis*, 97, 100.

[102] For the months of November and December see Archivio Sauli, no. 731, fos 59r–v, 67r. The bank records for 1518 do not survive.

modesty of his esteemed lifestyle' begins to make sense.[103] If de' Grassis over-stated his case it may have been to highlight a real and demonstrable truth, namely that Sauli died 'without title, and without benefices, and without honour'.[104]

[103] Giovio, *Le vite*, 270.
[104] 'sine titulo, & sine beneficio, & sine honore': Barb. Lat. 2683, fo. 269r.

5

Cardinal Sauli and Humanist Patronage

The honour that Sauli lacked in death was far from missing in life. He and his position as cardinal of the Catholic Church were celebrated, both directly and indirectly, in the works of the humanists of whom he was patron. Such patronage, like that of his household, was part of an established and deliberate pattern of magnificence but was not necessarily of such a fixed nature. A cardinal's material patronage of a humanist could range from a one-off payment in the form of money or a gift, the use of a cardinal's library or the payment of the publication costs of a work, to the provision of a place in the cardinal's household, with perhaps a benefice as well. Humanists were considered a positive influence: Cortesi advocated them as *famigliari* for, amongst other qualities, their more sober temperaments and their usefulness in tackling problems.[1] Whatever the nature of the patronal relationship, it was considered to be of mutual advantage: the humanist could pursue his studies, thus bringing glory to the cardinal's name and the cardinal would in turn improve his own erudition, promote learning and thus his own reputation and honour.

Sauli was part of a long-standing tradition of cardinal-patrons of humanists. He followed in the footsteps of, and was starting to take the place of, illustrious antecedents such as Cardinal Bessarion (1439–73); Cardinal Jacopo Ammanati-Piccolomini (1461–79) and Cardinal Francesco Todeschini Piccolomini (Pius III) (1460–1503).[2] Although a cardinal-patron did not necessarily have to be possessed of a great intellect, amongst Sauli's contemporaries some cardinals stand out for precisely this reason: Pietro Accolti (1511–32) was judged to be the most cultured member of the college of cardinals by the French chancellor Duprat, although details of his patronage are scant; Achille de' Grassis (1511–23), brother of the papal master of ceremonies, was a lawyer and had taught at the university of Bologna, while Bernardino Carvajal was famous for his intellect and the author of several *sermones* and *orationes*.[3] But perhaps the outstanding minds of the period were Cardinal Marco Vigerio and Cardinal Adriano Castellesi. Vigerio was recognised by Garimberto as a distinguished theologian, the author of the *Apologia* against

---

[1]   D'Amico, *Renaissance humanism*, 52, citing Cortesi, *De cardinalatu*.
[2]   Ibid. 53–5, 99.
[3]   B. Ulianich, 'Accolti, Pietro', *DBI* i (1960), 106–10 at p. 106; S. Tabacchi, 'Grassi, Achille', *DBI* lviii (2002), 587–91 at p. 588; Fragnito, 'Carvajal', 33.

the Council of Pisa and of the *Decachordum Christianum*.[4] Castellesi, one of the few humanists to become a cardinal, knew Latin, Greek and Hebrew, was the author of *De vera philosophia ex quattuor doctoribus ecclesiae* (1506) and *De sermone latino* (*c.* 1514) and in 1516 had begun to translate the first two books of the Bible from the Hebrew into Latin.[5]

Many of Sauli's peers were also patrons or were addressed as would-be patrons by humanists. A cursory examination reveals that Galeotto Franc-iotti della Rovere (1503–7) was friendly with Pietro Bembo and Baldassare Castiglione and himself wrote poetry in the *volgare*; his secretary for certain periods was Scipione Forteguerri (Carteromachus) who contributed to an edition of Ptolemy's *Geographia* (1507) and Girolamo Basso della Rovere (1477–1507) was the dedicatee of a work by Baptista Mantuanus.[6] Giovanni Francesco Pico dedicated his *De imitatione* to Cardinal Bibbiena (1513–20) and Sigismondo Gonzaga (1505–25) was the dedicatee of Pamphilius Saxus' *Epigrammatum libri IV*.[7] Cardinal Fieschi was the dedicatee of an *Apologia* by Bernardo de Vio (later Cardinal Cajetan, himself a noted scholar) and of Michele de Petra Sancta Serravezza's *Questio de promo cognito*.[8] Alessandro Farnese (later Pope Paul III) studied Greek in his youth, had as his secre-tary Scipione Forteguerri, featured in Paolo Cortesi's *De hominibus doctis* and had a series of poems written in his honour by Alessandro Cortesi.[9] Yet the great cardinal-patrons of the day in this field, as in many others, were Raffaele Riario and Oliviero Carafa. The latter had works dedicated to him by, to name only a few, Bernardino Carvajal, Jacopo Bonus, Francesco Elio Marchisi, Augustinus Niphus, Filippo Barbieri, Antonio Beccadelli and his secretary Andrea Brenta.[10] The list is equally long for Riario: for example, Lorenzo Buonincontri, Johannes Sulpitius, Petrus Marsus, Sebastianus Salvinus and Marsilio Ficino. Performances of Latin plays were put on in his palaces.[11]

Although much is known about the works dedicated to these cardinals, the circumstances in which they were written – whether as shots in the dark in an attempt to gain favour, which would not necessarily be granted, or as

4   Garimberto, *La prima parte*, 167–8; Cosenza, *Dictionary*, vi. 292.
5   D'Amico, *Renaissance humanism*, 16; G. Fragnito, 'Castellesi, Adriano', *DBI* xxi (1978), 665–71 at pp. 665, 670; Paschini, 'Tre illustri prelati', 108–15.
6   Cherubini, 'Franciotti della Rovere, Galeotto', *DBI* l (1998), 165–7 at p. 167; J. Haig Gaisser, *Piero Valeriano on the ill fortune of learned men: a Renaissance humanist and his world*, Anne Arbor, MI 1999, 291; F. Piovan, 'Forteguerra, Scipione', *DBI* xlix (1997), 163–7 at pp. 164–5; M. Miglio, 'Brenta, Andrea', *DBI* xiv (1972), 149–51 at p. 151; Cosenza, *Dictionary*, i. 813, 860–1; iv. 3107.
7   Cosenza, *Dictionary*, i. 583; ii. 1651.
8   F. Ascarelli, *Annali tipografici di Giacomo Mazzocchi*, Florence 1961, 64, 112.
9   D'Amico, *Renaissance humanism*, 46, 75–6, 97.
10 Petrucci, 'Carafa', 595.
11 Cosenza, *Dictionary*, v. 3037; A. Schiavo, *Il palazzo della Cancelleria*, Rome 1964, 55 n. 2.

thank-offerings from a grateful *famigliare* – are not always clear. Dependent on their patrons' good will and good health, humanists often moved from household to household: Scipione Forteguerri served Cardinals Domenico Grimani, Franciotti della Rovere, Alessandro Farnese (at times in tandem with della Rovere) and then Francesco Alidosi.[12] Precise details of the humanist members of the cardinals' households are also relatively scant. But, given the little surviving information, how does Cardinal Sauli compare? Sauli's own scholarly inclinations were certainly recognised in his own life-time. In 1515 the humanist Raffaele Brandolini described him as 'very wise', praised him for his intellect and noted that he read extensively.[13] When Sauli was exiled to Monterotondo in late 1517, Lippomano wrote that if Sauli wished, he would have space to study there.[14]

This picture of Sauli as a learned cardinal never totally disappeared. Indeed, in the historiography of Sauli his patronage of men of letters and his own intellect are, like his role in the plot to murder Leo X, a constant feature. His interests most clearly emerge in the 1574 eulogy written by Umberto Foglietta, the nephew of Agostino Foglietta, one of Sauli's fellow conclavists in 1513. Foglietta described him as possessing a lively mind and being a well-educated patron of men of letters, and listed Giovanni Maria Cattaneo and Paolo Giovio as part of his household (surprisingly, he omitted the name of another, well-known, Genoese humanist).[15] There can be little doubt that Foglietta's description formed the basis of that of later commentators, although some writers found further flesh to put on the bones of Sauli's intellectual interests. In 1630 Ciaconio had little to add other than an emphasis on Sauli's knowledge of many things, and that, even as a boy, he was especially well-versed in literature.[16] However, in 1652 Ughelli returned to earlier, then little known sources, to highlight that a 'monachus Severus', together with Cattaneo, Giovio and other great men of letters gathered in Sauli's court ('aula') to discuss theology.[17] Cardella, writing in 1793, described how Sauli held men of letters in high esteem and how those who interested him were well-renumerated; thus Sauli 'was able to make notable advancements in the study of the sciences, and holy learning'.[18] Given that Genoa has been consistently described as not being 'a culturally

---

[12] A. Chiti, *Scipione Forteguerri (il Carteromaco): studio biografico con una raccolta di epigrammi, sonetti e lettere di lui o a lui dirette*, Florence 1902, 17, 24, 27.

[13] 'prudentissimum': BCIS, MS K VI 73, fo. 3v. For Sauli's 'animo atque ingenio' and 'Legisti tu quidam pro summo tuo et vetustatis et optimarum artium studio' see fos 25r, 28r respectively.

[14] Lippomano to Sanuto, 21 Oct. 1517, Sanuto, *Diarii*, xxv. 66,.

[15] Folietae, *Clarorum ligurum*, 143.

[16] Ciaconio, *Vitae et res gestae pontificum*, 1385.

[17] F. Ughelli, *Italia sacra sive de episcopis Italiae et insularum adiacentium*, Rome 1644–62, iv. 1278.

[18] L. Cardella, *Memorie storiche de' cardinali della santa Romana Chiesa*, Rome 1793, iii. 356.

active or particularly important centre in the world of humanism', this paints a promising, and surprising, picture of Sauli as a cardinal-patron. How much of it was true?[19]

The humanist-secretary

Priscianese insisted, albeit with reference to a secular court, upon the importance of the secretary, a figure who could, literally, make or break his patron. He had to be loyal, diligent, eloquent, concise and wise.[20] Although at certain times Sauli had more than one secretary – for example Paolo Hieronimo de' Franchi acted as such at one time – the principal holder of this office was the humanist Giovanni Maria Cattaneo (after 1480–1529/30), a writer esteemed for his translations from Greek into Latin, who undoubtedly brought honour to Sauli's name.

Born in Novara and educated at Milan where he studied under Giorgio Merula and Demetrius Chalcondylas, Cattaneo first came to public attention with the highly successful publication in 1506 of his commentaries on the letters of Pliny the Younger.[21] Giovio, who knew him intimately in Sauli's household, believed that as a result of the fame and success resulting from this edition, Cattaneo came to Rome where, at an unknown date (but probably by 1509), Sauli took him into his household as 'secretary'.[22] His duties were principally to deal with the cardinal's correspondence, now unfortunately for the most part lost. But in other respects Cattaneo did not remain idle: he translated three of Lucian's dialogues, although just when is still open to debate, and in 1517 he published his translation of the *Preexercitamentorum libellus* of Aphthonius.[23] He was also an active member of the literary sodality – one of several in Rome at the time – which gathered around Hans Goritz (known as Corycius) and contributed to, and possibly edited, the *Coryciana*, poems written by its members.[24] His contributions to the *Coryciana* were the first signs of an interest in poetry and it was in this genre that he chose to celebrate Sauli.

Cattaneo must have accompanied Cardinal Sauli on a visit to Genoa, possibly that of July 1507, but more probably that of October 1509 to gather

[19] Petrucciani, 'Le biblioteche', 240.
[20] Priscianese, *Del governo*, 68.
[21] *C. Plinii Caecili secondi epistolarum libri IX: libellus epistol. ad Traianum cum rescriptis ed. principi: panegyricus Traiano dictus cum enarrationibus Io. Mar. Catanei*; G. Ballistreri, 'Cattaneo, Giovanni Maria', *DBI* xxii (1979), 468–71 at p. 468.
[22] P. Giovio, *Le iscrittioni poste sotto le vere imagini degli huomini famosi in lettere*, trans. H. Ohio, Venice 1558, 171; Archivio Urbano, sezione 66, protocollo 13, 109v, 31 Mar. 1514.
[23] Ballistreri, 'Cattaneo', 468, 469.
[24] Ibid. 468. The term 'sodality', adopted here, is used in Haig Gaisser, *Piero Valeriano*, passim where Goritz is considered in more detail.

material for what is his most famous work, the poem *Genua*.[25] It was published in 1514 and written, according to Giovio, 'at his Lord's instance' with a dedication to the cardinal's brother, Stefano Sauli. It described Genoa and its inhabitants and customs in verse and was, in Cattaneo's own words, unique: nobody had previously attemped such a feat. As such it is an important indication of Sauli's awareness of his own significance: this insistence upon flamboyant novelty will also figure in Sauli's artistic patronage.[26] In praising the Ligurian city, its people and their achievements Cattaneo naturally did not forget to promote the Sauli name. He noted how amongst the cardinals whom Genoa had produced, Bendinello had suffered the vicissitudes of fortune (presumably an allusion to his long wait for the cardinalate), but his heart burned with happy wisdom.[27] The poem ends, perhaps inevitably, with the hope that Bendinello might become pope and that war be waged against the Turks.[28] As Girolamo Bertolotto notes, the poem was well known in the *cinquecento* and was not forgotten by later commentators; its very originality seems to have brought it success and to have encouraged Cattaneo to further poetical efforts.[29] During Sauli's lifetime Cattaneo began to write a poem on the first crusade, *De solymnis*, which in turn was scathingly described by Giovio as 'a far from happy effort', a view shared, if Giovio is to be believed, by Pietro Bembo.[30] Yet Francesco Arsilli, in his *De poetis urbanis*, published in 1524, wondered, apparently without irony, 'what the muses would say if I didn't mention our Cattaneo?'[31]

Sauli's secretary was thus an esteemed translator of Pliny, Lucian (and also Isocrates), sufficiently well known and established in Rome to be a part of a thriving literary sodality and the author of a unique celebratory poem. He played an important role in Sauli's household, as secretary and *continuus commensalis*.[32] A sense of the prestige which the cardinal acquired by having so prominent a humanist as his secretary is demonstrated by the fact that Cattaneo is shown with Sauli in Sebastiano del Piombo's *Cardinal Bendinello Sauli and three companions* (1516) (*see* plate 1). Cattaneo was also rewarded

---

[25] See Notai Antichi, 1159, no.118, 7 July 1507; 1413, nos 326–7, 3 Oct. 1509, which detail Sauli dealing with business for the abbey of San Siro whilst in Genoa.
[26] 'nemo enim hactenus circumfertur, qui tale aliquod absolverit': Cataneo, *Genua*, i.
[27] Ibid. lines 327–30.
[28] 'O te maxime Serto/ BENDinelle decus virtutum tempora terno/ Aspiciam redimitum. O aurea tempora quando/ Tu concors Genua, atque in terris Maximus ille/ Cingetis gladios ad belli munera iustos:/Et Maumetanos contundet uterque furores': ibid. lines 461–6.
[29] G. Bertolotto, '*Genua* poemetto di Giovanni Maria Cataneo con introduzione e appendice storica a cura del socio Girolamo Bertolotto', *ASLSP* xxiv (1894), 729–818 at p. 732.
[30] Giovio, *Le iscrittioni*, 171, 172; Ballistreri, 'Cattaneo', 469; Giovio, *Dialogus de viris*, 234; P. Orth, 'Zur *Solymis* des Giovanni Maria Cattaneo', *Humanistica Lovaniensa: Journal of Neo-Latin Studies* l (2001), 131–41 at pp. 131–4, 136.
[31] *Poesie latine di Francesco Arsilli medico e poeta senigallese del secolo XVI: tratte da un codice autografo*, ed. R. Francolini, Senigallia 1837, 12–13.
[32] Notarile Ante-Cosimiano 1002, 17 Nov. 1513.

by help from his patron in acquiring at least four benefices, two of which were awarded in 1513 and 1514, and a pension of one hundred ducats a year on a canonry in Toledo.[33]

It is difficult to establish exactly what happened to Cattaneo following Sauli's arrest: did he leave the household immediately or stay with the cardinal until his death? It is clear, however, that uniquely amongst the humanists under Sauli's wing, the cardinal's disgrace had no effect on Cattaneo's literary and curial career. He remained in Rome, continued to write and enjoyed a position of some influence in the Curia, accruing what was believed to be a large number of benefices.[34]

The humanist doctor

Paolo Giovio (c. 1486–1552) is the best known of the humanists who gathered around Sauli, yet his stay in his household is poorly documented. Educated at Padua, Pavia and Milan, Giovio studied both the liberal arts and medicine.[35] He arrived in Rome in 1512 and joined Sauli's household at an unknown date. Sauli may well have known Ottobono Fieschi, a Genoese friend of Giovio's, or have met Giovio when Fieschi took him to Genoa as a young man. Alternatively Cattaneo, who was at Milan with Giovio, may have recommended him to Sauli.[36] The earliest notice of Giovio assisting the cardinal is on 3 September 1515 when as 'Paulo Jovio doctor' he witnessed a document drawn up in Sauli's palace.[37] Giovio's dislike of practising medicine is well-documented, although after Sauli's disgrace he went on to serve Cardinal de' Medici as cardinal and then pope in this role, and in 1522, Cardinal Cesarini, but he was also an accomplished humanist and may have served Sauli in this, still undocumented, capacity.[38]

No evidence survives of Giovio acquiring ecclesiastical benefices under Sauli, but as part of the cardinal's retinue in December 1515 he accompanied 'our monsignor de' Sauli' to Bologna for the meeting between Leo X

---

[33] Reg. Vat. 1037, fos 272r–275r, 17 May 1513; Archivio Urbano, sezione 66, protocollo 13, fo. 109v, 31 Mar. 1514. For the pension see Notarile Ante-Cosimiano, 1002, 17 Nov. 1513. In the same document Cattaneo is described as 'clericus Januensis', thus the holder of a so far unidentified benefice in Sauli's home town. Furthermore, in an attachment to this document of 12 Sept. 1513, he is described as 'clericus Novariensis' indicating that he held a so far unidentified benefice in this diocese as well.

[34] Ballistreri, 'Cattaneo', 469, 470. For some of the benefices he acquired after Sauli's death see F. Russo, *Regesto Vaticano per la Calabria*, Rome 1977, iii. 312, 339.

[35] T. C. P. Zimmerman, *Paolo Giovio: the historian and the crisis of sixteenth-century Italy*, Princeton 1995, 6–12.

[36] Ibid. 6, 14; Giovio, *Dialogus de viris*, 290.

[37] 'Paulo Jovio medico': Archivio Urbano, sezione 66, protocollo 14, fo. 167r.

[38] Zimmerman, *Paolo Giovio*, 14; P. Capparoni, *Paolo Giovio archiatra di papa Clemente VII*, Grottaferrata 1913, 4; *Lettere inedite di P. Giovio tratte dall'Archivio Gonzaga*, ed. A. Luzio, Mantua 1885, 21–3.

and Francis I of France, thus witnessing one of the most important historical events of the period.[39] He wrote to Marino Sanuto from Bologna that 'I have followed my lord, by whom I am petted'. Sauli's proximity to Leo probably benefitted Giovio: in the same letter Giovio noted that 'I am working on the Istoria [his Historiae] and think of nothing else but to finish it and publish it. The pope has ... praised it.'[40] In the next sentence he notes that he has been awarded the lectureship in natural philosophy at the University of Rome, although there is no evidence of intervention by Sauli to gain him this post.[41] His importance to Sauli, and the prestige that Sauli accorded him, is reflected in his inclusion with Cattaneo in Sebastiano del Piombo's painting.

Like Cattaneo Giovio was part of Roman intellectual life, but unlike Cattaneo he was affected by Sauli's disgrace: a letter of 3 July 1520 notes that 'if it had not been for the disgrace of the late Cardinal Sauli, perhaps we wouldn't have to struggle any more; and perhaps it will be for the best; and in truth I no longer count on the pope'.[42] Although three years after Sauli's disgrace Giovio was not receiving the favours he would have hoped for, he had joined the household of Cardinal de' Medici. The rare mentions of Sauli in Giovio's later works are gentle and a touch ironic, with the exception of the account of the plot in his Life of Leo. It is clear from this that some bitterness remained, presumably for the problems Giovio had suffered after Sauli's disgrace: he does not spare the cardinal's blushes.[43]

The humanist relative

Although Foglietta failed to mention him, there can be little doubt that Agostino Giustiniani (1470–1536) was for a time part of Sauli's household. He has been described as probably 'the foremost Genoese figure of high Renaissance humanism' and for much of the second decade of the cinque-cento was closely linked to members of the Sauli family. Giustiniani himself wrote that, although he and the cardinal were cousins, the cardinal loved and revered him for other reasons, enjoyed his conversation and wanted him to live in his household in Rome.[44]

Born in Genoa in 1470 as Pantaleone Giustiniani, Agostino was related to Sauli through the cardinal's mother, Mariola Giustiniani Longhi quondam

[39] Giovio to Marino Sanuto, 15 Dec. 1515, Paolo Giovio: lettere, i, no. 2 at p. 85.
[40] Ibid.
[41] Giovio first held the post in moral philosophy which he was awarded in 1514: Zimmerman, Paolo Giovio, 14–15; G. Sanuto to M. Sanuto, 15 Dec. 1515, Paolo Giovio: lettere, i, no. 2 at p. 85.
[42] P. Giovio to B. Giovio, 3 July 1520, Paolo Giovio: lettere, no. 3 at pp. 86–7.
[43] Zimmerman, Paolo Giovio, 15, 29.
[44] Musso, 'La cultura genovese', 152; Giustiniani, Castigatissimi annali, c. 224r.

Giacomi.[45] A genuinely religious man, he joined the reformed Dominican Lombard congregation in 1488, taking the name of Fra Agostino.[46] His years in the congregation were spent in study and teaching, mostly in Bologna where he made many humanist friends.[47] There is no concrete proof of any contact with members of the Sauli family until two of the cardinal's close relations, his cousin, Filippo, and his brother, Stefano, arrived at Bologna to pursue their studies, and, perhaps not coincidentally, until Bendinello Sauli was made a cardinal and thus become a figure of importance and influence. In 1513 Giustiniani dedicated his first published work, an edition of Ambrogio Traversari's translation of *De immortalitate animorum* by Aeneas of Gaza, to Filippo Sauli, and in the same year he dedicated his first autograph work, the cabalistic *Praecatio pietatis plena ad deum omnipotentem composita ex duobus et septuaginta nominibus divinis, Hebraicis et Latinis una cum interprete* to Stefano Sauli. The dedicatory letter of the *De immortalitate animorum* makes it clear that Giustiniani's aim was to curry favour with his cousin, Cardinal Sauli; Aurelio Cevolotto is correct to suppose that the true dedicatee of the two works was the cardinal himself.[48]

What did Giustiniani hope to gain from this? Undoubtedly it was support for a project on which he had been working since least 1506, namely a polyglot Bible.[49] Gesner published part of an undated (lost) letter, of about 1516–17, from Giustiniani to Bendinello in which the scholar indirectly invited the cardinal, as the person who had encouraged him to undertake this work, to help it reach completion, presumably through his financial intervention, but conceivably, given what is known of Sauli, through his intellectual help as well.[50] This patronage was not forthcoming and in November 1516 Giustiniani published in Genoa, at his own expense, 2,000 copies of the

---

45 See Giustiniani, *Castigatissimi annali*, c. 223r: he was the son of Paolo Giustiniani Banca and Bartholomea Giustiniani Longa.

46 Ibid. c. 223v.

47 A. Cevolotto, *Agostino Giustiniani un umanista tra bibbia e cabala*, Genoa 1992, 20.

48 *Aenae Platonici Greci Christianissimi: De immortalitate animorum, deque corporum resurrectione, aureus libellus, cui titulus est Theophrastus*, Venice 1513, i v–ii r; Cevolotto, *Agostino Giustiniani*, 36.

49 For the letter from the humanist Jacopo Antiquario to Giustiniani in which his interest in languages and in the project of a polyglot Bible was established see L. Bossi, *Vita e pontificato di Leone X di Guglielmo Roscoe: tradotto e corredata di annotazioni e di alcuni documenti inediti dal conte Cav. Luigi Bossi*, Milan 1816–17, iv. 166–8.

50 'nobis animadvertimus: qui mihi est author, is ac adiutor ac perfector sit operis': C. Gesner, *Bibliotheca universalis, sive catalogus omnium scriptorum locupletissimus, in tribus linguis, Latina, Graeca ac Hebraica: extantium et non extantium, veterum et recentiorum in hunc usq diem, doctorum et indoctorum, publicatorum et in bibliothecis latentium: opus novum, et non bibliothecis tantum publicis privatisve instituendis necessarium, sed studiosis omnibus cuiuscunq artis aut scientiae ad studia melius formanda utilissimum*, Tiguri 1545, i. 105r, and Cevolotto, *Agostino Giustiniani*, 43, who, however, fails to identify Sauli's role as initial supporter of the work. Gesner had access to two letters but only in the first (cf. Cevolotto) is the request for support made.

*Psalterium Hebraeum, Graecum, Arabicum et Chaldeum, cum tribus latinis inter-
pretationibus et glossis.*[51] Unique because it was written in five languages, this
was a foretaste of the larger work and was highly praised, but met with little
success; many of the volumes remaining unsold. The complete Old and New
Testaments were never to see the light of day. Giovanni Battista Spotorno
argued convincingly that Giustiniani was ahead of the team of scholars under
Cardinal Ximenes who were working in Spain on the *Complutensian Bible*,
probably in conception and certainly in completing the project in manuscript by 1515, but lack of patronage to help with printing costs meant that
the appearance of the final volume of the *Complutensian* probably sounded
the death knell for Giustiniani's own Bible.[52]

On 21 September 1514 Giustiniani, as 'kinsman' of Cardinal Sauli, was
granted the see of Nebbio in Corsica.[53] Although the income was not very
high – 400 ducats – this was the only time that Sauli intervened to gain a
bishopric for one of his friends or *famigliari* and shows the esteem in which
he held Giustiniani. The latter was present in Genoa in June and November
of 1514 but at some point after this, as he himself implies, he visited Sauli
in Rome, presumably to thank him for the benefice and to seek support for
the polyglot Bible.[54] Such a visit must have taken place: despite the failure
of his attempt to attract Sauli's patronage for his project, Giustiniani states
that after the publication of the *Psalterium* he returned (rather than went)
to Rome to please Sauli and to serve 'my Lord'.[55]

The very fact that the cardinal had encouraged Giustiniani to undertake work on a polyglot Bible demonstrates his own interest in exegesis and
perhaps in languages. Why was Sauli's support for the Bible not forthcoming
and why did Giustiniani have to finance the publication of the *Psalterium*
himself? Was Sauli unable to bear the cost? His debts were never excessive.
Did he, then, want Giustiniani to finance the *Psalterium* himself to test the
waters and intend, if its publication were successful, to finance the complete
edition? Was this plan aborted due to the cardinal's disgrace and subsequent
death? Or did he already feel that duty had been done by providing his
protégé with the see of Nebbio? Perhaps, as an astute businessman, he realised that the *Complutensian Bible*, albeit a linguistically inferior production,

[51] A. Giulia Cavagna, 'Tipografia ed editoria d'antico regime a Genova', in D. Puncuh
(ed.), 'Storia della cultura ligure', *ASLSP* xlv/1 (2005), iii. 355–419 at pp. 371–2.
[52] G. B. Spotorno, *Della bibbia poliglotta di Monsignor Agostino Giustiniani vescovo di
Nebbio: ragionamento del P. Don Giambattista Spotorno Barnabita*, Genoa 1820, 9–11;
Cavagna, 'Tipografia ed editoria', 359–60.
[53] Reg. Lat. 1293, fo. 296v; cf. A. Cevolotto, 'Giustiniani, Agostino', *DBI* lvii (2001),
301–6 at p. 302.
[54] Giustiniani, *Castigatissimi annali*, c. 224r. For his presence at the Dominican convent
of Santa Maria di Castello on 22 June. 1514 see Cevolotto, *Giustiniani*, 39, and the
unpublished documents in Notai Antichi, 1163, nos 249, 251, 253, 15, 16 Nov. 1514.
[55] Giustiniani, *Castigatissimi annali*, c. 224r.

had already cornered the market and that his investment would never be recovered.

The cardinal and his cousin had other interests in common. Cevolotto believes that by making his literary debut with the *Praecatio* of 1513 Giustiniani 'was putting himself forward for a leading role in the reform movement centered around biblical-theological studies and the renewal of Christian spirituality'.[56] Giustiniani was close to that enigmatic Genoese humanist and exponent of Christian humanism, Battista Fieschi (1471– after 1535). Fieschi was a witness on 15 November 1514 to the two documents which outline Giustiniani's appointment of a *vicario generale* to run the bishopric of Nebbio, and the following day the document authorising Giustiniani's appointment to the bishopric was drawn up in Fieschi's house.[57] In 1516 the same Fieschi provided the corrections to the *Psalterium*.[58] He has been described as part of the movement of spiritual and cultural renewal prevalent in Genoa: in fact Fieschi was a founder and staunch defender of the Genoese *Ospedale degli incurabili* and in 1524 was listed as a member of the *Compagnia del divino amore* in Rome.[59]

Giustiniani himself was a devout friar with a genuine religious vocation and there are indications that he was a keen advocate of church reform, an interest seemingly shared by Cardinal Sauli. He intervened in the Fifth Lateran Council, attending sessions on 19 December 1516, and 13 and 16 March 1517.[60] He also tried to reform his own bishopric: he spent nine years there in the 1520s, repaired the cathedral, built a house next to it for the clergy to live in and a substantial house for the bishop, added to the income of the episcopal *mensa* and translated several works into Italian so that they could be read by his clergy. Perhaps under the influence of Filippo Sauli, he refused to consecrate illiterate priests.[61]

It seems likely that he spent the period during which he attended the Lateran Council in Sauli's household, a stay eventually brought to an end by the discovery of Sauli's involvement in the plot to murder Leo x. While Sauli was imprisoned, disgraced and then briefly exiled to Monterotondo, Giustiniani remained in Rome, sheltering with Cardinal Ferrero (1517–43) and hoping for the preferment which the pope had earlier promised him.[62] His career in Rome has been described as 'permanently ended' by Sauli's disgrace.[63] Indeed, early in 1518 he was invited by Francis I, a supporter of

---

56 Cevolotto, *Giustiniani*, 39.

57 Notai Antichi, 1163, nos 249, 251, 253.

58 Cevolotto, *Giustiniani*, 40.

59 Ibid; A. Cevolotto, 'Fieschi, Battista', *DBI* xlvii (1997), 433–4 at p. 433; Solfaroli Camillocci, *I devoti*, 272–3.

60 Mansi, *Sacrorum conciliorum*, xxxii. 941, 978, 982, 993; Cevolotto, *Giustiniani*, 75.

61 Giustiniani, *Castigatissimi annali*, c. 224v; Cevolotto, *Giustiniani*, 104.

62 Cevolotto, *Giustiniani*, 76. He was still in Rome on 20 Oct. 1517: Archivio Urbano, sezione 66, protocollo 19, fo. 144v.

63 Cevolotto, *Giustiniani*, 76.

Cardinal Sauli, to teach Hebrew at the University of Paris and accepted, beginning the intellectually most prolific period of his life. He died at sea in 1536.[64] Giustiniani did not forget his debts to the Sauli: they are mentioned favourably in the *Castigatissimi annali*, but, like Giovio, he was in Rome in the period leading up to the discovery of the plot and Sauli's arrest and suffered as a result. He was, perhaps as a result, lukewarm in his defence of Sauli in his *Annali*.

Cattaneo, Giovio and Giustiniani were all members of Sauli's household; the cardinal's patronage, like that of other cardinals, also extended to figures who passed in and out of his orbit.

The pope's surgeon

If Giovio was Sauli's personal physician during his cardinalate, there is no doubt that from an early age he also had links with another physician, Giovanni da Vigo (*c.* 1460–1525), who, in his efforts to promote learning amongst doctors, honoured Sauli in print. Born at Rapallo near Genoa, da Vigo served as a doctor in Saluzzo, Genoa and Savona, was part of the entourage of Julius' *nipote* Cardinal Girolamo Basso della Rovere and then entered the *famiglia* of Julius II. He became Julius' surgeon near the beginning of his pontificate, and in 1503, as he wrote to his son, began to write a compendium of his knowledge, prompted by public demand.[65] He served the pope until his death, when he joined the household of another papal *nipote*, the invalid Cardinal Sisto Gara della Rovere.

Da Vigo was famous in his lifetime and after for his treatment of gunshot wounds, his discovery that the size of man's brain was proportionally greater when compared to the rest of his body than that of other mammals, and for his cure for venereal disease through the use of mercury. All these advances were included in the work which he took ten years to write, the *Practica in chirurgia copiosa in arte chirurgica nuper edita* (Bologna 1514), written in the belief that doctors should be educated men, and dedicated to Cardinal Sauli. The dedication speaks of the cardinal's largesse towards Da Vigo and the ongoing friendship between the two men, part of the Sauli family's patronage of both doctors and good men.[66] Having been a member of the Sauli household from an early age – perhaps, given the cardinal's disability,

---

[64] Ibid. 76–7.

[65] G. Marini, *Degli archiatri pontificii*, Rome 1784, i. 301; V. Malacarne, *Delle opere de'medici, e de' ceruschi che nacquero, o fiorirono prima del secolo XVI negli stati della real casa di Savoia*, Turin 1786, 188–9; G. Bonino, *Biografia medica Piemontese*, Turin 1824, i. 109; D. Giordano, *Scritti e discorsi pertinenti alla storia della medicina e ad argomenti diversi*, Milan 1930, 218.

[66] 'tanta est etenim magnitudo quorum erga me beneficiorum' and 'continuam familiaritatem in qua semper tecum a teneris annis domesticisque tuis versatus sum: tum quia domus Saulea ac medicorum ac bonorum virorum semper amatrix fuit': G. Da Vigo,

already practising his medical skills – this patronage continued in Rome, so that he might complete his book.[67] Such protection indicates an interest in medicine on the cardinal's part, and also reflects the role of Sauli's *famiglia*, as Vigo himself noted, as a haven for Ligurians.[68] The *Practica* was a great success, going through more than forty editions and being translated into five languages, thus immortalising Sauli's name.[69]

The pope's professor of rhetoric

Raffaele Lippo Brandolini (1465–1517), a perenially impoverished humanist resident at the papal court, was a (blind) scholar with a keen nose for a potential patron. He was the brother of the poet and orator Aurelio Lippo Brandolini (1454–97) and, before moving to Rome in 1495, had been in Naples and Florence. He was first a member of the Augustinian order and then a priest.[70] In Rome he was, in effect, a freelance orator excelling in funeral oratory, but he also worked as a tutor, teaching the future pope Julius III (Giovanni Maria del Monte) and Marcantonio Flaminio.[71] He received evidence of papal favour, being appointed a papal *cubicularius* by Julius and eventually professor of rhetoric at the University of Rome by Leo. Like Cattaneo, he was a member of Goritz's sodality.[72]

Throughout his time in Rome Brandolini was a prolific correspondent, his letters ranging from commentary on contemporary events to the inevitable flattering and/or begging letters. He seems to have been succesful in this persistent letter-writing: he wrote four times to Cardinal Galeotto della Rovere and in one letter thanked him for assigning him an annual income of fifty ducats.[73] Much of his correspondence is now lost, but a mid-*cinquecento* inventory drawn up by the brother of Julius III makes interesting reading. Many cardinals are listed, but his most favoured recipients were (with the exception of the del Monte family) Cardinal Francesco Soderini and Bendinello Sauli.[74] Unlike Soderini, Sauli became a cardinal somewhat late in Brandolini's career, yet the correspondence began when Sauli was

---

Pratica in chirurgia copiosa in arte chirurgica nuper edita a Ioanne de Vigo Iuli secondi Pon. Max. olim chirurgico que infrascripta novem continet volumina, Bologna 1514, 2r.

[67] 'non dubitavi sub protectione alarum tuarum his temporibus de professione iam dicta pro communi hominum utilitate ad scribendum animum intendere': ibid.

[68] Ibid.

[69] A. Castiglioni, *A history of medicine*, New York 1947, 470.

[70] G. Ballistreri, 'Brandolini, Raffaele Lippo', *DBI* xiv (1972), 40–2 at p. 40.

[71] D'Amico, *Renaissance humanism*, 59.

[72] Ibid. 59, 108; Ballistreri, 'Brandolini', 40–1; F. M. Renazzi, *Storia dell'università degli studi di Roma*, Rome 1803–6, ii. 238.

[73] Vat. Lat. 3570, fo. 22r.

[74] For Soderini see ibid. fos 8v, 12v, 17v, 21v; for Sauli see fos 7v, 12r, 21r, 27r, 32r, 33r–v, 205r.

still a mere *protonotario* and thus probably around 1503–6. All but one of the letters is lost, but the inventory lists their contents as, first, a letter to Sauli as *protonotario* accusing him of taciturnity and advising him that in the presence of the pope silence would be more damaging to him than speech; then a letter to Sauli as bishop of Gerace congratulating him on his elevation to the cardinalate (1511); a letter to Cardinal Sauli consoling him on the death of his younger brother Pasquale (1515); shortly afterwards a letter praising the liberality of Cardinal Sauli and the learning of his brother Stefano; a letter praising Sauli's treatment of him and finally another letter simply praising Sauli.[75] Unless other letters sent between the first and second listed above were lost by the mid-*cinquecento*, it is obvious that Brandolini's first letter to Sauli *protonotario* met with little response or encouragement. The same cannot be said of the only letter which has survived, that which aimed to console Sauli on Pasquale's death and which can be dated to late 1515 as it mentions the loss of the post of *depositario generale*.[76] This type of letter was far from unusual: Brandolini had earlier written a similar, albeit shorter, letter to Cardinal Fieschi on the death of his nephew.[77]

Little is known about Pasquale Sauli *quondam* Pasquali. He was born in about 1493 and died at some point between 12 August 1514 and 9 August 1515.[78] He was involved in the family business of banking and mercantile activities and had been a young man of some ambition: he had planned to build a second Sauli chapel in the Genoese church of San Domenico.[79] He was only twenty-one when he died and Cardinal Sauli was suitably distraught. Ostensibly the main aim of Brandolini's long letter – forty-four pages recto and verso – is to console the cardinal by reminding him of far worse public calamities, of historical and literary figures who had suffered similar or worse losses and of contemporaries who were not postrated with grief at the loss of a relative (including Sauli's redoubtable Genoese contemporary, Andrea Gentile, who apparently took a mere two days off work following the death of his eldest son).[80] But it also offered Brandolini the chance to approach

---

[75] Ibid. fo. 21r: bk ii: '(153) Bandinellum Saulium taciturnitatis accusat: plus illi apud Pontificem nociturum silentium dicit quam interpellationem'; fo. 27r: bk iv: '(114) Saulio Giracen Card. Creato gratulatur'; fo. 32r: bk v: '(156) Bandinellum Saulium Card de Pascasij fratris morte consolatur: Sauliam gentem laudat.'; fo. 33r: '(201) Bandinelli Saulij Card liberalitatem, et Stephani eius fratris doctrinam laudat'; '(205) Bandinelli Sauli beneficia erga se narrat: Urbanas res persequitu'; fo. 33v: 'B. Saulium Card laudat'.

[76] BCIS, MS K VI 73, fo. 25v.

[77] J. W. O'Malley, *Praise and blame in Renaissance Rome: rhetoric, doctrine, and reform in the sacred orators of the papal court* c. 1450–1521, Durham, NC 1979, 171; Biblioteca Angelica, Rome, MS 252, 25 Jan. 1512.

[78] So little known is he that he does not feature in the reconstruction of the Sauli family tree in Bologna: 'L'archivio della famiglia Sauli', 630. He is the child described in Notai Antichi, 950, no. 96, the will of Pasquale Sauli of 21 June 1493 as 'ac ventrem mariole sue uxoris': Archivio Urbano, sezione 66, protocollo 14, fo. 166v.

[79] Notai Antichi, 1284, no. 532, 27 Aug. 1515.

[80] BCIS, MS K VI 73, fos 4r–v, 5r, 32r–35v.

Sauli again, to flatter and commemorate him and his family in what is a highly skilful rhetorical exercise.[81] Given the lost letters which follow this one, Sauli obviously showed his appreciation in some way.

Il monaco Severo (c.1470–c.1549?)

There were other forms of 'occasional' patronage. In his *Orlando Furioso* Ludovico Ariosto cited as famous poets:

> 'Lascari, and Mussuro, and Navagero,
> And Andrea Marone, and the monk Severo'

In 1549 Severo was identified in a gloss written by Simone Fornari as Don Severo da Firenzuola, a Cistercian brother who was well-educated in, and practised, *belles lettres* and who lived for some time in Sauli's household. Fornari then adds that because Sauli was found guilty of being involved in the plot against Leo, Severo, aware of the plot, fled to Germany and had recently died there, although this detail is open to debate.[82] This is the earliest report of any relationship between a 'monaco Severo' and Cardinal Sauli and undoubtedly, together with a manuscript written by Niccolò Bacceti in the early seventeenth century, but not published until 1724, formed the basis of Ughelli's assertion that a Severo, Cattaneo, Giovio and others gathered in Sauli's palace to discuss theology. Nicolo' Bacceti supported Fornari's identification of Severo as a Cistercian and provided further biographical details: 'il monaco Severo' was most probably the Cistercian Severo Varini.[83] His biography is both complicated and incomplete. Perhaps born in 1470, he took his vows at Ferrara on 26 May 1493.[84] According to Bacceti he taught for a time at the abbey of San Salvatore Settimo and received many visitors because of his fame, including Ariosto, whom he helped in the completion of the *Orlando furioso*.[85] In 1503 he was elected abbot of San Salvatore and was president of the Cistercian congregation in Italy.[86] At some point

81 Ibid. fos 1r–2r, 4v, 12r–v, 24r–v.

82 L. Ariosto, *Orlando furioso di M. Lodovico Ariosto con cinque nuovi canti del medesimo*, Venice 1566, 553, canto 46, stanza 13; S. Fornari, *La spositione di M. Simon Fornari da Rheggio sopra l'Orlando Furioso di M. Ludovico Ariosto*, Florence 1549, 772.

83 Ughelli, *Italia sacra*, iv. 1277; *Nicolai Baccetii Fiorentini ex ordine Cistercensi, Abbatis Septimianae historiae libri VII: hanc notis, variis observationibus, et praefatione illustravit, necnon a temporis ludibriis vindicabit editor*, Rome 1724, 229.

84 A. Cesari, *Severo Varini (frate umanista) ricerche di Augusto Cesari*, Bologna 1894, 3, 10; Tiraboschi, *Storia della letteratura*, iv. 129; C. Minieri Ricci, *Biografie degli accademici Alfonsini detti poi Pontaniani dal 1442 al 1543*, Naples 1881, 173.

85 Bacceti, *Abbatis Septimianae*, 228.

86 G. Jongelinus, *Notizia abbatiarum ordinis Cistertiensis per orbem universum: libros X completa*, Coloniae Agrippinae 1640, 34.

in the late *quattrocento* he went to Rome where he became tutor to Paolo Cortesi, wrote the preface to his *De cardinalatu* (and is mentioned in the text) and also knew and helped his relative, and later Sauli family intimate, Gregorio Cortese.[87] He then moved to Siena where he taught Greek and Latin to Alfonso, the son of the ruler of Siena, Pandolfo Petrucci, later to become a cardinal (1511–17) and the main conspirator in the plot to murder Leo X. He was also sent as an ambassador to Louis XII on behalf of the Sienese Republic.[88] Varini can be traced for the most part to Siena from 1506 until the summer of 1516 as reader in oratory at the university, abbot of San Michele at Quarto outside Siena and then also as secretary to Cardinal Petrucci.[89] Yet he maintained his links with Rome: like Cattaneo, he was a member of Goritz's sodality and contributed a poem to the *Coryciana*.[90]

What evidence is there to suppose that he formed a part, whether permanent or temporary, of Sauli's household? He is not mentioned as such in surviving documents and the earliest record is that of Fornari, who should, however, not be dismissed out of hand: although born at Reggio Calabria, he was a member of a branch of the Genoese de' Fornari family which had settled there during the *quattrocento*.[91] He may well have maintained links with Genoa and known surviving Sauli members such as Stefano Sauli who was very much alive in 1549. Fornari was certainly regarded as a Ligurian by writers such as Soprani.[92] Perhaps most important, in order to write the glosses on *Orlando furioso* he went to Ferrara to meet Ariosto's *famigliari*, so some degree of reliability can be assumed.[93] Fornari does not state the exact nature of Varini's position in Sauli's household: that is left to Bacceti: he believes that Varini frequented Sauli's household as a theologian during the time of Leo X (and was himself dear to the pope).[94] This is then expanded by Ughelli into the discussions on theology held with Cattaneo, Giovio and other men of letters.

The fact that, if Bacceti is to be believed, this occurred during Leo's pontificate, opens up certain possibilities, but also raises certain questions. Leo became pope on 11 March 1513 and Sauli can be firmly placed in Rome for nearly all his pontificate, with the exception of the entry into Florence of

---

[87] Cesari, *Severo Varini*, 9–10, 44–5. For the full texts of letters between Cortese and Varini see *Gregorii Cortesii*, ii, nos 93–4, 121 at pp. 145–7, 178–9.

[88] Haig Gaisser, *Piero Valeriano*, 96.

[89] ASS, Balia 52, fos 96r, 112r; written communication from Philippa Jackson. S. Varini to M. Maffei, 15 Feb. 1510, Biblioteca Nazionale Vittorio Emmanuele, Rome, Fondo Autografi, A 97/41; Archivio Urbano, sezione 66, protocollo 23, fo. 188r.

[90] Haig Gaisser, *Piero Valeriano*, 97 n. 19; F. Ubaldini, 'Vita di Mons. Angelo Colocci: edizione del testo originale Italiano, Barb. Lat. 4882, ed. V. Fanelli, Vatican City 1969, 114.

[91] R. Contarino, 'Fornari, Simone', *DBI* xlix (1997), 80–2 at p. 80.

[92] R. Soprani, *Li scrittori della Liguria e particolarmente della Maritima*, Genoa 1667, 257.

[93] Contarino, 'Fornari', 81.

[94] Bacceti, *Abbatis Septiminianae*, 228.

1515, the journey to Bologna of the same year, a visit to Genoa in early 1516 and the hunting trips on which he accompanied Leo. Yet Bacceti confirms that it was in Rome that Sauli and Varini conversed. How does this correlate with Varini's known movements? He was not permanently tied to Siena: correspondence between Varini and Gregorio Cortese shows that at some point in late 1515 he was also in Flanders, on Benedictine business, and there are doubts as to whether he fulfilled his teaching commitments at the university in 1516.[95] But he then returned to Petrucci's service and is mentioned as such in letters of January and May 1516. The Sienese historian Sigismondo Tizio believed that he accompanied Petrucci from Genazzano to Rome (where Petrucci was subsequently arrested) in May 1517.[96]

There are thus two possibilities: either that he was with Sauli after the summer of 1516 when his post at the university definitely ended, he is last mentioned in the Petrucci letters and Sauli had returned from Genoa at some point in 1517 or that he visited Sauli on a more casual basis whenever Petrucci was in Rome. If there was a more permanent stay, this period would also seem to be the one proposed by Bacceti, who, in his attempts to refute Fornari's belief that Varini was guilty of taking part in the plot to murder Leo, states that Varini was known to Sauli as a theologian, was continually involved in his business and had open access to his ears, but meanwhile Sauli was conspiring to murder Leo, and innocent familiars, fearing for themselves, fled, with Varini escaping to Flanders.[97] The plot, if at this point its existence is accepted, was nurtured in 1516, but officially discovered in April/May 1517. The years 1516–17 were also a period in Sauli's life for which we have some evidence of a heightened interest in religion and reform: Ettore Vernazza was in Rome, receiving alms and perhaps other help from Sauli, and Silvestro Prierias, the pope's *magister sacri palatii* was resident at Santa Sabina and perhaps already Sauli's confessor.

Yet it seems more likely that the relationship between Sauli and Varini was a fluid one. In fact Bacceti specifically uses the verb 'versabatur' to describe it, a verb which indicates frequentation rather than residence.[98] Perhaps when in Rome, either independently or with Petrucci, Varini frequented Sauli's palace, having close access to him not just for his own qualities but because he was still intimate with Petrucci. If there was a relationship between the cardinal and Severo, what did Varini bring to it? Varini was a poet and a scholar well-versed in Greek and Latin, and was expert in literature and at

[95] Cesari, *Severo Varini*, 38; Tiraboschi, *Storia della letteratura*, iv. 129; *Gregorii Cortesii*, ii, no. 94 at pp. 146–7; A. Petrucci to B. Petrucci, 29 Dec. 1515, ASS, Concistoro, 2426, fo. 19r; written communication from Philippa Jackson.

[96] Ferrajoli, *La congiura*, 198–9 n. 4, 200; Archivio Urbano, sezione 66, protocollo 23, fo. 188r.

[97] Bacceti, *Abbatis Septiminianae*, 229–30.

[98] Ibid. 228. 'Versabatur in aula Bandinelli Sauli Cardinalis pro theologo noster Severus negotiis interterat assiduus, ad aures domini patentissimum habebat accessum': ibid. 229.

judging other people's writings, yet Bacceti emphasises his role as a theologian.[99] It is the latter quality which remains the most puzzling – what aspect of theology interested him? Was he interested in reform? Any hint of Lutheran leanings raised by his fleeing to Flanders and the possibility that he was at some point in Germany, perhaps dying there, is counteracted by his presence in the more than orthodox Spain, teaching at court. By 1519 Varini was in Spain – perhaps, as the Spanish had supported Petrucci before the discovery of the plot, to plead the Petrucci/Sauli cause – and was still abroad in 1520, according to some remaining there until his death in 1549. At some point during his time there he taught Fernando Alvarez, the future duke of Alba, and may well be the Severo mentioned as a historiographer at the court of Charles V in letters of the early 1520s.[100] His reputation in Spain is attested by his mention in the *Eglogas* of Garcilaso de la Vega (1503–36), written in the 1530s and featuring members of the Spanish court, in which Varini is depicted as a famous teacher, especially of the spiritual life.[101] Yet if little is known about his theological interests, even less is known about his literary achievements: he has been described as one of the few Cistercians from central Italy to have made a fairly important contribution to humanism: he was a translator of, amongst other things, Aristotle's *Ethics*, yet none of his writings was ever published.[102]

Hellenic studies, Cardinal Sauli and Domenico Sauli

Cattaneo (translator of Isocrates and Lucian), Varini (Petrucci's Greek teacher and translator of Aristotle) and Giustiniani (author of the *Psalterium* and exegist of a polyglot Bible) are all linked by an interest in the Greek language. Was this chance or did Sauli too share their interest, one, furthermore, which Filippo and Stefano Sauli were in turn to manifest?

The study of Greek in the early *cinquecento* is now thought to have been reasonably widespread: the ability to read Greek was not a 'particularly original or exceptional accomplishment' and Giovio was later to write that 'everybody needs to know Greek'.[103] The links between Genoa, and more specifically the Sauli, and Chios may have fostered an interest on the part of a young Bendinello. Indeed, when Giustiniani wrote to Sauli about his polyglot Bible he stated that Greek had long been almost common knowledge

[99] Ibid. 228; *Poesie latine*, 14–15.

[100] Ferrajoli, *La congiura*, 200; Cesari, *Severo Varini*, 47–8; *Gregorii Cortesii*, i. 13, 101; written communication from Philippa Jackson.

[101] J. Rubio y Balaguer, *Las eglogas de Garcilaso de la Vega*, Barcelona 1945, p. xvii.

[102] E. Brouette, A. Dimier and E. Manning (eds), *Dictionnaire des auteurs cisterciens*, i, Rochefort 1975, 715.

[103] J. Whittaker, 'Giles of Viterbo as classical scholar', in *Egidio da Viterbo, OSA e il suo tempo: atti del V convegno dell'Istituto Storico Agostiniano, Roma-Viterbo, 20–23 Ottobre 1982*, Rome 1983, 85–105 at p. 85; Giovio, *Dialogus de viris*, 239.

and his use of the first person plural makes it very likely that the cardinal knew Greek.[104] Under Leo Hellenic studies were to flower in Rome. On his election he had called the Greek scholar Janus Lascaris (1445–1535) to Rome, founded a Greek college and increased the number of chairs in Greek at the university to three. In 1516 he also founded a Greek press in the city which was under the supervision of the Greek scholar Marcus Musurus (1470–1517).[105] Rome had somewhat lagged behind in the cultivation of Greek in general and the publication of Greek texts in particular – for example, books had begun to be printed in Greek in Venice in c. 1471 and Padua had flourished for many years as an important centre of Greek studies – but this was not the first Greek press in Rome.[106] In 1511 a letter of Angelo Colocci relates that the printer Iacomo Mazzocchi, at the instigation of another printer, Evangelista Tosini known as Mercurio, was considering publishing Greek texts in Rome with the help of the Greek printer Zacharias Calliergis who was then working in Venice. Although this plan came to nothing, it was of continuing significance.[107]

Subsequently, in 1515, the Sienese banker Agostino Chigi provided the funds for the foundation of a Greek press under the aegis of the humanist Cornelio Benigno (active 1505–20) and that same Calliergis. Benigno, who was Chigi's chancellor, had been recommended as a humanist by Cortesi in his *De cardinalatu* and had previously collaborated with other humanists on an edition of the Latin version of Ptolemy's *Geographia* (1507).[108] On 13 August 1515 Benigno and Calliergis published, on a press established in one of Chigi's houses, the first Greek work to be published in Rome, an edition of Pindar with *scholia*. This was followed on 15 January 1516 by an annotated edition of the *Idylls* of Theocritus.[109] How is this relevant to Sauli?

104 Petrucciani, 'Le biblioteche', 243; 'Nam Graeca omnia iamdudum esse in propatulo non ignoramus': Gesner, *Bibliotheca universalis*, 106r.

105 V. Fanelli, 'Il ginnasio greco di Leone X a Roma', *Studi Romani* ix (1961), 379–93 at pp. 379–81, 384; Whittaker, 'Giles of Viterbo', 85; J. O. Riedl, *A catalogue of Renaissance philosophers (1350–1650)*, Milwaukee 1940, 52.

106 N. G. Wilson, *From Byzantium to Italy: Greek studies in the Renaissance*, London 1992, 96, 133.

107 'A presso Iacomo mazzocchio gia mercurio vol condurre la stampa greca in roma et gia promecte stampar lo Eustathio sopra omero et vorria condurre compositori. M. Johanni Antonio Marostico dice che lui poi disponere di quello Zacharia qui fece lo Ethymo-logico. Informatevi chi e quello': A. Colocci to S. Carteromacho, 15 May 1511, Vat. Lat. 4104, fo. 41v, cited in Fanelli, 'Il ginnasio Greco', 381, and J. Ruysschaert, 'Trois Recher-ches sur le XIVe siècle romain', *ASRSP* lciv (1971), 10–29 at p. 12. For Calliergis see D. J. Geanakoplos, *Greek scholars in Venice: studies in the dissemination of Greek learning from Byzantium to Western Europe*, Cambridge, MA 1962, 201–14; for Mazzocchi see Ascarelli, *Annali tipografici*, 14, 16, 18–19.

108 D'Amico, *Renaissance humanism*, 58, 279 n. 81; Haig Gaisser, *Piero Valeriano*, 267; M. Gigante, 'Benigno, Cornelio', *DBI* viii (1966), 513–14; Ruysschaert, 'Trois Recher-ches', 19–20.

109 Geanakoplos, *Greek scholars*, 213, 217.

A document in the Vatican Library records that on 25 September 1516 Calliergis and Benigno sold the remaining copies of Pindar and Theocritus to a Pavian bookseller, Francesco Calvo, for the sum of 450 cameral ducats (430 to Benigno and 20 to Calliergis) and that this document was drawn up in the house of Cardinal Sauli. Calliergis received his money that same day and Benigno received thirty ducats on 2 October.[110] The notary was Francesco Vigorosi and a cancelled version is to be found in his *filza* of 1517, dated 25 September 1517. Other unrelated documents in the same *filza* can be securely dated to that year. The cancelled version is puzzling: it does not give the name of the witnesses and gives the payment to Benigno as undated but the discrepancy in the dating between the Vatican document and that in the notary's own files can perhaps be explained by the need for a copy to be drawn up after Sauli's disgrace (when payment to Benigno may have looked less likely) and reflects the date the copy was made, or it may be a result of problems in providing Calvo with the books which in turn delayed payment to Benigno.

Whatever the explanation, Sauli is not cited as present in either version and was almost certainly at Viterbo with Leo, but one of the witnesses to the document was his doctor, Paolo Giovio. Why draw up the document in Sauli's palace rather than in that of Chigi or the lawyer's own studio? It seems that the sum to be paid by Calvo was to be provided (at least on paper) by Domenico Sauli, who recognises that he is 'debtor in full' of the amount to be paid. In reality the final sum was not paid by the bankers Vincenzo, Giovanni and Agostino Sauli until 13 April 1518, a fortnight after Cardinal Sauli's death.[111]

There are further links between the Sauli and Francesco Calvo. Calvo was apparently a friend of Paolo Giovio – but this friendship can only be firmly fixed to the 1520s.[112] He had become a bookseller thanks to financial help from Domenico Sauli and in 1516 was active as such in Pavia. Early in 1517, however, he and Domenico had signed a contract to set up a printing press in Genoa.[113] The project came to nothing but the idea was that the

---

[110] Vat. Lat. 1173, fos 112r–113r, cited in Ruysschaert, 'Trois Recherches', 22, and Wilson, *From Byzantium*, 188–9 n. 76, but with no mention of the location; Notai del Tribunale, AC 7156, fo. 482r–v.

[111] Vat. Lat. 1173, fo. 112v; Notai del Tribunale, AC 7156, fo. 482v.

[112] G. Mercati, 'Francesco Calvo e Fausto Sabeo alla cerca di codici nell'Europa setten-trionale', *Rendiconti della Pontifica Accademia Romana di Archeologia* xiii (1937), 149–78 at pp. 150–1; F. Barberi, 'Le edizioni romane di Francesco Minizio Calvo', *Miscellanea di scritti di bibliografia ed erudizione in memoria di Luigi Ferrari*, Florence 1952, 57–98 at p. 58, and 'Calvo, Francesco', *DBI* xvii (1974), 38–41 at p. 39.

[113] Barberi, 'Calvo', 39. This is mentioned in a letter to Johannes Froben of 10 Feb. 1517 and then in a letter from the Beato Renano to Erasmus of 10 May of that year: *Opus epis-tolarum Des. Erasmi Roterodami*, ed. P. S. Allen, Oxford, 1906–47, ii, no. 581 at pp. 557–8. The letter is reproduced in part by A. Cataldi Palau, 'Catalogo dei manoscritti greci della Biblioteca Franzoniana (Genova) (Urbani 21–40)', *Bollettino dei Classici: Accademia Nazi-onale dei Lincei* supplement xvii (1996), 1–235 at pp. 190–1.

press should print Greek, Latin and Hebrew texts.[114] Sauli and Calvo were presumably hoping to fill a gap in the market: the first printing press had been established in Genoa in 1471 (with the financial backing of two Genoese *nobili*) and was swiftly followed by two others, but the market simply did not exist and printing within the city disappeared in the 1480s only to reappear briefly (and afterwards immediately disappear) when Agostino Giustiniani imported a printer from Turin, Pietro Paolo Porro, to publish his *Psalterium* in November 1516.[115]

Little is known of the early years of Domenico Sauli, although his later prominent role in Milanese politics and finances and his fame as the father of Sant'Alessandro Sauli is well documented.[116] He was an *anziano* and then a member of the *ufficio di mare* in Genoa in 1518, and was a friend and patron of humanists throughout his life, including the writer Matteo Bandello (1485–1561), Marcantonio Flaminio and Giulio Camillo.[117] Like his father, Antonio Sauli, he was a businessman and by 1513 had been sublet the rental of Cardinal Sauli's benefice of San Simpliciano in Milan. He was obviously successful in this field and by 1516 was the lessee of the abbey of Santa Maria de Cereto in the diocese of Lodi held by Cardinal Leonardo Grosso della Rovere.[118] Did the commercial failure of Giustiniani's *Psalterium* convince the pragmatic Domenico that the market for a Genoese printing press was still not there? Or is it pure coincidence that the venture failed in the year that Cardinal Sauli was disgraced and all available Sauli funds were spent on raising the fine which ensured his release from prison? Close links between Domenico and Cardinal Sauli, other than the rental of San Simpliciano, are difficult to establish and, given that Calvo names Domenico, rather than the cardinal, as his partner, it does not, at first glance, appear likely that Cardinal Sauli was involved in the establishing of a Greek press.

Yet the situation is not quite as clear-cut as it at first seems. The second witness to the Vatican document on the sale of Greek books to Calvo was a certain Giovanni Antonio Marostica (sometimes given as Marostico), who, unknown to later commentators, was like Giovio one of the cardinal's *famigliare*. Marostica is also mentioned in the Sauli accounts on 28 May 1516 when a third party is reimbursed for twenty-five ducats which Marostica had received.[119] He was highly praised by Giovio who described him as a 'learned and very open man who spent almost all his life on Greek letters,

---

114 Cataldi Palau, 'Catalogo (1996)', 191.
115 Cavagna, 'Tipografia ed editoria', 355–60, 368.
116 F. Chabod, 'L'epoca di Carlo V', *Storia di Milano*, ix, Milan 1961, 6, 301, 325, 335; O. Premoli, 'Domenico Sauli ed i Gesuiti', *Archivio Storico Lombardo* xv (1911), 147–55.
117 ASG, MS 798, fo. 166v; MS 10, fo. 135v; Cataldi Palau, 'Catalogo', 15; Pastore, *Marcantonio Flaminio*, 55; *Tutte le opere*, i. 700–1.
118 Notai Antichi, 1283, no. 664; 1285, no. 88, 22 Mar. 1516; Notai del Tribunale, AC 7157, fos 391r–392v.
119 Vat. Lat. 1173, fo. 112v; Archivio Sauli, no. 730, fo. 40r.

in the end almost forgetting Latin'.[120] His real name was Giovanni Antonio Matteazzi and he was a native of Marostica near Vicenza. From 1502 to 1505 he is recorded as at the University of Padua, where he seems to have graduated, returning to teach there in 1517 after the cardinal's disgrace. He was a friend of Buonamico, soon to be tutor in Greek and Latin to Stefano Sauli, and was also an intimate of Angelo Colocci.[121] Praised by Valeriano for his oratory, famous for his learning and a member of Goritz's sodality, after Sauli's disgrace he eventually became secretary to Cardinal Francesco Pisano (1517–70) but died from plague on 26 February 1523 and all his writings, including a defence of the Venetian Republic and a *encomium* of Leo X, were burned.[122] He is of interest not just because he was yet another *famigliare* of Cardinal Sauli with a keen interest in Greek, but because he is mentioned in Colocci's letter of 1511, which outlines the attempt to establish a Greek press in Rome, as someone who was aware of the project and of the possibility of luring Calliergis to Rome: 'Messer Iohanni Antonio Marostico says that he can get hold of that Zacharia.'[123]

It is difficult to establish Marostica's exact role: was the 'he' referred to in this letter Tosini/Mercurio, and Marostica merely Colocci's informant, as José Ruysschaert believes, or was it Marostica himself who knew Calliergis sufficiently well to bring him to Rome? The text is open to both interpretations, but the fact that Marostica has been identified as a friend of Janus Lascaris would seem to favour the latter.[124] What is clear is that Marostica was interested in the promotion of Greek, was a Sauli intimate by 1516 and a witness to a document involving the sale of Greek books drawn up in Sauli's palace. If anybody was likely to encourage the Sauli to set up a printing press whose output would include Greek texts, then Marostica was surely that person. Furthermore Iacomo Mazzocchi, also mentioned in the letter of 1511 as involved in the setting up of a Greek press, was no stranger to Sauli: in 1514 the printer dedicated the Latin edition by Giovanni Lorenzi (c.1440– c.1501) of Plutarch's *Quomodo ab adulatore discernatur amicus* to Sauli, apparently hoping that it would persuade Sauli to ignore false flattery.[125] No definite conclusion can be reached, but it seems likely that Cardinal Sauli knew Greek, was interested in Greek literature and was possibly linked to,

---

[120] Giovio, *Dialogus de viris*, 239.

[121] *Acta graduum academicorum ab anno 1501 ad annum 1525*, ed. E. Martellozzo Forin, Padua 1969, 55–6, 58, 125, 128–9, 395; Marangoni, 'Buonamico', 131.

[122] Haig Gaisser, *Piero Valeriano*, 308; Bembo to L. Buonamico, 30 Nov. 1523, *Lettere: Pietro Bembo*, ii, no. 463 at p. 198; Marangoni, 'Buonamico', 131.

[123] Ruysschaert, 'Trois Recherches', 12.

[124] Ibid. 23; Haig Gaisser, *Piero Valeriano*, 308.

[125] Ascarelli, *Annali tipografici*, 76; '& Reverendissime D Vestrae dicavimus que' apprime intelligit q sit perniciosa adulatio principum perpetuum malum: quorum opes & famam saepius assentatio q hostis evertat': *Plutarchi Libellus aureus quomodo ab adulatore discernatur amicus: Joanne Laurenzio Veneto viro doctissimo interprete nuper ad utilitatem legentium summa diligentia publicatus*, p. i.

or at the least aware of, the idea of founding a press in Genoa which would print Greek texts.

In comparison to many of the cardinals named earlier in this chapter, Sauli's life and cardinalate were cut short, but it is safe to say that he had strong humanistic patronal inclinations. This was recognised by Foglietta: the other Ligurian cardinals he cited were noted for their intellect alone. Only Sauli was also celebrated for his activities as a patron and it is as a patron (and plotter) that he is known to most modern commentators. What emerges from this study is that Sauli, noted for his learning in his own lifetime and thus naturally inclined towards humanist patronage, was a more liberal patron than earlier commentators believed, and that his elevation to the cardinalate marked a turning point, not only in his choice of residence, but also in his patronage of humanists: Giovio, Giustiniani and Marostica joined his household and Brandolini wrote four letters to Sauli, all after 1511. Both he, and the humanists who surrounded him, recognised the importance of his promotion and the potential patronage that he had to offer. Sauli can also be seen as a cardinal who carefully gave his moral and financial support to ventures which would bring glory to his name and, if his failed backing of Giustiniani's polyglot Bible is indicative, money into his pockets. Those under his wing, for however brief a period, included a follower of traditional humanism – Cattaneo, translator of and commentator on classical texts, who, in turn, celebrated his patron in a unique way; two physicians – Giovio and da Vigo; a learned Cistercian with whom it is likely that he discussed theology; the biblical commentator Agostino Giustiniani; and the Greek scholar Marostica. He did not forget his Genoese roots – both da Vigo and Giustiniani were Ligurians and Cattaneo's poem exalted Genoa and the Genoese – but his patronage centred for the most part on Rome, now his home and powerbase and where the image he projected – that of an astute and educated patron – reflected positively on his role as a prince of the Church.

6

Portraits of Cardinal Sauli

If the patronage of humanists allowed a patron, whether a cardinal or not, to demonstrate magnificence and liberality, it also allowed him to be celebrated for posterity in their works. There were also other, more visual, ways for a cardinal to ensure that his name was not forgotten: he could build palaces or endow chapels, churches or monasteries and have them decorated, commemorating his donation through inscriptions, coats of arms or portraits (either painted or sculpted) of himself. In Rome, on the façade of the Palazzo della Cancelleria, is an inscription which proclaims the status and wealth of Cardinal Riario, and the Carafa Chapel in Santa Maria sopra Minerva commemorates its patron (Cardinal Carafa) in the same way through its altarpiece and frescoes.[1] At Santa Sabina Cardinal Sauli had the roof of the north wing of the cloister replaced and his coat of arms fixed in the vault. The walls were decorated with frescoes, including one of Sauli kneeling before the Virgin and St Dominic, and although these frescoes have been lost, the coat of arms remains and to this day Sauli's name is known to any inquiring visitor to that part of the convent.

Alternatively, a cardinal could have his portrait painted. In general portraits of individuals in the late *quattrocento* and early *cinquecento* had three possible functions: they could be memorial, commissioned either in life or after death and displayed in the home or in public to keep alive the memory of the sitter, as for example Botticelli's *Giuliano de' Medici*.[2] They could also be commemorative or celebratory, commissioned to celebrate the love or fidelity of the sitter or to celebrate betrothals or weddings, for example Filippo Lippi's *Double portrait* of c. 1440.[3] They could also, in the case of rulers (and a cardinal was, after all, the ruler of his household), be used as a form of propaganda. In the latter case, as Bruce Cole notes, such portraits 'say much about the sitter's self-image and the way he or she wished this image projected to the spectator'.[4] These functions also applied to portraits of ecclesiastics: although, in theory, no churchman could be betrothed or married the need for commemoration, celebration and propaganda was the same. If the Renaissance artist has been described as 'an image maker in every sense', it can be argued that he was never more so than

---

[1] Hollingsworth, *Patronage*, 293–4.
[2] Samuel H. Kress Collection, National Gallery of Art, Washington.
[3] Metropolitan Museum of Art, New York.
[4] B. Cole, *Italian art, 1250–1500*, New York 1987, 227.

when executing a portrait.[5] For this reason alone the known contemporary portraits of Cardinal Sauli are worthy of separate examination from his other patronage: they represent the possibility of seeing the public *persona* that Sauli, the commissioner of the work, wished to project.

In the early *cinquecento* the conventions for the portrayal of cardinals in free-standing portraits kept pace with the portrayal of lay sitters. In the *quattrocento* the rediscovery of the classical portrait bust, together with the influence of Netherlandish art, had seen the development of a more realistic and intimate portrayal of the sitter in a three-quarter or full face pose. This can be seen in portraits of cardinals as diverse as Ippolito d'Este, Alfonso Petrucci and Georges d'Amboise.[6] Yet portraits of churchmen, and cardinals in particular, were in fact more limited in their scope precisely because the sitter was a man of the Church. Whereas lay people could advertise their status and wealth through the detail of the painting: the clothes and fabrics that they wore and other objects portrayed, churchmen wore the robes proper to their ecclesiastical status. It has to be said that often the cardinal was satisfied with just this: for example Raphael's *Portrait of a cardinal* (*c.* 1511) or his *Cardinal Bibbiena* (*c.* 1516).[7] After all, the status of cardinal as denoted by the sitter's red robes would have more than adequately advertised his success and prestige. But where there are additional objects in portraits of cardinals – whether a bell, a piece of paper or a book – or, as in the case of *Cardinal Bendinello Sauli and three companions* (*see* plate 1), other people, these take on an added significance. They offer us a key to understanding the image the cardinal-sitter wished to project, one the viewer would have been able to unlock.

Perhaps equally important was the choice of artist: did the cardinal choose a minor artist, one who was cheaper than a famous name, or did he choose a painter who was already well-known (and consequently more expensive) to portray his likeness? Did the choice of artist reflect the cardinal's own inclinations, producing a traditional and thus non-controversial celebration of his status, or did he opt for an innovatory artist, someone who could produce a work which perhaps would startle the onlooker and prove so ground-breaking that its influence would be mirrored in portrayals of later ecclesiastics? Cardinals were the big fish in the small pond that was curial Rome and the resonances of portraits which were put on public display and caught the public's eye would have been, and were, widely felt.

All these factors play a part in the examination of the two surviving free-standing portraits of Cardinal Sauli, Sebastiano del Piombo's *Cardinal*

---

5 Ibid. 217.
6 J. Pope-Hennessy, *The portrait in the Renaissance*, New York 1966, 72–85; Cole, *Italian art*, 25. Reproductions of these portraits can be found in A. Haidacher, *Geschichte der Päpste in Bildern: eine Dokumentation zur Papstgeschichte von Ludwig von Pastor*, Heidelberg 1965, 232, 265, 231.
7 Galleria Palatina, Florence.

Bendinello Sauli and three companions (and the copy) and Raphael's *Portrait of a cardinal* (*see* plate 3). Commissioned five years apart, they offer an important reading of Cardinal Sauli's public *persona* at the beginning and at the peak of his brief cardinalate.

The Washington portrait

In del Piombo's *Cardinal Bendinello Sauli and three companions* the cardinal is shown three-quarter length, accompanied by three men in a room which contains a chair and a table covered by an oriental carpet upon which lie a bell and a book with maps. Originally painted in oil on wood and measuring 121.8 x 150.4 cm, it is signed and dated '1516 ... S Faciebat' on the *cartello* on the front of the table carpet.[8] The bell is inscribed with the letters 'EN. TO. R' and the words 'B. DE. SAVLIS. CAR'. Since 1951 the figure of the cardinal has been accepted as being that of Cardinal Bendinello Sauli.[9] The painting followed a circuitous route via inheritance and sales from the Sauli family to Washington.[10] At some point the surface of the painting suffered considerable damage and restoration, a fact often ignored by scholars anxious to identify other portraits of Cardinal Sauli.[11]

By 1516, the year the work was painted, Sauli was at the peak of his influence in Rome.[12] Although his family had lost the positions of *depositarii generali* and the flow of benefices had decreased, he and his relatives were well-established within the Church: Filippo was bishop of Brugnato and Stefano was a *protonotario apostolico* and *commendatario* of the important abbey of San Simpliciano in Milan. In 1514 Sauli had been celebrated in print by his secretary, Giovanni Maria Cattaneo, in his unique poem *Genua* and he had established himself as a patron of humanists of the calibre

---

[8]   The painting was transferred onto fabric in 1943–4. For the acceptance of Sebastiano's authorship of the work in the critical literature see M. Lucco, 'Catalogo delle opere', in M. Lucco and C. Volpe (eds), *L'opera completa di Sebastiano del Piombo*, Milan 1980, 90–144 at pp. 106–7. More recently it been discussed by F. R. Shapley, *Catalogue of the Italian paintings: National Gallery of Art, Washington*, Washington 1979, i. 422; M. Hirst, *Sebastiano del Piombo*, Oxford 1981, 99; C. Davis, 'Un appunto per Sebastiano del Piombo ritrattista', *Mitteilungen des Kunsthistorisches Institutes in Florenz* xxvi (1982), 383–8; and Jungic, 'Prophecies', 345–70.
[9]   Lucco, 'Catalogo', 106. The meaning of EN. TO. R. remains a mystery.
[10] P. Boccardo, 'Materiali per una storia del collezionismo artistico a Genova nel XVII secolo', unpubl. PhD diss. Milan 1989, 122–5, 133; P. Boccardo and L. Magnani, *Il palazzo dell'università di Genova: il collegio dei Gesuiti nella strada dei Balbi*, Savona 1987, 85 n. 128; P. Humfrey, 'Cardinal Bendinello Sauli and three companions', in *National Gallery of Art systematic catalogue: sixteenth century Italy*', forthcoming; Lucco, 'Catalogo', 106–7.
[11] 'Examination summary' of the condition of the painting undertaken by the conservation department of the National Gallery, Washington in 1988, 1. I am grateful to William Breazeale of the National Gallery for forwarding this information to me in 1995.
[12] Also noted by Hirst, *Sebastiano del Piombo*, 99.

of Cattaneo, Giovio, Giustiniani and Marostica. In April 1515 he had acquired the tenancy of a suitably magnificent residence, the present-day Palazzo Doria-Pamphilij. At the end of that year Sauli had, like other cardinals, accompanied the pope to Bologna to meet Francis I and had played a significant role in proceedings there. It was time for a visual celebration of his success, a celebration which was presumably to hang in the sumptuous surroundings of the palace at Santa Maria in Via Lata.

Why did Sauli choose Sebastiano del Piombo? The choice of artist reflects Sauli's sense of prestige. Sebastiano had been brought to Rome from his native Venice in August 1511 by Agostino Chigi and was quickly set to work amongst the leading figures of Roman society.[13] By the end of 1511 he had painted eight lunettes and a figure of *Polyphemus* in the loggia of Chigi's villa.[14] Other important works which can be assigned to the years before the Washington portrait are the *Dead Adonis* probably also painted for Chigi;[15] *Ferry Carondelet and his secretary* of early 1512[16] and the *Pietà* of c. 1513 for Giovanni Botonti.[17] Another *Pietà* also bears the date 1516 on its *cartello*.[18]

Sauli may well have chosen Sebastiano because he was clearly in demand, a popularity which was attributed by Vasari to his use of colour and the success of the Viterbo *Pietà*.[19] Two of his known patrons during this period were involved in finance: Chigi as a banker and farmer of the papal alum and Botonti as a clerk in the *camera apostolica*.[20] Sauli may well have known both of them, but especially Agostino Chigi whose business dealings would have necessitated contact with the Sauli.[21] Chigi has been described as 'a patron who, if we allow for a few minor lapses provoked by Sienese *campanilismo*, wanted the best'.[22] If Sauli artistic patronage in Genoa was often based upon the principle of imitation, then in Rome there can have been no better example to follow in choosing an artist than Chigi.

Sauli may also have been influenced by the fact that at the time Sebastiano was viewed as an innovatory artist: at the Villa Farnesina he had executed his frescoes within a month and had introduced technical and stylistic innovations.[23] This may well have been important: as in the case of *Genua*, Sauli was

13 He was born Sebastiano Luciani in Venice in about 1485: M. Lucco, 'Sebastiano del Piombo', in J. Turner (ed.), *The Grove dictionary of art*, xxviii, New York 1996, 331–6 at p. 331. For his arrival in Rome see Lucco, 'Catalogo', 87, and Hirst, *Sebastiano del Piombo*, 33–4.

14 Hirst, *Sebastiano del Piombo*, 34; Lucco, 'Catalogo', 87, 99.

15 Galleria Uffizi, Florence.

16 Thyssen-Bornemisza Collection, Madrid.

17 Viterbo, Museo Civico. See Lucco, 'Sebastiano del Piombo', 332–3.

18 Hermitage, St Petersburg.

19 G. Vasari, *The lives of the painters, sculptors and architects*, trans. A. Hinds, rev. edn, New York 1963, iii. 113.

20 Hirst, *Sebastiano del Piombo*, 43, 50.

21 F. Gilbert, *The pope, his banker and Venice*, London 1980, 77–88.

22 Hirst, *Sebastiano del Piombo*, 4.

23 For del Piombo's innovations such as painting freehand on fresh plaster instead of

aiming for a celebratory work that, despite its echoes of earlier (papal and group) portraits, was above all innovatory. And indeed *Cardinal Bendinello Sauli and three companions* has been described as 'the most quantitatively ambitious venture in easel painting so far undertaken in the Roman school'.[24] If its size were unusual, and evidence of Sauli's wish to impress, so was the composition. The portrait has been seen as a *conversazione profana*, using a group format generally reserved for sacred subjects or for portraits of musicians.[25] In the case of the Sauli portrait, Sebastiano seems to have drawn on a composition that he had used in an earlier, now lost, painting, the *Portrait of Verdelot and Obrecht* done at the beginning of his career. He then developed his handling of the subject further in his *Ferry Carondelet,* and for the Sauli portrait enlarged the composition to include four sitters.[26] However, Sebastiano did not just refine a compositional device – the group portrait – which he had used earlier: he perhaps also turned to works by other artists for inspiration: for example, Jean Fouquet's (lost) *Eugenius IV* portrayed the pope with two of his followers.[27] Furthermore, Sauli's seated pose is similar to that used in Raphael's *Portrait of Julius II* (c. 1511),[28] although Sauli's upper torso is turned slightly to face the viewer and his left hand is outstretched. A green background is used in both paintings and both sitters are dressed in rochet and *mozzetta*.[29] Sauli was thus confirming in paint his links with Julius II, the pope from whom he had received important benefices and the cardinalate. The cardinal and the approaching figure on the left do not so much recall the two figures in *Ferry Carondelet* – where the second figure on the left seems to have rushed onto the scene at the last minute and to have no relationship with Carondelet – as Mantegna's portrait of Lodovico Gonzaga and his secretary in the 'Camera picta' in the Palazzo Ducale at Mantua.[30] Sauli's lack of interaction with the other figures in the portrait is remarkable and his aloofness recalls Brandolini's comment to him that 'you who show yourself privately and publicly to have a regal loftiness of character'.[31] It seems obvious, given such references, that, albeit on a smaller scale, Sauli, like Gonzaga and the della Rovere pope, was to be seen as a ruler. And it is in this that the portrait's real innovation lies: for the first

pouncing the cartoon, and his use of more intense colours, see Lucco, 'Sebastiano del Piombo', 332.

[24] S. J. Freedberg, *Painting of the high Renaissance in Rome and Florence*, Cambridge, MA 1961, 374.

[25] R. Pallucchini, *Sebastiano Viniziano*, Milan 1944, 41. For group portraits of musicians see E. H. Ramsden, *Come, take this lute*, Bristol 1983, 5–77.

[26] Lucco, 'Catalogo', 127; Freedberg, *Painting of the high Renaissance*, 374.

[27] Humfrey, 'Cardinal Bendinello Sauli'.

[28] National Gallery, London.

[29] Jungic, 'Prophecies', 349–50.

[30] Hirst, *Sebastiano del Piombo*, 99.

[31] 'Qui regiam animi celsitudinem in amplissima ista dignitate et privatim, et publice ostendis': BCIS, MS K VI 73, fo. 34v.

time a cardinal is shown surrounded by members of his household. It is thus an illustration of Cardinal Sauli's everyday reality and the roles and *personae* that he, and those portrayed with him, adopted within that reality.[32]

Cardinal Sauli: head of household and patron of men of letters

Michael Hirst was the first to identify the figure on the right of the Washington portrait as Paolo Giovio and to suggest that the figure on the far left is that of Giovanni Maria Cattaneo.[33] Charles Davis supported the identification of Giovio, which is further confirmed by a medal portrait of Giovio of 1552, but established that the figure sitting next to him was Giovanni Maria Cattaneo.[34] So who is the figure on the extreme left? It is tempting to suggest that this is another humanist close to Sauli, Agostino Giustiniani, but this is confuted by Giustiniani's own description of himself as having blue eyes.[35] Nor is Josephine Jungic's tentative identification of him as Stefano Sauli, the cardinal's brother, acceptable: there is simply no resemblance between the figure in the portrait and the (albeit later) portrait medal in the British Museum. The figure is probably that of a servant.[36] He will remain anonymous: the household servant who was closest to Sauli and benefited most from his patronage was Domenico de' Caffis, but as no known portrait of him survives any confirmation is impossible.

Thus in *Cardinal Sauli and three companions* a cardinal is for the first time shown surrounded by three of his *famigliari* – his servant, his secretary and his doctor – and hence as a ruler of his household. Sebastiano, presumably with Sauli's approval, had brought to a portrait of a cardinal the concept of a subject shown 'engaged in his usual business, in a setting and with companions emphasizing his public persona' which he had introduced to Italian portraiture in *Ferry Carondelet*.[37] Yet in addition to the roles of Cattaneo and Giovio as Sauli's secretary and doctor, they were also men of letters and known as such at the time. Giovio had already begun his *Historiae* which had elicited Leo x's approval in 1515 and Cattaneo's output in Rome was considerable. He was perhaps best known at the time and in the following decades for his poem *Genua*: Davis has suggested that the book of text and maps which is open in front of him, and on the edge of which his right hand rests, 'may allude to the theme of the Latin poem ... *Genua*'.[38] The question

---

[32] Cf. Jungic, 'Prophecies', passim.

[33] Hirst, *Sebastiano del Piombo*, 99–100.

[34] Davis, 'Un appunto', 383–4. For an illustration of the medal, probably designed by Francesco da Sangallo, see Capparoni, *Paolo Giovio*, 6.

[35] Giustiniani, *Castigatissimi annali*, c. 225r.

[36] P. D'Achiardi, *Sebastiano del Piombo*, Rome 1908, 190.

[37] Hirst, *Sebastiano del Piombo*, 98.

[38] Davis, 'Un appunto', 383.

is, why did Sebastiano, presumably at Sauli's request, prefer to show maps and some text rather than just maps or just text in the book as would have been more common at the time? The book in the portrait is unique and has confounded all attempts at identification. Is the combination of maps and text a reference to Cardinal Sauli's origins and public *persona* or to those of Cattaneo? There is no surviving record of any interest on the part of Sauli or of Cattaneo in exploration. It could perhaps be argued that maps – an obvious reference to travel and exploration – allude to Sauli's Genoese roots and to the most famous Genoese of the period, Christopher Columbus. Yet Cattaneo's right hand rests on the edge of the book of maps, signifying some sort of possession or relationship to it. It thus seems probable that Davis is right: the poem *Genua* celebrates Genoa (in text) and, consequently, its marine exploits (alluded to through the maps).

The curious conversation and interaction between Cattaneo and Giovio adds a narrative element to the painting.[39] Cattaneo's hand rests just below the main map and he is turned towards Giovio who in turn looks at him and gestures upwards with the index finger of his right hand. There can be little doubt that Sebastiano was requested to make a specific point through the hands of these two scholars: an infra-red examination undertaken at Washington revealed that 'the artist reworked the position of the fingers of the right hand geographer [sic]'.[40] Indeed, the position of their hands seem to denote their positions within Sauli's household: Cattaneo is shown to be the secretary by his hand on a book, which in itself probably alludes to his most famous work, whereas Giovio was Sauli's doctor and as such would have been trained in, and in fact had a passionate interest in, the study of the heavens, namely astrology.[41] It has already been demonstrated that the manuscript is a possible allusion to *Genua*; and it could also be argued that the gestures of Cattaneo and Giovio also illustrate the passage in the poem in which Cattaneo rails against those who study the heavens and do not explore the earth, a preference indicated by Giovio's upraised finger, while Cattaneo, whose hand is firmly earthbound and placed on the maps, confirms his preference for the exploration of the earth over the heavens.[42] Given Giovio's fascination with astrology, it is thus also likely that this passage in the poem is a lighthearted jibe at Giovio and his interests.

Their gestures can be viewed on still another level. Giovio's raised hand has been seen as a direct quotation from Leonardo da Vinci's *Last*

---

[39] Humfrey, 'Cardinal Bendinello Sauli'.
[40] 'Examination summary', 3.
[41] Zimmerman, *Paolo Giovio*, 6; S. J. Tester, *A history of western astrology*, Woodbridge 1987, 186–7; E. Garin, *Astrology in the Renaissance: the zodiac of life*, trans. C. Jackson, J. Allen and C. Robertson, London 1983, 93–4.
[42] 'O vani quorum astra animos, caelumque fatigant [sic]? / Qui supra captum humanum caelestia regna / Quaeritis, at terram quae vos producit alitque/ Nescitis, solum nebulas captatis inanes ... Sabatii melius, qui per commercia partes / Divisas orbi iungant ad comoda vitae': *Genua*, lines 408–11, 412–13.

Supper,[43] while it, and that of Cattaneo, recall another fresco which would certainly have been known to Sauli and probably to Sebastiano: Raphael's *School of Athens (see* plate 2).[44] This adorned one of the walls of Julius II's private library, a room which by 1513 had become known as the *stanza della segnatura*, the room in which the pope signed papal bulls, and which would have been known to papal intimates. The four frescoes in the room – the *Parnassus*, the *Disputa*, the *School of Athens* and *Gregory IX handing the Decretals to Raimondo of Penaforte* – represent the classifications then to be found in contemporary libraries.[45] The *School of Athens* signified Philosophy and the two most conspicuous figures within it were Plato and Aristotle whose hands are echoed in those of Giovio and Cattaneo. This reference would stress still further the importance of Sauli's patronage: he is the patron of two humanists whom he believes to be the modern equivalents of the two ancient philosophers.

Thus, as Michael Hirst rightly posited, within *Cardinal Bendinello Sauli and three companions* Sauli is also celebrated as a patron of men of letters.[46] Giovanni Maria Cattaneo and Paolo Giovio, like the secretary and messenger in *Ferry Carondelet*, contribute to Sauli's public *persona* as a head of household and patron of humanists. The latter was a role for which he remained famous after his death, through both later commentators and this portrait.

Sauli as cardinal-priest

But this is not the only aspect of Sauli's public *persona* celebrated within the portrait: he is also shown as a cardinal-priest. On the more obvious level he is dressed in rochet and *mozzetta*, the vestments of a cardinal, and to the right of his left hand is a small hand bell which can be identified as the Sanctus bell.[47] Bells are rarely featured in Renaissance portraits, but some similar to the one in the Sauli portrait can be seen in later ecclesiastical portraits: Raphael's *Pope Leo X with cardinals Giulio de' Medici and Luigi de' Rossi* (1518);[48] Joos van Cleve's *Portrait of Bernardo Clesio* (1530s);[49] the *Portrait of Cardinal Marcello Cervini degli Spannocchi* by an anonymous Florentine master (c. 1540)[50]; the copy by an anonymous Italian of the *Portrait of*

---

43 Santa Maria delle Grazie, Milan. See Hirst, *Sebastiano del Piombo*, 99.
44 Vatican Museums, Vatican City.
45 I. D. Rowland, 'The intellectual background of the "School of Athens": tracking divine wisdom in the Rome of Julius II', in M. Hall (ed.), *Raphael's School of Athens*, Cambridge 997, 131, 136, 161 n. 1.
46 Hirst, 'Sebastiano del Piombo', 99.
47 Jungic, 'Prophecies', 350, 352.
48 Galleria Uffizi, Florence.
49 Galleria Corsini, Rome.
50 Galleria Borghese, Rome.

Cardinal Domenico Grimani;[51] and Tintoretto's *Portrait of a priest*.[52] In the latter two cases the bell is undecorated as it is in the Sauli portrait.

The role of the bell within the eucharistic rite can be traced back to the thirteenth century when a bell was rung at the elevation of the host. From the sixteenth century onwards the bell used was a small hand bell, rung at the altar.[53] Sauli's identification with the priesthood is shown by the fact that the bell is engraved with his name and the letters 'EN. T. OR.', a feature repeated in the *Portrait of Domenico Grimani*. The bell, and Sauli's identification with it, are pivotal to the painting: it is the axis of the ninety degree angle between the hands of Giovio and the cardinal, while a space for his name on the bell was an intrinsic part of the original structure of the painting and was 'conceived as an important compositional element'.[54]

The portrait is also noteworthy because it is the first to survive in which a cardinal is holding a glove.[55] Gloves were part of the vestments for clerics of the rank of bishop and above, but were particularly seen as an 'item worn by bishops'.[56] The glove may thus be an allusion to his role as bishop of Gerace and Oppido and of Albenga and also to the priesthood given that 'gloves were worn by officiating priests when consecrating the holy sacrament'.[57] Sauli regularly celebrated mass on Easter Saturday for the pope and other cardinals; Paris de' Grassis noted that Sauli had celebrated mass 'quite well' and 'quite competently and modestly'.[58]

Extraneous to such interpretations of Sauli as a patron and a man of the Church is the carpet which covers the table and the fly on the cardinal's robes. The carpet has been identified as an Arabesque Ushak, also known as a Lotto carpet, with a Kufic border. This is the first surviving painting in which such a carpet is recorded.[59] Oriental carpets feature in Italian paintings from *c.* 1300 onwards and are used in a variety of ways in different types of pictures such as the *Virgin and child* and the *Annunciation*.[60] There is no reason to suppose that they are an allusion to the East in either these pictures, the Sauli portrait or indeed in the two pictures by Lorenzo Lotto

---

[51] Windsor Castle.
[52] Galleria Doria Pamphilij, Rome.
[53] A. Jungmann, *The mass of the Roman rite: its origins and development*, New York 1950, i. 131, 210.
[54] 'Examination summary', 3.
[55] Jungic, 'Prophecies', 350.
[56] Moroni, *Dizionario*, xxxiii. 93, 95.
[57] Jungic, 'Prophecies', 350; Moroni, *Dizionario*, xxxiii. 94.
[58] Barb. Lat. 2683, fos 99r, 158v.
[59] J. Mills, *Carpets in paintings*, London 1983, 28–30; O. Ydema, *Carpets and their datings in Netherlandish paintings, 1540–1700*, Woodbridge 1991, 227.
[60] J. Mills, 'The coming of the carpet to the west', in D. King and D. Sylvester (eds), *The eastern carpet in the western world from the 15th to the 17th century*, London 1983, 11–23 at pp. 12, 13–14.

in which the same type of carpet is used: the *Portrait of Giovanni della Volta and family* (1547) and the *St Antoninus altarpiece* (1541–2).[61] So what would be the reason for depicting an oriental carpet of this type? In everyday life in fifteenth- and sixteenth-century Italy, carpets were used on floors and on furniture and were often exhibited on special occasions.[62] Here the oriental carpet is what it seems: a furnishing to cover the table which forms the compositional focus of the right hand half of the painting. Certainly the predominant colour of the carpet, red, was a compositional aid: in the case of the Sauli portrait it allowed Sebastiano to link the red of Sauli's rochet and cuff with Giovio's costume, thus taking the onlooker through the painting from left to right. This device is also repeated in Lotto's *St Antoninus altarpiece* where the carpet helps to take the onlooker's eye anti-clockwise around the picture.

The depiction of flies in Renaissance paintings has been the object of scant study. They have been interpreted simply as a demonstration of a painter's skill, as a *memento mori* or as a talisman to keep real flies away from the painting.[63] There was an established tradition of insects in paintings in both Netherlandish and North Italian painting of the fifteenth century, and Sebastiano would doubtless have known Dürer's *Feast of the rosegarlands* (1505–6)[64] painted for San Bartolomeo di Rialto in Venice, in which the fly is placed on the main figure's left knee as in the Washington portrait. In about 1508 Sebastiano had painted the organ wings showing *SS Bartolomeo, Sebastiano, Ludovico di Tolosa e Sinibaldo* for this very church.[65] In the Sauli portrait the fly has been set against the white of the cardinal's robe as if to emphasise its darkness and thus its reality and, given its proximity to the *cartellino* in which Sebastiano had signed the work, it seems most likely that the fly is to be seen as conspicuous proof of the artist's skill: if he could paint a fly with such conviction, then his portraits too would show equally skilfully the physiognomies of the sitters.

What can be learned of Sauli's tastes from this examination of the Washington portrait? The rich details of the portrait – the fly, the book, the carpet – show that Sauli probably shared the taste of his uncle, Vincenzo Sauli, for Netherlandish details. Furthermore, he had chosen a prominent painter who had worked for the upper echelons of Roman society. He requested, and got, a large, ambitious and innovatory portrait which introduced a new format for the portrayal of a cardinal and a new visual concept of the cardinal as a patron and as a ruler of his household.

The portrait is dated 1516 on the *cartellino*, but it is possible to date it a

---

61 National Gallery, London; SS Giovanni e Paolo, Venice.
62 Mills, *Carpets*, 20 and passim.
63 A. Chastel, *Musca depicta*, Milan 1994, 14, 36; A. Pigler, 'La Mouche peinte: un talisman', *Bulletin des Musées Hongrois des Beaux-Arts* xxiv (1964), 47–64 at p. 61.
64 National Gallery, Prague
65 Accademia, Venice. See Humfrey, '*Cardinal Bendinello Sauli*'.

little more precisely. It had been completed by 6 June 1516 when thirty ducats are recorded as being paid 'to Sebastiano veneto painter for the remainder of the works'.[66] This is, obviously, only a part payment on completion. No other record of payment could be located in the Archivio Sauli and, given that Cardinal Sauli's banking records for 1515 are lost, this suggests that the work was begun prior to his departure for Bologna in November 1515 and that most of the painter's fee was paid at that point. The portrait was then completed after Sauli's return to Rome in mid-March 1516.

The influence of the Washington portrait

Sauli (and presumably Sebastiano) had hoped to gain prestige from such a portrait and indeed prestige was conferred on the painting despite its many incoherencies and a lack of unity which has been stressed by modern critics.[67] *Cardinal Bendinello Sauli and three companions* exerted considerable influence in the following years on portraits of ecclesiastics. As late as 1540 Jacopo da Ponte copied the fly against a white background.[68] In later portraits the bell becomes a constant feature and a book is often found close to it, as for example in the *Portrait of Domenico Grimani* and the *Portrait of Marcello Cervini*. The popularity of the bell and book motifs may be due to the painting in which the influence of the Washington portrait is most seen, Raphael's *Portrait of Leo X with Cardinals Giulio de' Medici and Luigi de' Rossi*.[69] This too is a large portrait, aiming to impress with its size (154 x 119 cm) and, like the Sebastiano, recalls Raphael's earlier *Portrait of Julius II* in the pose of the main sitter, which here is reversed. The book and bell clearly derive from the Sauli portrait, but here the book is the Hamilton Bible open at the Gospel of St John, an allusion to the pope's baptismal name.[70] The glove held by Sauli is not used by Raphael, and hence the motif did not enjoy the same subsequent success. Raphael, however, was more successful in giving a sense of unity to the picture and here, through the proximity of Cardinal de' Medici to the pope and the hands of Cardinal de' Rossi on the

---

66 'videlicet ducatos 30 sebastiano veneto pictori pro residuo laborum': Archivio Sauli, no. 730, fo. 72r.
67 Lucco, 'Catalogo', 107; Palluchini, *Sebastiano Viniziano*, 41; Hirst, *Sebastiano del Piombo*, 99–100; Freedberg, *Painting of the high Renaissance*, 374.
68 Lucco, 'Catalogo', 107.
69 Davis, 'Un appunto', 386; Freedberg, *Painting of the high Renaissance*, 341; Jungic, 'Prophecies', 369–70; T. Borenius, 'A portrait group by Sebastiano del Piombo', *Burlington Magazine* xxxvii (1920), 169–70 at p. 169; V. Guazzoni, 'La tradizione della ritrattistica papale nel Rinascimento e il *Leone X* di Raffaello', in *Raffaello e il ritratto di Papa Leone: per il ristauro del 'Leone X con due cardinali' nella Galleria degli Uffizi*, Milan 1996, 89–133 at p. 110; Minnich, 'Raphael's portrait', 1008–9, 1019.
70 Minnich, 'Raphael's portrait', 1009; Jungic, 'Prophecies', 369; R. Jones and N. Penny, *Raphael*, New Haven 1983, 166.

back of his chair, the onlooker gets the impression of a coherent family unit, even if, as is now generally believed, the two cardinals did not form part of the original design of the painting.[71] Did Raphael want to show that he was more skilful than Sebastiano, or did Leo X, for his own personal reasons, ask him to emulate the Sauli portrait? No conclusive answer can be given.

The copy of the Washington portrait

It has long been known that a painting which can best be described as an old copy of *Cardinal Bendinello Sauli and three companions* existed in a private collection in Rome. In 1764 Paolo Fidanza attributed it to Mantegna and identified the sitters as Cardinal Giovanni Borgia, Cesare Borgia, Niccolò Macchiavelli and a henchman (*sicario*) of Cesare Borgia.[72] In 1916 and 1917 Mario Menotti signalled agreement with the identification of Cesare Borgia and Macchiavelli, but believed the cardinal to be Pier Luigi Borgia and the figure on the left his secretary don Micheletto Corella.[73] From the mid-*settecento* to the beginning of the *novecento* the painting was part of the Albani collection in Urbino, where its presence had been duly noted by Fidanza, and it was then sold to the family of its current owner.[74] It was exhibited as part of the exhibition *I Borgia* at the Palazzo Ruspoli in Rome in 2002 and Menotti's identification of the sitters was maintained in the catalogue entry.

The present owner's thesis is that the Albani portrait shows a cardinal, perhaps Pier Luigi Borgia (1500–11), who witnesses the meeting between Cesare Borgia and Niccolò Macchiavelli and their discussion of Borgia's conquests and the unification of Italy. He believes that in 1516 Sauli asked Sebastiano to copy the portrait, replacing the cardinal's portrait with his own and changing the book of maps and the writing on the bell.[75] The

---

[71] P. De Vecchi, 'Raffaello e il ritratto "di naturale"', in *Raffaello e il ritratto di Papa Leone*, 9–50 at p. 44.

[72] P. Fidanza, *Teste scelte di personaggi illustri in lettere e in armi cavate già dall'antico, o dall'originale e dipinte nel Vaticano da Raffaello di Urbino e da altri valenti pittori ora esattamente disegnate, incise in rame secondo la loro grandezza e divise in due tomi da Paolo Fidanza pittore e incisore romano*, Rome 1757–74, v. 33–6.

[73] M. Menotti, 'Vannozza Cattanei e i Borgia', *Nuova Antologia* (Nov.–Dec. 1916), 471–86 at p. 480, and *I Borgia: storia e iconografia*, Rome 1917, 124–32.

[74] Written communication from the owner, 30 Oct. 2003; Menotti, 'Vannozza Cattanei', 480; Anon., 'Ritratto di Cesare Borgia Il Valentino e Niccolò Macchiavelli in conversazione davanti al cardinale Pedro Loys Borgia e al segretario don Micheletto Corella', in M. Menotti, *I Borgia*, Rome 2002, 215, where the painting is reproduced. The painting is in oil on canvas, 150 x 118 cm.

[75] Anon., 'Ritratto di Cesare Borgia', 215; written communication from the owner, 20 Mar. 2003. It is difficult to know how much weight to give to the catalogue entry: although anonymous it was presumably written by the current owner, who remains adamant that the Albani portrait is the original work.

Albani *cartellino* is of no help in identifying the cardinal: it is now illegible but at one time 'perhaps featured a signature and the date of 1503', ironically the year in which Cardinal Giovanni Borgia, cited by Fidanza as the main sitter, died.[76] The ring on the cardinal's own right hand also provides no answers: it is identical in both cases, featuring a stylised animal of some sort. This could as easily be the Sauli eagle rampant as 'a stylised quadruped which could probably be a bull' (the emblem of the Borgia).[77] Indeed, if the Albani portrait is compared to that in Washington it is, at first glance, difficult to refute the identification of the cardinal as Sauli, but it should be remembered that the face in the Washington portrait was, at an unknown date, 'extensively reworked as revealed during examination with ultra-violet light' and is 'the most damaged out of the four figures and has been heavily overpainted'.[78] In the Albani portrait the cardinal is definitely older, but the nose, eyebrows and mouth are seemingly those of Sauli as portrayed in Washington. A drawing which forms part of the Chatsworth Collection (*see* frontispiece) provides the answer.[79] Generally accepted as being subsequent to the Washington portrait rather than a preparatory drawing, its *terminus ante quem* is 1680 and it is undoubtedly taken from the Washington portrait, as can be seen in the nose and hair, both longer than in the Albani portrait, and in the absence of the white undershirt.[80] The drawing was obviously made before the repainting of Sauli's face to its present bland state and a comparison of the Chatsworth drawing with the Albani portrait confirms that the Albani cardinal is in fact Sauli: the shape of the face, including eyes, nose, mouth and eyebrows are the same, but belong to an older, more careworn man. Sauli died on 29 March 1518; less than two years had passed between the Washington portrait and his death, but they had been traumatic years, encompassing imprisonment in very poor conditions, disgrace and, most important, the ill-health which eventually led to his death.

If the cardinal in the Albani portrait is Sauli, then it is highly improbable that he would have wished to be shown with either Cesare Borgia or Macchiavelli, with whom he had no known links. There can be little doubt that the figures to the right of both paintings are in fact Cattaneo and Giovio:

---

[76] Ibid. 215.

[77] Written communication from the owner, 24 Mar. 2003: 'un quadrupede stilizzato che verosimilmente potrebbe essere un toro'.

[78] 'Examination summary', 1, 4; Davis, 'Un appunto', 386.

[79] Chatsworth Collection, no. 341; there is also a drawing of the cardinal's hand (no. 340). Davis, 'Un appunto', 386, highlights the importance of the Chatsworth drawing; other scholars have for the most part ignored it. The drawing is in black chalk and measures 371 x 250 mm.

[80] Humfrey, 'Cardinal Bendinello Sauli'. For the details of the drawing and its provenance see M. Jaffé, *The Devonshire collection of Italian drawings: Venetian and North Italian schools*, London 1994, 126. Jaffé attributes it to an anonymous North Italian artist. See Davis, 'Un appunto', 386, and Rusk Shapley, *Catalogue*, i. 422. Kempers, 'Canonical portrait', 21 n. 19, is the only critic to believe it may be an autograph study.

Cesare Borgia is nearly always shown with a beard and a brief glance at the drawings by Leonardo da Vinci,[81] the *Portrait of Cesare Borgia*[82] and *Cesare Borgia*[83] reveals that there is quite simply no similarity between the more delicate facial features of Cesare and the somewhat coarser ones of the bull-necked Cattaneo. Nor is Giovio in fact Macchiavelli: Giovio's nose was unique, as confirmed by other representations of him such as the da Sangallo medal. Cattaneo was probably with Sauli by *c.* 1509 and Giovio joined his household in *c.* 1512. Why should they figure together in an earlier or later portrayal of any other cardinal and his household given that that the only patron that they had in common was Sauli?

There are also artistic arguments against the Washington portrait being a copy of the Albani. There is only a limited amount of under-drawing in the former, concentrated for the most part on the heads of the four figures and the position of Sauli's throne.[84] This suggests that the heads were drawn from life or from closer detailed drawings that Sebastiano had already made and this, and the *pentimenti* – for example the change in the position of the cardinal's own right eye; the nose of the second figure from the right, the original location of the head of the figure on the far right at a lower level and the position of his fingers – suggest that it is not a copy.[85] Radiographic examination has also revealed *pentimenti* in the Albani portrait, most specifically in reference to Giovio's finger, but these may be a result of the second artist's difficulty in accommodating the problematic scale and detail of Sebastiano's original; indeed Sebastiano himself had problems with Giovio's hand in the Washington portrait.[86] The Albani portrait, which is in good condition, is also artistically of a poorer standard: the brushwork in the shading is pedestrian and lacks finesse, and all the hands are more coarsely painted and lack characterisation. There was of course a difference in medium which may account for this: the Washington portrait was initially painted on wood, the Albani copy on canvas and was painted '*in prima tela*'.[87] But the smoothness and luxury of the Washington portrait are missing, and although nearly all the details are reproduced to a more or less faithful degree (and indeed, in the case of the white undershirts worn by the sitters in the Albani portrait, added), they are simply that: reproductions which do not attain the heights of the original.[88] Only the head of the cardinal is skilfully executed and may, perhaps, be by another hand.

[81] Biblioteca Reale, Turin.

[82] Palazzo Venezia, Rome.

[83] Kunsthistorisches Museum, Vienna.

[84] 'Examination summary', 2.

[85] Ibid. 3.

[86] Anon, 'Ritratto di Cesare Borgia', 215; written, and final, communication from the owner, 30 Oct. 2003.

[87] Anon., 'Ritratto di Cesare Borgia', 215.

[88] Undershirts, although common in Renaissance portraits, were not 'de rigeur'. See, for example, Raphael's *Portrait of a cardinal*.

Given the identification of the main sitters as Sauli, Cattaneo and Giovio, the differences in the cardinal's features which can be explained by the traumatic events of 1517 and the lower artistic standard, it seems likely that the Albani portrait is an early memorial copy, commissioned to commemorate Sauli and including a portrait of him executed shortly before his death. It was commissioned by an unknown patron, perhaps by a member of his family, and was certainly executed before the damage occurred to Sauli's face in the Washington portrait.

Raphael's portrayal of a cardinal

Raphael's *Portrait of a cardinal* (1511) (*see* plate 3) has been the subject of high praise and numerous identifications, the latter ranging from Francesco Alidosi to Luigi d'Aragona, with none finding a general consensus.[89] Information about provenance is scarce: it was purchased by Charles IV and by 1818 was at Aranjuez, subsequently finding its way to the Prado. The painting, but most specifically the green background, has been restored.[90] Wilhelm Suida proposed Cardinal Sauli as the sitter on the basis of similarities with the Washington portrait, but his identification received little critical attention.[91] This 'old but neglected idea' was more recently resurrected by Anton Haidacher, Charles Davis and Bram Kempers, the latter basing his attribution on the similarities in age and features between the Prado and Washington portraits, especially the eyes, nose and lips.[92] Once again, the Chatsworth drawing is ignored by all except Davis, but it is only through a comparison between this and the Prado portrait that one can definitely state that the two sitters are the same: although the positions of the two heads are different, their lips, nose, cheekbones, lines around the mouth and above all the eyebrows are identical.

Thus, at a very early point in his cardinalate, and perhaps, given the date generally assigned to the work, to celebrate his elevation, Sauli picked the foremost artist in Rome, Raphael, to paint his portrait. He felt that he deserved the best, and indeed could afford it. Having been immortalised, alone, in a free-standing portrait in which his red cardinal robes tell the onlooker all that needs to be known about him, the innovation of the group

[89] Museo del Prado, Madrid. For discussion see, for example, Pope-Hennessy, *The portrait*, 113; *Museo del Prado: catalogo de las pinturas*, Madrid 1985, 527; E. Camasca (ed.), *Tutta la pittura di Raffaello: i quadri*, Milan 1956, i. 55; Kempers, 'Canonical portrait', 7.

[90] *Museo del Prado*, 528; Camasca, *Tutta la pittura*, 55.

[91] W. E. Suida, *Paintings and sculptures from the Kress Collection, National Gallery of Art*, Washington, DC 1951, 104; *Museo del Prado*, 527.

[92] Haidacher, *Geschichte der Päpste in Bildern*, 266; Davis, 'Un appunto', 388 n. 14; Kempers, 'Canonical portrait', 7, 11, 13.

portrait of *Cardinal Bendinello Sauli and three companions* some five years later becomes more understandable: it was something different.

There is a well-established critical link between the Madrid *Portrait of a cardinal* and the bishop looking out on the left of Raphael's *Disputa* in the Stanza della Segnatura (1509–10) (*see* plate 4), the identification of the latter depending on that of the former.[93] The frescoed figure is dressed as a bishop, as Sauli was at the time, and the similarities with the Madrid portrait – hair, eyes, eyebrows, cheekbones are the same – are striking. The bishop portrayed is thus almost certainly Sauli. His inclusion in the fresco confirms his position as a favourite of Julius II and, given that the fresco is devoted to the subject of religion and the revelation of divine truth to man, perhaps indicates his interest in theology, an interest already encountered in his discussions with humanists.[94] Perhaps Sauli's satisfaction with Raphael's depiction of him in the *Disputa* led to the slightly later commissioning of the Madrid portrait. Bram Kempers also believes that the young, curly-haired cardinal who is second on the left in the fresco of *Gregory IX handing the Decretals to Raimondo de Penaforte* in the same room is also Sauli.[95] The similarities there are less obvious, however, not least in the hair and eyebrows; and why, if Raphael could paint such a detailed portrait of Sauli as that now in Madrid, should this one be such an approximation?

Sebastiano del Piombo and Stefano Sauli

It is generally believed that after Raphael's death Sebastiano was regarded as the most skilful artist in Rome.[96] His portraits, until the Sack of Rome in 1527, took on a manifest new power and strength. During this period he painted, for example, the *Flagellation* for Giovanni Botonti,[97] *Clement VII*,[98] *Andrea Doria*[99] and *Pietro Aretino*,[100] names which testify to the degree of success he had achieved.[101]

Yet relations between Sebastiano and his patrons did not always run

---

[93] S. Ferino Pagden and M. A. Zancan, *Raffaello: catalogo completo dei dipinti*, Florence 1989, 89; Camesasca, *Tutta la pittura*, 55; Kempers, 'Canonical portrait', 8; Jones and Penny, *Raphael*, 159.

[94] For the interpretation of the fresco see G. Reale, *Raffaello: la Disputa*, Milan 1998, 7.

[95] Kempers ('Canonical portrait', 18) also notes that the hair is blonder and the facial expression is different.

[96] For a letter from Michelangelo to Sebastiano of that year in which this opinion of Sebastiano is confirmed see Lucco, 'Catalogo', 88.

[97] Museo Civico, Viterbo.

[98] Gallerie Nazionali di Capodimonte, Naples.

[99] Palazzo de' Principi, Genoa.

[100] Palazzo Communale, Arezzo.

[101] Lucco, 'Sebastiano del Piombo', 334.

smoothly. The *Raising of Lazarus*, commissioned by Cardinal de' Medici for his cathedral at Narbonne, was completed in late 1519 and was well-received.[102] But by 15 January 1520 Sebastiano and de' Medici were at loggerheads over the price and although Baldassare Peruzzi was called in to mediate, Sebastiano had still not been paid by the end of March of that year.[103] A similar situation arose over the fee to be paid for the *Flagellation*. Sebastiano had finished the work in early 1525 but Botonti wanted to send it to Florence so that Michelangelo could arbitrate on the price.[104] The painter was obviously aware of his worth and his reputation.

It is thus interesting that a previously unknown reference in a letter from Stefano Sauli to Sebastiano Sauli further confirms the painter's prickly character when it came to the matter of payment (and indeed Stefano Sauli's careful attention to money). On 23 February 1527 Stefano wrote to his brother that 'you can happily tell Sebastiano the painter that I don't want to give him anything more'.[105] 'Altro', in the Italian can, of course, be translated as 'anything else' and could thus refer to another commission, but it seems most unlikely that an artist of Sebastiano's fame would actually be asking for work. The use of 'liberamente' ('happily') denotes Stefano Sauli's irritation and it may thus be assumed that 'altro' refers to money. To what payment does this refer? It seems unlikely that it relates to *Cardinal Bendinello Sauli and three companions*, which is clearly dated 1516 and for which the final payment had been made in that year. The two earlier quibbles over price related to works which had been completed recently. Given that the quarrel can be dated to early 1527, then, based on the earlier examples this unknown work may have been completed in *c.* 1526. It is known that Sebastiano was in Rome and by the end of May of that year had painted a portrait of Clement VII (probably the Naples one).[106] He also painted the *Andrea Doria*, to which the pope was greatly attached, and was commissioned by the heirs of Agostino Chigi to paint an *Assumption* for Chigi's chapel in Santa Maria del Popolo, but this was never completed.[107] So what was this (presumably) lost work which Stefano Sauli had commissioned? The Albani copy has no traceable Genoese provenance – Stefano Sauli lived in Genoa for much of his life after 1521 – and it is less skilfully painted than the Washington original and thus unlikely to have been painted by Sebastiano. There are no surviving works datable to this period with a Genoese provenance and the details of this lost work are probably destined to remain undiscovered. All traces of the

102 National Gallery, London. See Lucco, 'Catalogo', 110.
103 Ibid. 87, 111.
104 Ibid. 115.
105 'a' Sebastiano pittor' dicte liberamente che non voglio darli altro': Archivio Sauli, i no. 1568, fo. 19r.
106 Lucco, 'Catalogo', 88.
107 Idem, 'Sebastiano del Piombo', 335.

quarrel disappear from Stefano's correspondence – and it thus seems likely that Sebastiano decided to accept Stefano's (lost) original offer.

What has been learned from this examination of contemporary portrayals of Cardinal Sauli? The unique nature of the Washington painting, as a group portrait of a cardinal with members of his household celebrating his role as ruler, patron and priest, has been established. It demonstrates Sauli's sense of prestige and pride in his position and a taste for innovation. It has also been seen how, using the Chatsworth drawing as a more accurate means of identification, the Albani copy of the Washington portrait can be dated to about 1518 or later as a representation of an older, more careworn Cardinal Sauli, perhaps commissioned by a member of his family. The Chatsworth drawing also allows a firm identification of Sauli as the sitter for Raphael's *Portrait of a cardinal* and, by extension, confirms his presence in the *Disputa*. Both the Washington and the Madrid paintings show Sauli's taste for celebration, in both cases by the two foremost artists of the day, his love of rich details and his satisfaction with all that he had achieved. This would change with his implication in the plot to murder Leo.

Plate 1. Sebastiano del Piombo, *Cardinal Bendinello Sauli and three companions* (1516) (Samuel H. Kress Collection, National Gallery of Art, Washington). Photograph © Board of Trustees, National Gallery of Art, Washington.

Plate 2. Raphael, *School of Athens* (detail) (c. 1508) (Vatican Museums, Vatican City). Photograph © Vatican Museums, Vatican City.

Plate 3. Raphael, *Portrait of a cardinal* (c. 1511) (Museo Prado, Madrid). Photograph ©
Museo Nacional del Prado, Madrid.

Plate 4. Raphael, *Disputa* (detail) (1509–10) (Vatican Museums, Vatican City). Photograph © Vatican Museums, Vatican City.

PART III

THE PLOT TO KILL THE POPE

7

The Plot to Kill Leo X

On 19 May 1517 Cardinal Sauli and Cardinal Petrucci were arrested in the papal antechamber of the *palazzo apostolico* and taken to separate cells in the Castel Sant'Angelo. They were placed in custody 'it was said because they had planned to poison the pope'.[1]

How did Sauli, a young cardinal, petted by Leo and showered with benefices, find himself in prison and in danger of his life? Had he, as some believed and still believe, been set up, or had he really thought that he, Cardinal Riario, Cardinal Soderini, Cardinal Castellesi and others still unidentified could stand by and watch the murder of a pope on Petrucci's orders via a third party and see him replaced by their candidate? Or was he the victim of his own lack of common sense: had he listened to Petrucci's ramblings about revenge for the loss of Siena and perhaps, for his own reasons, half-heartedly lent his support, but without taking him seriously?[2]

How the plot was uncovered

Evidence of a plot emerged in April 1517 during the interrogation of the *famigliari* of Cardinal Petrucci regarding the cardinal's political crimes. The background is complex. In 1512 the French had been defeated, the Papal States consolidated (and indeed extended) and relations with the Holy Roman Emperor and Spain were, on the whole, on a sound footing. Leo, on his election, initially attempted to remain neutral when faced with the various proposed alliances between the main powers, which aimed to foster their own ambitions and further limit the claims of France on Milan but then, as was his nature, vacillated between one power and another. In

---

[1] 'ut dicitur, quod venenum contra personam santissimi D N Papae machinati essent': Barb. Lat. 2683, fo. 200r.

[2] For the theory that the plot was 'probably spurious' see K. J. P. Lowe, 'The political crime of conspiracy in fifteenth- and sixteenth-century Rome', in T. Dean and K. J. P. Lowe (eds), *Crime, society and the law in Renaissance Italy*, Cambridge 1994, 184–203 at p. 185. See also G. B. Picotti, 'La congiura dei cardinali contro Leone X', *Rivista Storica Italiana* n.s. i (1923), 249–67; Jungic, 'Prophecies', 345–70; M. Gattoni, *Leone X e la geopolitica dello stato pontificio*, Vatican City 2000, passim; and K. J. P. Lowe, 'An alternative account of the alleged cardinals' conspiracy of 1517 against pope Leo X', *Roma moderna e contemporanea: Rivista interdisciplinare di Storia* xi (2003), 53–77, and *Church and politics*, 104–13.

1515 the French regained Milan and in December Francis I and Leo met at Bologna to ratify the peace agreement. Yet relations between the papacy and both France and Spain remained strained. Some indication of Leo's intentions had been signalled in June 1515 when Giuliano, and then later Lorenzo de' Medici (a papal nephew), became commander of the papal troops. Family matters had always been important to Leo, as indeed they had been to previous popes, but Leo had the added impetus of needing to protect the interests of Florence, to which the Medici had been restored in 1512. In 1516 he chose to combine family and papal interests by adopting what has been described as a 'macro state' policy: in March he attempted to fortify his political position by replacing Borghese Petrucci as ruler of Siena and forming what has been called a papal protectorate, thus withdrawing the city from the orbit of its traditional supporter, Spain. More was to follow: later in the same year Lorenzo de' Medici replaced the pro-French Francesco Maria della Rovere as duke of Urbino in a similar coup.[3]

A disgusted Cardinal Petrucci left Rome in July 1516 and from then until May 1517 conducted political negotiations to recover Siena with, amongst others, Spain, with whom he concluded a treaty, della Rovere and the Baglioni of Perugia. Such moves against the pope, which especially contravened a bull of 20 January 1517 prohibiting negotiations with della Rovere, meant that Petrucci was guilty of *lèse majesté*.[4] At the behest of Leo, who had used two *famigliari* of Cardinal Sauli and Cardinal Cornaro (1500–24) as intermediaries, Petrucci returned to Rome on 11 February 1517 in an attempt to clarify the situation, only to flee secretly on 7 or 8 March.[5] Leo then adopted a three-pronged approach: he wrote to Petrucci, warning him to desist from his negotiations, and he extended the powers of the *procuratore fiscale* empowering him to act against all crimes against the state. In addition he began negotiations to settle two-thirds of the patrimony of the late Pandolfo Petrucci upon the cardinal.[6]

Then, on 15 April, Marc'Antonio Nini, Petrucci's *maestro di casa*, his cousin Scipione Petrucci, Lorenzo Suares his business agent, and the papal groom Nicolò Masi da Romena were arrested and imprisoned in the Castel Sant'Angelo. They were interrogated by Domenico Coletta, the *vicecastellano*, Gian Giacomo Gambarana, the *uditore generale* of the governor of

---

3 For the background to what was eventually the war of Urbino see Gattoni, *Leone X*, 187, 158–9, 188ff., and Pastor, *History of the popes*, vii. 147ff.
4 Ferrajoli, *La congiura*, 13; Giovio, *Le vite*, 265; Real Accademia de la Historia, Madrid, Salazar y Castro, MS 76, fos 213v, 214r, 218r; M. Zorzi to Venetian government, 7, 9 Feb. 1517, Sanuto, *Diarii*, xxiii. 584, 585; H. Lippomano to Venetian government, 13 May 1517, ibid. xxiv. 197.
5 Zorzi to Venetian government, 12 Feb. 1517, Sanuto, *Diarii*, xxiii. 591; Ferrajoli, *La congiura*, 15; Salazar y Castro, MS 76, fo. 218r–v.
6 Ferrajoli, *La congiura*, 15–16; F. Winspeare, *La congiura dei cardinali contro Leone X*, Florence 1957, 40–1.

Rome and the *procuratore fiscale*, Mario Peruschi.[7] The surviving draft of their trial, taken down by, amongst others, the notary Giovanpietro Perac-chia, also includes interrogations of other minor figures and forms the basis of much of what is known about the charges later faced by the three cardi-nals. Other sources include contemporary accounts by onlookers such as Paris de' Grassis, the slightly later account written by a Portuguese servant of Petrucci, the orators' reports (which did not simply regurgitate Leo's opin-ions, but also reported other sources, rumours and the *vox populi*), and the official version to be found in the consistorial records written by the vice-chancellor Cardinal de' Medici. The latter are at times in conflict with more immediate evidence. Greater reliance, in this account, has thus been placed on eyewitness evidence and the Sauli account books when possible.[8]

The interrogations, based on letters in Peruschi's possession, concentrated at first on Petrucci's political dealings to regain Siena. These were confirmed by Nini who named members of the Curia and Cardinal Sauli and Cardinal Cornaro as aware of these negotiations.[9] Scipione Petrucci in turn revealed that Lattanzio Petrucci, bishop of Sovana and Petrucci's mainstay in his political negotiations, had had dealings with Cardinal Soderini ('Palea' according to the codenames that the cardinals had seemingly given them-selves), Sauli ('Paritas') and an unidentified cardinal 'Sansome', although at one stage their support for Petrucci was not certain.[10]

In the interrogation of 22 April the climate changed: it became clear that in July and August 1516, when Leo had suffered a recurrence of his problem-atic anal fistula and had been gravely ill, Cardinal Castellesi and a cardinal known as 'Exiguus' (generally supposed to be Marco Cornaro) had shown a lively interest in the progress of the pope's illness, sharing this with Nini.[11] This is the first time that the pope's death is mentioned in the interrogations; the information supplied by Nini appears in between discussions of Petruc-ci's political dealings and has no connection to them. It thus seems probable that he was prompted to expand on the subject and furnished these titbits in the hope of satisfying his interrogators. At this point the political aspect of

[7] Ferrajoli, *La congiura*, 17–18. The dates in this chapter are those to be found in contemporary documents and the writings of contemporary commentators rather than those supplied by more recent authors.

[8] A.A. Arm. I–XVIII, 2243, much of it is transcribed in Ferrajoli, *La congiura*, 221–322. Gattoni, *Leone X*, 192–4 n. 37, publishes a further part of the document. For the consis-torial records see Picotti, 'La congiura', 253–4. The Portuguese diary is Salazar y Castro, MS 76, fos 136r–230v: I am very grateful to Philippa Jackson for this valuable reference.

[9] A.A. Arm. I–XVIII, 2243, fos 3r–v, 5r, 9v, 10r–15v, 16v, 18r, 19v; Ferrajoli, *La congiura*, 221–3, 226–36, 239–41, 243.

[10] A.A. Arm. I–XVIII, 2243, fos 69r–71r; Ferrajoli, *La congiura*, 290–2, 293. For the fate of Lattanzio, who escaped arrest but was deprived of his bishopric in Nov. 1517, see Ferrajoli, *La congiura*, 116–17, 170, and Arch. Concist., Acta Vicecanc. 2, fos 56v, 59r.

[11] Barb. Lat. 2683, fo. 166v; A.A. Arm. I–XVIII, 2243, fo. 19r; Ferrajoli, *La congiura*, 28, 241–3. For the supposition that 'Exiguus' is Cornaro see Winspeare, *La congiura*, 171.

his interrogations ended, Nini was taken back to his cell, and from then on was only interrogated about an even more serious matter, the possibility of a plot to poison the pope. That same day saw the first official announcement of the arrest of Nini and a warning from the pope that he intended to proceed against Petrucci because he had treated with his enemies.[12]

Nini was interrogated again six days later: much of the questioning from this point onwards was based on eighteen letters written by him and Cardinal Petrucci between 4 April 1516 and 11 April 1517. They had presumably come into Peruschi's possession during the course of the interrogations.[13] Seemingly prompted by Peruschi, an interest in the pope's death on the part of Petrucci and the possibility of the existence of a plot first emerged in this interrogation when Nini was asked about a partly coded letter from himself to Petrucci of 11 August 1516.[14] Asked to explain the beginning of the letter, which was mostly in code, he said that it concerned the pope's illness during that period and that he had seemed near death, a death desired by Nini and Petrucci for the good of Siena and because it would mean a new pope. He was then asked about another part of the letter mostly in code which began 'I spoke with Vercelli'. He replied that anyone with common sense who knew of Petrucci's hatred for Leo and his wish for his demise would interpret the letter as alluding to the fact that (Giovanni) Battista Vercelli, a surgeon and Petrucci intimate, was trying to enter the pope's service to replace the pope's doctor Jacopo (da Brescia) in the hope of doing Petrucci a service by poisoning the pope with his medicines.[15] He continued that the truth was actually that Petrucci had asked Nini to invite Vercelli to Genazzano; Vercelli had declined because he was busy trying to enter the pope's service. Vercelli, a skilful surgeon and a good man, wanted to help both himself and Siena: he was to aid Petrucci by passing information to the cardinal and by praising Petrucci to the pope. Nini continued to maintain these claims under torture, until finally admitting that Vercelli was intent on killing the pope and had expressed this intention to him.[16] It is unlikely, as Alessandro Ferrajoli notes, that Nini should offer a criminal interpretation of the letter

---

12 M. Minio to Venetian government, 22 Apr. 1517, Sanuto, *Diarii*, xxiv. 195.
13 A.A. Arm. I–XVIII, 2243, fo. 20v; Ferrajoli, *La congiura*, 244. For the letters see Giovio, *Le vite*, 265; *Corpo diplomatico Portuguez contendo os actos e relacoes politicas e diplomaticas de Portugal com as diversas potencias do mundo, desde o seculo XVI at, nosso dias*, ed. L. A. Rebello da Silva, Lisbon 1862–91, i. 469; Winspeare, *La congiura*, 40–1, 86–7; Ferrajoli, *La congiura*, 34, 223, 236; and B. Costabili to A. d'Este, 24 June 1517, in P. Capparoni, 'Giov. Battista da Vercelli, sifilioatra squartato sotto Leone x', *Bollettino dell'Istituto Storico Italiano dell'Arte Sanitaria* i (1921), 3–36 at p. 34.
14 Ferrajoli, *La congiura*, 25, 256.
15 'parlai cum Vercelli': A.A. Arm. I–XVIII, 2243, fo. 21r–v; Ferrajoli, *La congiura*, 245. For Vercelli see Ferrajoli, *La congiura*, 201–7; Capparoni, 'Giov. Battista da Vercelli', 3–24; and Winspeare, *La congiura*, 105–9. See also Salazar y Castro, MS 76, fo. 220r.
16 A.A. Arm. I–XVIII, 2243, fos 22r–24r; Ferrajoli, *La congiura*, 246–9.

without prompting from Peruschi, first admit that this interpretation was possible, then deny it only to confirm it in later interrogations, but it is also clear that Vercelli was eager to enter Leo's service: this is not denied at any point, even under torture.

Nini made further claims in the course of further interrogations and an increasingly dark picture emerges. He stated that in early March 1517 (three or four days before Petrucci left Rome), Sauli, via his brother, had personally lent the impecunious cardinal 1,000 ducats, doing his best to ensure that the matter did not come to the pope's attention. Soderini had also lent Petrucci money in August 1516 and, via the offices of Lattanzio Petrucci, was fully aware of and supported Petrucci's aims and like Cardinal Riario ('Carcioffo') advised on his affairs. 'Exiguus', Castellesi ('Rubeus') and Sauli were closely tied to Petrucci and passed on news, especially regarding the election of the new pope. In August 1516, while the pope was ill, both Sauli and Petrucci had agreed on their choice for a new pope and had informed an unidentified cardinal, 'Comes'. Vercelli had repeatedly expressed evil intentions towards the pope and all Petrucci's *famigliari* hoped for Leo's death.[17] The *coup de grâce* came on 2 May when he revealed that in July 1516, before Petrucci's departure from Rome, he had been summoned at lunchtime to Petrucci's bedroom and told that the cardinal had agreed with Vercelli that the latter would try to gain entry to the pope's service and would then apply poison to the pope's fistula, thus causing his death. This was confirmed to him by Vercelli. Riario, Sauli and Soderini were aware of his plans; they all wanted the pope's death and had chosen Riario to be the new pope. Nini was to discuss this only with Sauli.[18] There is, of course, an inconsistency here (which Nini recognised) with his earlier admission that in August 1516 only Sauli, Petrucci and 'Comes' had agreed on the choice of a new pope. Had he previously avoided revealing all because it strengthened the case against him as an accomplice and not just a witness, or was he now simply lying?

The accusations increased in both volume and seriousness, implicating Sauli even further. Nini asserted that in August 1516 he had discussed the deal with Vercelli with Sauli who had reiterated his support for Petrucci and the election of a new pope. At the beginning of September he returned once again to talk to Sauli and to tell him that the plan had not succeeded and Sauli replied, 'Fate has not been kind to us; we will trust in God, wait to live and be patient.'[19] In the meantime, and apparently until recently, Nini and Sauli frequently conferred about Petrucci's other business and the war of Urbino, with Sauli passing on news to Nini. Three letters of August 1516,

---

[17] A.A. Arm. I–XVIII, 2243, fos 24v, 25r–v, 26v, 27v–28r; Ferrajoli, *La congiura*, 250–6.
[18] A.A. Arm. I–XVIII, 2243, fos 29r–30v; Ferrajoli, *La congiura*,. 257–8, 260.
[19] 'Orsu la sorte nostra non ha voluto; recomendaresimo a Dio, attenderemo a vivere e haveremo pacientia': A.A. Arm. I–XVIII , 2243, fos 30v–31r; Ferrajoli, *La congiura*, 260–1.

as interpreted by Nini, confirmed Sauli's awareness and involvement in the matter of the pope's death.[20]

This was heady stuff. Initially Leo chose to act on the very real political crimes which had been confirmed independently by both Nini, Scipione Petrucci and later by the Petrucci henchman Pochintesta and were common knowledge in Rome.[21] They involved the negotiation of a treaty with Spain which was signed by both parties; attempts to provoke a revolt in Siena; and negotiations with various *condottieri*, especially Francesco Maria della Rovere. Leo then lured Petrucci to Rome: on 16 May the agreement mooted in April with Sauli's help which would reinstate Petrucci in Siena, return some of his patrimony and keep Siena under the pope's protection, was drawn up and ratified by Petrucci on the following day. Leo then sent Petrucci a safe conduct which covered protection from recriminations for political crimes and by the evening of 18 May 1517 he was in Rome, in his own palace.[22]

The arrest of the conspirators

With the arrest of Petrucci and Sauli on 19 May Leo had violated this same safe conduct. Protests by one of the Spanish orators were ignored.[23] On the same day other Petrucci *famigliari*, who were waiting outside the *palazzo*, were held; Vercelli was arrested in Florence and subsequently transferred to Rome.[24] The pope immediately summoned the cardinals, and then the orators, to announce what had happened and why, namely that he, by means of Nini's confession, had learned that Petrucci and Vercelli had planned to poison the pope's fistula and had communicated this to Cardinal Sauli and other accomplices. They had been arrested so that further investigations could be conducted. Leo appointed three cardinals, Farnese, Accolti and Remolino, to oversee the trial and 'advise the pope'.[25] Briefs were sent out to nuncios in Venice and France and also to Henry VIII and the king of Portugal which promised that copies of the trial documents would later follow.[26]

20 A.A. Arm. I–XVIII, 2243, fos 31r–32v; Ferrajoli, *La congiura*, 261–4.
21 Ferrajoli, *La congiura*, 16 n. 4, 17 n. 4, 297, 300–7, 310–15, 317, 319; A.A. Arm. I–XVIII, 2243, fos 79r–96v; Salazar y Castro, MS 76, fos 214r–v, 218r.
22 Minio to Venetian government, 9, 13 May 1517, Sanuto, *Diarii*, xxiv, 230, 274; Gattoni, *Leone* X, 194–5; Ferrajoli, *La congiura*, 43, 329ff; Barb. Lat. 2683, fo. 200r; Salazar y Castro, MS 76, fo. 220v.
23 Gattoni, *Leone* X, 197 n. 46; Cardinal de' Medici to bishop of Bayeux, 19 May 1517, in 'I manoscritti Torrigiani donati al R. Archivio Centrale di Stato di Firenze: descrizione e saggio', ed. C. Guasti, ASI xx (1874), 19–50, 228–55, 367–408 at pp. 394–5.
24 Winspeare, *La congiura*, 125; BAV, Chigiana G. II. 38, fo. 91v; G. Gheri to F. Guicciardini, 21 May 1517, in *F. Guicciardini: le lettere*, ed. P. Jodogne, Rome 1986–2005, ii, no. 386 at p. 535.
25 'ut Sanctitate Sue consulere possent': Arch. Concist., Acta Misc. 31, fo. 69v.
26 See, for example, Bembo to L. Giovenale, 19 May 1517, *Lettere: Pietro Bembo*, ii, no. 383 at p. 126.

On 21 May a *motu proprio* appointed the same judges and prosecutor (Coletta, Gamberana and Peruschi) to try the two cardinals. Torture was to be allowed and the trial proceedings would be presented in consistory, which would determine the sentence. Petrucci was described as guilty of political crimes and he and Sauli were accused of *lèse majesté*: planning to murder the pope and appoint another in his place. The document also confirmed that other cardinals were involved and were to be subject to investigation.[27] On 29 May, to everyone's surprise, Riario was arrested. He was kept under arrest at the *palazzo apostolico* for a week, with Cardinal de' Medici to interrogate him.[28] Riario's relatives wrote to the government of Venice and to Henry VIII, asking them to intercede.[29] By 2 June Paolo Agostini, Bernardino da Perugia (both Petrucci *famigliari*) and Vercelli had seemingly confessed to the existence of a plot and Scipione Petrucci had independently confirmed the hatred of Petrucci and his *famiglia* for Leo, that Vercelli was trying to gain entry into Leo's service and that he himself had initially urged Vercelli to apply the wrong type of medicine to Leo's fistula, because if he would not, then others would. The surgeon had agreed.[30]

In the consistory of 3 June Cardinal Farnese read out handwritten confessions in which the cardinals acknowledged part of their errors and asked for mercy. Afterwards Remolino and Farnese remained for two hours, probably to confer with Accolti about the case.[31] On 4 June Riario, who had refused to confess any further despite being implicated by Petrucci and Sauli, was transferred, in a state of shock, to the Castel Sant'Angelo.[32] Leo told the orators that Riario had retracted what he had earlier confessed to Cardinal de' Medici, namely that he was aware of Petrucci's desire for Leo's death, but Leo had witnesses who confirmed Riario's wish to be the next pope.[33] It is possible that Riario had endeavoured to maintain his innocence on the advice of a nephew, who had seen him and urged that his lawyers advise

[27] Vat. Lat. 7109, fo. 95; Ferrajoli, *La congiura*, 332–4.

[28] Barb. Lat. 2683, fo. 203r; *Diario romano*, 372; Minio to Venetian government, 29 May 1517, Sanuto, *Diarii*, xxiv. 323–4; BAV, MSS Ottoboniani Latini, 3552, fo. 29r.

[29] Winspeare, *La congiura*, 13; Minio to Venetian government, 29 May 1517, Sanuto, *Diarii*, xxiv. 323–4; Barb. Lat. 2683, fo. 203r; Ottaviano, Cesare, Galeazzo and Francesco (Sforzino) Riario to Venetian government, 29 May 1517, Sanuto, *Diarii*, xxiv. 326.

[30] Gattoni, *Leone X*, 197 n. 49, citing Minio of 27 May. For Vercelli's confession see Minio to Venetian government, 5 June 1517, Sanuto, *Diarii*, xxiv. 353–4, and Ferrajoli, *La congiura*, 38 n. 1; for Scipione's interrogations see Ferrajoli, *La congiura*, 294–6 with A.A. Arm. I–XVIII, 2243, fos 71r–72r–v. Scipio then disappears from the trial records: fo. 102v.

[31] Arch. Concist., Acta Vicecanc. 2, fo. 33v; Ferrajoli, *La congiura*, 58.

[32] Arch. Concist., Acta Vicecanc 2, fo. 35r; Minio to Venetian government, 29 May, 5 June 1517, Sanuto, *Diarii*, xxiv. 324, 354; A. Luzio, 'Isabella d'Este e Leone X dal congresso di Bologna alla presa di Milano (1515–1521), *ASI* xl (1907), 18–97 at p. 70; *Diario romano*, 372.

[33] Minio to Venetian government, 5 June 1517, Sanuto, *Diarii*, xxiv. 353–4.

against confessing, given that 'it took a lot to convict a cardinal'.[34] His relatives took immediate steps to have him released: Cesare Riario and other
members of the Riario clan wrote again to Henry VIII asking for help and
Marco Minio, the Venetian ambassador, reported that Cesare 'lent' the pope
12,000 ducats and returned items previously pawned to a value of 8,000
ducats in order to get Riario released. Other sources confirm that some
money changed hands at this point.[35]

Cardinal Soderini and Cardinal Castellesi

On 8 June a further consistory took place and Leo informed the assembly
that two more cardinals were cited in the trial documents and, promising
mercy, invited them to confess. After being publicly accused, and initially
denying their involvement, Soderini, and then Castellesi, both prompted by
the cardinal-advisors and threatened with prison, eventually threw themselves on the pope's mercy, admitting that they had heard Petrucci speak of
his wish for the pope's death. They were publicly pardoned and ordered to
remain in Rome and pay a fine, probably of 12,500 ducats each. The involvement of two cardinals was then announced to the orators, but their identities
were not revealed and rumours abounded.[36]

Attempts at mediation

The Sauli family had swiftly realised the seriousness of their cardinal's situation. On 7 July Giovanni Gioacchino da Passano (1465–1551), a man
of some importance within Genoa and 'major domo' to Louise of Savoy,
arrived in Paris to ask that Francis I intervene on Sauli's behalf.[37] Jacopo
Sauli, normally resident at Lyons, had also gone to the king and Domenico
d'Ancona, who had been in France since May on other business for the

34 Costabili to d'Este, 8 June 1517, Ferrajoli, La congiura, 59 n. 3.
35 For the full text see Bossi, Vita, viii. 102–4; for the loan see Luzio, 'Isabella d'Este', 71,
and Minio to the Venetian government, 5 June 1517, Sanuto, Diarii, xxiv. 354. This was
confirmed in part by Tedallini in his Diario romano, 372, and Salazar y Castro, MS 76, fo.
223v.
36 Lowe, Church and politics, 105 n. 7, 107; cf. Calendar of state papers and manuscripts
relating to English affairs, existing in the archives and collections of Venice, and in other libraries
of northern Italy, ed. L. Rawdon Brown, London 1864, 391–3, and Minio to Venetian
government, 9, 22 June 1517, Sanuto, Diarii, xxiv, 355, 412–13; Ferrajoli, La congiura, 74,
76 n. 5; Arch. Concist., Acta Vicecanc. 2, fos 35v–36r; Barb. Lat. 2683, fos 204r–6v.
37 Venetian orator in France to Venetian government, 7 June 1517, Sanuto, Diarii, xxiv.
394; A. Lercari, 'Da Passano (dei Signori), Giovanni Gioacchino', in W. Piastra (ed.),
Dizionario biografico dei Liguri dalle origini ai nostri giorni, iv, Genoa 1998, 210–17 at p. 214.
For the payment of his expenses see Archivio Sauli, no. 707, fo. 45r; no. 731, fo. 46r.

cardinal, also remained there to help plead for him.[38] The family continued to agitate and on 10 June a French orator, Monsignor Villa Brama, accompanied by d'Ancona, was sent to Leo to ask for Sauli's release. On 12 June Francis I ordered that a letter be written by the bishop of Bayeux to Cardinal de' Medici in which Francis pleaded for mercy, unable to believe, given Sauli's character, that he should have thought, let alone attempted, such a thing. On 4 July the king also intervened on Soderini's behalf with the Florentine government.[39] The Genoese government was also far from inactive: they wrote a letter of accreditation on behalf of Vincenzo Sauli, who went to Lorenzo de' Medici, duke of Urbino, to plead for his nephew.[40] Vincenzo then proceeded to Rome, presumably to advise the brothers.[41] For the first time there were rumours that both Sauli and Riario would be freed on the payment of a fine; estimates of the amounts to be paid circulated until the end of July.[42] In Rome the Sauli brothers were absorbed in trying to free the cardinal and to raise the money to pay a fine; they had no time for other business.[43]

By 15 June the Genoese government had already decided to send Tommaso Cattaneo as special orator to the pope to plead the cause of one who is 'venerated by his homeland. So much so that there is nobody who can believe that such as he would do anything which was not good and right' and had begun to compose letters to Leo, Cardinal Fieschi, Franceschetto Cibo and Maddalena Cibo (the pope's sister and Franceschetto's wife). The government could not believe that the evidence was such that Sauli would not be freed. Cattaneo was also to plead Riario's cause as he saw fit.[44]

On 19 June Minio made representations on Riario's behalf to Leo and at some point the imperial orator, Alberto Pio da Carpi, also successfully intervened.[45] By 20 June Lorenzo de' Medici had arrived in Rome, perhaps

---

[38] Archivio Sauli no. 731, fos 46r, 59r; no. 707, fo. 45r.
[39] G. G. da Passano to G. G. Trivulzio, 12 June 1517, Sanuto, *Diarii*, xxiv. 411; G. Ruscelli, *Delle lettere di principi, le quali si scrivono da principi, o a principi, o ragionano di principi*, Venice 1581, 21; Lowe, *Church and politics*, 114.
[40] Genoese government to L. de' Medici, 12 June 1517, Archivio Segreto 2822.
[41] Archivio Sauli, no. 731, fo. 46r.
[42] Minio to Venetian government, 15, 23, 27, 30 June 1517, Sanuto, *Diarii*, xxiv. 376, 418, 421, 448, 449. For Costabili to d'Este, 12, 18, 25 June 1517, see Capparoni, 'Giov. Battista da Vercelli', 34, and Pastor, *History of the popes*, vii. 181, 185, 190. See also Winspeare, *La congiura*, 160–1; *Corpo diplomatico Portuguez*, i. 471.
[43] J. Gentile to G. De Auria, S. Giustiniano and A. Grimaldi, 17 June 1517, ASG, Archivio Segreto, Litterarum Fogliazzi, 1959.
[44] 'quanto sia ornata e venerata da questa patria. In modo che non e chi possia estimar che da tale homo e signore reverendissimo possi proceder si non cossa conveniente e justificata' and 'e le cause de la detentione non dover essere tale che non potessimo sperare in brievi la liberatione del detto reverendissimo nostro Cardinale': Fregoso to T. Cattaneo, 15–17 June 1517, Archivio Segreto 2707 C.
[45] Minio to Venetian government, 20 June 1517, Sanuto, *Diarii*, xxiv. 403; K. M. Setton, *The papacy and the Levant (1204–1571)*, Philadelphia 1976–84, iii. 168.

to bolster Leo's resolve, and on the same night Castellesi, having paid part of his fine, fled in disguise, taking a circuitous route to Venice. From there relations with the pope worsened, due in part to the acquisitive intervention of Cardinal Wolsey (1515–30), and Castellesi was eventually found guilty, amongst other things, of knowing but not revealing the plot and agreeing on a new pope. On 5 July he was duly deprived of his benefices and stripped of the cardinalate.[46] A few hours before Castellesi's flight Soderini had fled to Palestrina, and thence to Fondi. By 25 June Leo had declared himself happy with Soderini's movements and he was eventually allowed to live in the kingdom of Naples, but was kept under close observation and possible threat.[47]

On the morning of 22 June a consistory was held at which all the cardinals with the exception of Leonardo Grosso della Rovere (who claimed illness) were present, as were the judges and Peruschi. The transcript was read out and the consistory continued, with much dissension, until very late.[48] The cardinals were asked for their judgement on the accused and all, with the exception of Cardinal Grimani (1493–1523), found them guilty. The charges were that Sauli and Petrucci had had dealings with Francesco Maria della Rovere, had promised the papacy to Riario, who knew of their plans, early in Leo's papacy, and had then plotted against the pope's life. The sentence was read and Riario, Sauli and Petrucci were stripped of their goods, benefices, offices and rank and turned over to secular justice, and thus the risk of execution, 'to the great surprise of the curia'.[49]

On 25 June Leo summoned the orators to inform them of the sentence and the transcript, or parts of it, were read. This removed any lingering doubts in the orators' minds, although there was some concern that initially the cardinals' confessions had not been spontaneous.[50] The pope also announced that he felt it necessary to create new cardinals and duly created thirty-one on 1 July, amongst whom were men of varying degrees of worthiness, ranging from Adrian of Utrecht (later Adrian VI), Egidio di Viterbo and Cristoforo Numai to Ferdinando Ponzetti, Raffaele Petrucci and Francesco Armellini and other Medici lap-dogs, probably with deep pockets.[51]

---

46 Ferrajoli, La congiura, 76 n. 2, 78, 122–3, 128–31, 340–5; Calendar of state papers, 403–4, 411–12, 414–16, 420–1, 440–3; Cardinal de' Medici to papal nuncio in Venice, 29 Oct. 1517, 'Manoscritti Torrigiani', ASI xx. 404–6.
47 Barb. Lat. 2683, fo. 206r; Calendar of state papers, 395; Lowe, Church and politics, 114–20; Gattoni, Leone X, 202 n. 59; Ferrajoli, La congiura, 78–9.
48 Barb. Lat. 2683, fo. 207v.
49 Ibid; Arch. Concist., Acta Vicecanc. 2, fos 37v–38v; Cam. Ap., Div. Cam. 65, fo. 218v; Ferrajoli, La congiura, 89; Capparoni, 'Giov. Battista Vercelli', 17 n. 4; cf. Salazar y Castro, MS 76, fos 222v, 223v; Diario romano, 372.
50 Capparoni, 'Giov. Battista da Vercelli', 34; Costabili to d'Este, 24 June 1517, Pastor, History of the popes, vii. 465–6; Minio to Venetian government, 25 June 1517, Sanuto, Diarii, xxiv. 419; Gattoni, Leone X, 199 n. 52.
51 Barb. Lat. 2683, fos 208v, 210r–v; Arch. Concist., Acta Vicecanc. 2, fo. 40r–v; Minio to Venetian government, 4 July 1517, Sanuto, Diarii, xxiv. 462.

The fate of the conspirators

Things were looking less hopeful for Petrucci and his *famigliari*: on 23 June Nini was deprived of his benefices and then turned over to secular justice. On 27 June he and Vercelli were hanged, drawn and quartered after being paraded naked on a cart around Rome and publicly tortured.[52]

The French orator and Tommaso Cattaneo arrived on 25 June and Monsignor Villa Brama immediately went to the pope. Cattaneo lodged in the house of Giovanni Franco Martelli: the rent and all expenses, including new costumes, were met by the Sauli.[53] Genoese hopes of a complete pardon seemed remote and Cattaneo's letter of 30 June was far from optimistic. He had procured a private audience with Leo and on 27 June had pleaded for mercy for Sauli and Riario, asking for them to be restored to the cardinalate. Leo had said that the 'matter was so important and of such a nature' that there was little that he could do and he would prefer the Genoese to press no further. Cardinal Fieschi and Cardinal Cibo had also tried to persuade the pope and eventually he agreed to think about it, but said that he thought mercy was unlikely. Cattaneo reported that he had heard since then that Leo had decided against mercy and the best hope seemed to lie with a financial settlement which the relatives and servants of the two cardinals were trying to organise.[54] Yet if, as Ferrajoli suggests, Leo had already decided to pardon Sauli and Riario, his rancour against Sauli remained intact. On 29 June the abbey of San Siro in Genoa was given to Cardinal Cibo and Sauli and Petrucci were placed in foul prisons, their servants dismissed and it is possible that they were not allowed food. On 1 July Sauli lost his titular church of Santa Maria in Trastevere to Cardinal de' Grassis, who also received a monastery previously belonging to Petrucci. Prior to this Pietro Bembo had received Petrucci's abbey of Villa Nuova near Verona.[55] The situation seemed grim; to some the possibility of execution was real.[56]

On 4 July Petrucci was secretly strangled in the Castel Sant'Angelo; Sauli was then transferred to a better prison, probably that previously occupied by Petrucci.[57] On 6 July the first monies were pledged to pay for Riario's release and on 7 July his capitulation document began to be drafted. He was to pay

---

[52] Ferrajoli, *La congiura*, 110–11, 322, 336–7. See also Costabili to d'Este, 29 June 1517, Capparoni, 'Giov. Battista Vercelli', 35, and *Corpo diplomatico Portuguez*, i. 471.

[53] Cattaneo to O. Fregoso, 30 June 1517, Archivio Segreto 2342; Ferrajoli, *La congiura*, 96; Archivio Sauli, no. 731, fos 46v–47r, 59r; no. 707, fo. 45r; 26 July 1517 unfoliated.

[54] 'essendo la causa tanto importante et di tal sorte che le paria che per VS non se dovesse fare sopra de questo alcuna requesta': Cattaneo to O. Fregoso, 30 June 1517, Archivio Segreto 2342.

[55] Minio to Venetian government, 30 June 1517, Sanuto, *Diarii*, xxiv. 449; ibid. 470–1; Ferrajoli, *La congiura*, 95; Barb. Lat. 2683, fo. 208v.

[56] Lowe, *Church and politics*, 105 n. 8.

[57] For the discrepancies in the sources as to how Petrucci died see Gattoni, *Leone X*, 204–5, and Salazar y Castro, MS 76, fo. 225r. His Portuguese servant believed that he

a deposit of 150,000 ducats and a fine of the same amount in three instalments. He was to confess his guilt and guarantee that he would not leave the place to which the pope assigned him without papal permission; he would be a loyal servant to the pope and not act or plot against him, the Church or his family in any way. In return, he would be restored to the cardinalate, but with no active or passive vote in consistory. He would keep his benefices (with the exception of San Lorenzo in Damaso) which he was allowed to rent out for a maximum of six years to help raise money. The cardinals and orators swore to guarantee his good behaviour and his list of financial guarantors was impressive, including Agostino Chigi, much of the Roman nobility and many curial officials.[58]

Despite Petrucci's fate, there was still hope for Sauli and a fine seemed likely. But Leo vacillated.[59] From 5 July the Sauli actively collected pledges for the deposit to be paid to secure his release.[60] On 6 July Bendinello lost Santa Sabina to the newly-created (Sienese) Cardinal Piccolomini and Peruschi's son was awarded one of Petrucci's bishoprics.[61] News of events reached Genoa and on 9 July Ottaviano Fregoso wrote to thank Franceschetto Cibo for his ardent efforts on Sauli's behalf, asking him to do his best to ensure that Sauli remained in the pope's good graces.[62] Cattaneo's letter of 10 July stated that the matter was settled: Riario and Sauli would be freed, although conditions were not yet completely settled. He planned to leave Rome in a few days.[63] Yet Leo's anger towards Sauli was unabated: on the same day he awarded 4,200 ducats of pensions previously held by Sauli to members of the Curia, and 500 ducats of Sauli's income to Peruschi's son.[64] On 12 July, despite Leo's vacillations as reported by Minio, the drafting of Sauli's capitulations began. The Vatican copy is incomplete and obviously only a draft. Cattaneo wrote again to Fregoso on 12 July stating that further requests for the full restoration of Sauli to the cardinalate and his benefices were out of the question and that Fregoso should write to thank the pope: the situation and the punishment, as detailed in the (lost) attached capitulations, was to be accepted. He outlined the promises to be given by the orators and their rulers (these are missing in the surviving draft, which

---

was hanged. See Ferrajoli, *La congiura*, 96; Minio to Venetian government, 7 July 1517, Sanuto, *Diarii*, xxiv. 463.

58 A.A. Arm. I–XVIII 1443, fos 158r, 160v, 162v, 164r, 165v, 166v–167r, 168r, 170r, 171v; Gattoni, *Leone X*, 207 n. 71; Ferrajoli, *La congiura*, 91; Pastor, *History of the popes*, vii. 189, 190. The fine had been paid in full by 10 Feb. 1518: Notai del Tribunale, AC 7157, fo. 313r–v.

59 Minio to Venetian government, 4, 7 July 1517, Sanuto, *Diarii*, xxiv. 462–3.

60 MS Ferr. 424, fos 161r–v.

61 Arch. Concist., Acta Vicecanc. 2, fos 42v–43r.

62 O. Fregoso to F. Cibo, 9 July 1517, Archivio Segreto 2822.

63 Cattaneo to Fregoso, 10 July 1517, Lit. Fogl. 1959.

64 Ferrajoli, *La congiura*, 97 n. 3, citing ASV, Reg. Supp. 1562, fos 153, 162. This register could not be consulted due to its fragile condition.

merely specifies a deposit of 80,000 ducats).[65] Sauli was also to make the same promises of good behaviour as Riario and, like him, was deprived of voting powers in consistory and in the election of a new pope.[66]

On 17 July, when the negotiations for Sauli were obviously near completion, Monsignor Villa Brama left Rome.[67] On the same day the conditions for release were read to Riario in the Castel Sant'Angelo; on Friday 24 July his bull of restoration was drawn up and he was released amidst the rejoicing of the Roman populace and the college of cardinals.[68] Paris de' Grassis paints a picture of a reasonably benevolent pope, who, although he was perhaps freeing Riario unwillingly, was even prepared to restore his vote in consistory, subject to his good behaviour.[69] Riario confessed his guilt, saying that he was unable to defend it and had indeed sinned to a greater degree than he had acknowledged, and thanked the pope for his great mercy.[70] He was then well received by the pope, who said he would forget past offences, and confined to the Vatican palace, where he received many visitors over the following days.[71] In the same consistory Leo supposedly asked whether Sauli should be restored, and although the cardinals agreed, the pope decided against it.[72] In fact his bull of restoration is of this date and on 26 July a sum of 904 ducats were deposited by the Sauli with a holding bank 'for his release'.[73] His brothers were still actively collecting the necessary remaining oaths to be given by the orators (some mistrust was shown, notably by Minio who wanted a written guarantee from Sauli that he would behave). The taking of the orators' oaths does not, however, seem to have been a mandatory condition for Riario's release: several did not swear to his good behaviour until six days after his release.[74]

---

[65] For Leo's vacillations see Minio to Venetian government, 9 July 1517, Sanuto, *Diarii*, xxiv. 477–8, and Ferrajoli, *La congiura*, 92. Sauli's incomplete capitulations are to be found in A.A. Arm. I–XVIII, 4770 (fo. 1r for the initial date) as noted by Ferrajoli, *La congiura*, 97 n. 2 and Gattoni, *Leone X*, 348. See also Cattaneo to Fregoso, 12 July 1517, Archivio Segreto 2342.
[66] A.A. Arm. I–XVIII, 4770, fo. 1r.
[67] Minio to the Venetian government, Sanuto, *Diarii*, xxiv. 493, 17 July 1517.
[68] A.A. Arm. I–XVIII, 1443, fos 167v–168v; Arch. Concist., Acta Vicecanc. 2, fo. 45r; Barb. Lat. 2683, fo. 215v; Reg. Vat. 1203, fo. 15v; Pastor, *History of the popes*, vii. 488–9.
[69] Barb. Lat. 2683, fos 215v, 216v.
[70] Ibid. fo. 218r–v, especially 218v: 'peccavi, peccavi, peccavi. Et in quam peccavi plus quam in iudiciali confessione mea expressum sit '; *Diario romano*, 373–5; Gheri to Guicciardini, 27 July 1517, *Francesco Guicciardini: le lettere*, iii, no. 473 at pp. 56–7.
[71] Barb. Lat. 2683, fos 216v, 219r; Minio to Venetian government, 30 July 1517, Sanuto, *Diarii*, xxiv. 518.
[72] Arch. Concist., Acta Vicecanc. 2, fo. 45r. This is not mentioned by Paris de' Grassis.
[73] 'pro liberatione sua': Archivio Sauli, no. 731, fo. 46v.
[74] Minio to Venetian government, 30 July. 1517, Sanuto, *Diarii*, xxiv. 518. For the bull see A.A. Arm. I–XVIII, 1903; for the visit by Cesare Riario of 30 July to several of the orators see ibid. 1443, fos 169v–170r.

On 31 July, just a day after telling Paris de' Grassis that Sauli was to remain in prison, Leo ordered his release.[75] The description of the ensuing restoration highlights the fact that Sauli was publicly humiliated. He was told that if he did not openly confess his sins, or offered an excuse, he would not be released, to which he agreed. Then, unlike Riario, he was accompanied to the consistory, dressed as a simple priest, by de' Grassis and Peruschi. He knelt at the pope's feet, remained kneeling for much of the consistory, and confessed that he had been persuaded by the devil, Petrucci and others, that he had plotted with della Rovere and given him money and advice and that he had plotted with Petrucci and other accomplices against the pope's life through Vercelli, who was to administer poisons to the pope but had been unable to do so because the plot was discovered. He said that the judgement passed on him had been correct, that he would never contradict it, and promised to be a loyal servant to Leo. The pope listened uncomfortably and said that he doubted whether Sauli's words reflected what was in his heart, and that he feared that he would return to his evil ways. Sauli protested, took the necessary oaths, and was eventually pardoned and restored to the cardinalate, although he was to be confined to the main sacristy of the palace. The crowds outside, although not as great as for Riario, exulted.[76]

The financial penalty to be paid was insignificant compared to Riario's – a deposit of 80,000 ducats to guarantee his good behaviour and a fine of 25,000 ducats. Some of the Roman notables who had pledged money for Riario's good behaviour did the same for Sauli.[77] The Sauli family had paid 8,000 ducats, the first instalment of the fine, by 20 August, and the two further instalments were registered on 20 November 1517 and 14 May 1518.[78] Both deposit and fine constituted large sums of money and finding the ready cash was difficult: by 27 August Sauli's brothers has sold the cardinal's silver and had raised 1,685 ducats and on the following day 2,095 ducats left the Sauli accounts as part of the earlier payment for Bendinello's release.[79] Money was also borrowed from the cardinal's uncle, Antonio Sauli, in Genoa.[80]

However, conditions were in one respect much harsher for Sauli than for Riario who retained nearly all his benefices. Sauli was left with only the sees of Gerace and Oppide and Albenga and any benefices which had not been given away by the pope during his imprisonment. He was to have an income which totalled a mere 2,000 ducats and consisted of two pensions. Given the number of benefices that he had previously possessed, this was severe

---

75 Barb. Lat. 2683, fo. 219v; Arch. Concist., Acta Vicecanc. 2, fo. 45v.
76 Barb. Lat. 2683, fos 220r–221v; Minio to Venetian government, 31 July 1517, Sanuto, *Diarii*, xxiv. 545. For the 'discovery' of the plot interfering with its execution see chapter 8 below.
77 A.A. Arm. I–XVIII, 4770, fos 1r–2v.
78 Cam. Ap., Div. Cam. 67, fos 121v–122r.
79 Archivio Sauli, no. 731, fo. 58r.
80 Notai Antichi, 1285, no. 739, 8 Oct. 1517; 1522bis, no. 135, 3 Feb. 1518.

punishment.[81] Leo was implacable. The few remaining benefices which still belonged to Sauli were swiftly disposed of: on 1 August, one day after his release, Sauli agreed to resign the monastery of San Dionigi in Milan to Ricardo Malaspina and Serapica, two of the pope's *famigliari*. On 6 August he resigned the *commenda* of San Nicolò di Casale in the diocese of Otranto to Theodico de' Carpi, bishop of Mondovì.[82] This was hardly going to help Sauli survive: in prison his debts had increased by 5,000 ducats. Between 14 July and 22 November his brothers debited 1,950 ducats from his account for expenses incurred in sending messengers, paying the orators' expenses and other necessities. Messengers to Francis I alone accounted for 579 ducats.[83]

On 6 August the Genoese government wrote to thank Leo for the release of the two cardinals and promising to sign the capitulations.[84] Only on 13 August did Sauli write to thank the Genoese government and the city which had 'twice brought me to the light of day, both publicly and privately' for their help, most specifically in engaging the support of Francis I and sending their own orator to Rome. He promised to do what little was in his power to repay his debt.[85] When Ottaviano Fregoso wrote to Riario after his release, his letter overran with 'the boundless joy and subsequent sense of relief we experienced at your release'.[86] His letter to Cardinal Sauli was far more circumspect: Fregoso stated that the Genoese appreciated his gratitude, but that it was superfluous as Genoa had done what she had because of Sauli's personal qualities and the advantages of having a Genoese cardinal and had thus done her duty. Sauli would be advised to look after his health carefully, forgetting the past and looking to the future.[87]

The lukewarm support of his government was matched by the pope's behaviour: while Riario was allowed a sort of freedom in the *palazzo apostolico* and was often with the pope, Sauli was a virtual prisoner, apart from short walks, and received no sign of benevolence from Leo, who reportedly did not wish to speak to him.[88] By the end of September it had been decided that Riario could go to his villa at Caprarola and then return to his palace in Rome; Sauli, apparently, could return to his palace at Santa Maria in Via Lata for a few days.[89] This was to prove a temporary reprieve. By 21

---

[81] A.A. Arm. I–XVIII, 1903, fo. 1v; Barb. Lat. 2683, fo. 221v.

[82] Cam. Ap., Resignationes 17, fo. 253v; 20, fo. 20r.

[83] Archivio Sauli, no. 731, fos 46r–v; 47r; 59r–v.

[84] O. Fregoso to Leo X, 6 Aug. 1517, and T. Pecunia to O. Fregoso, n.d., Archivio Segreto 2822, 2342.

[85] 'patria quae me bis in lucem edidit, cum publice, tum privatum', Cardinal Sauli to O. Fregoso, 13 Aug. 1517, ibid. 2805.

[86] 'e siamo supra mortale gaudium relegrati de la sua liberatione et subinde de ea quiete de l'animo', O. Fregoso to Cardinal Riario, 6 Aug. 1517, ibid. 2822.

[87] O. Fregoso to Cardinal Sauli, 20 Aug. 1517, ibid..

[88] Minio to Venetian government, 7 Sept. 1517, Sanuto, *Diarii*, xxiv. 668–9; Ferrajoli, *La congiura*, 99 n. 2.

[89] Ferrajoli, *La congiura*, 102, 122.

October Riario was once again taking part in public consistories, but Sauli had been exiled by Leo to Monterotondo, part of the Orsini dominions, and outside Rome.[90] There he contracted tertiary fever and had returned to Rome, escorted by Stefano Sauli, by 6 November. Doctors were paid on 22 November.[91] He then lived with what remained of his *famiglia* in a house in the parish of San Salvatore in Campo which belonged to the Santacroce family.

Even then Sauli was not allowed any peace: on 19 November, at the pope's insistence, he 'resigned' the bishopric of Gerace and Oppide to the Medici favourite Cardinal Armellini, and that of Albenga to Cardinal de' Medici.[92] There is then no further news until 9 February 1518 when he resigned some minor benefices in the diocese of Milan to his *famigliare* Domenico de' Caffis.[93] The money the family had raised by selling his silver and borrowing from their uncle had clearly proved insufficient and on 10 February the pope allowed him to rent out the fruits of Gerace and Oppide and Albenga (which he had held on to, despite resigning the bishoprics) for six years to a group of merchants which included his uncles Antonio and Giovanni Battista Sauli, in order the more easily to pay his fine, the money for which had been found by the Genoese banker Ansaldo Grimaldi.[94] In the following days he was reported as seriously ill, suffering from dropsy, and not expected to live. Dropsy is a swelling due to the accumulation of fluid in the tissues and although its causes can be many, the most common is heart failure. However it can also be caused by starvation or malnutrition, and certainly neglect, unsanitary conditions (and the tertiary fever contracted at Monterotondo) would have aggravated any pre-existing illnesses such as heart problems. The poor conditions of his imprisonment in the Castel Sant'Angelo make Leo responsible, at least in part, for Sauli's death. He died on 29 March with a reported income of 1,500 ducats.[95] As Denis Hay notes (albeit in a different context), 'the cardinal … if he played his cards well and was loyal to the pope who had promoted him, could reach great wealth and much public esteem, if little power'.[96] In one year Sauli had fallen far: guilty or innocent, his fate was an example of the power of the pope.

[90] Lippomano to Sanuto, 21 Oct. 1517, Sanuto, *Diarii*, xxv. 66.

[91] Giustiniani, *Castigatissimi annali*, 224r; Archivio Sauli, no. 731, fo. 59r.

[92] Arch. Concist., Acta Vicecanc. 2, fo. 58v; Reg. Vat. 1105, fos 75r–76v. De' Medici resigned Albenga to Gian Giacopo Gambarana on 5 May 1518: Arch. Concist., Acta Misc. 6, fo. 219r.

[93] Cam. Ap., Resignationes 20, fo. 86v.

[94] Arm. xxxix, 39, fos 19v–20r; Ferrajoli, *La congiura*, 97 n. 2.

[95] 'E stato lungamente infermo di male quasi incurabile': Minio, 6 Apr. 1518; Ferrajoli, *La congiura*, 100 n. 5, 322, 338, 348. I am grateful to Thomas Dormandy for his help in explaining the causes of dropsy.

[96] Hay, 'Renaissance cardinals', 45.

Justice or revenge?

From the time of his flight Cardinal Soderini had sporadically contested Leo's actions against him.[97] When the pope died in late 1521 he hurried to Rome, arriving on the 5 December for the conclave. On various occasions in December he attacked Leo in consistory, albeit not specifically regarding the plot, meeting with some opposition.[98] There can be little doubt that his long-standing anti-Medicean sentiments were at the heart of this and that his main aim was to avoid a new Medici pope: the election of Adrian VI on 9 January briefly secured this. He then proclaimed his innocence of any involvement in the plot and by 2 February 1522 Peracchia, the notary who had transcribed the trial, had been arrested and a review committee comprised of Cardinals Fieschi, Cesi and Jacobazzi had been appointed. As one of the cardinal governors during the wait for Adrian to arrive (in late August) Soderini was obviously in a position to exert considerable pressure.[99] But things moved slowly: only on 10 April were the trial documents, 634 pages in all, given to Fieschi, who was to allow nobody to see them except Cesi and Jacobazzi.[100] Nor did things go as Soderini had planned: a consistory of 13 July saw moves to free Peracchia, thus perhaps implying that the commission had found that the trial was valid.[101] Soderini was furious, insisted that the notary should be detained until Adrian arrived and in the end carried the day over the other cardinals.[102] On 31 July 1522 Mario Peruschi lodged a formal protest about Peracchia's arrest and demanded his release from the Tor de' Nona. He also insisted that a certain Alfonso Paragrano, who had slandered him in a public consistory on 11 July, should retract his words.[103] Paragrano was a servant in Soderini's household and it is thus no surprise that Peruschi's request, which was heard by Soderini and eight other cardinals, was refused.[104]

Soderini was not alone in agitating for a review: Stefano Sauli left Rome after his brother's death and spent much of 1518–21 between Padua and Genoa pursuing his studies, although he did return briefly to Rome on non-related business.[105] A poem by Flaminio places the author and Stefano in

97 Ferrajoli, La congiura, 62–3.
98 Lowe, Church and politics, 121–2; Venetian orator in Rome to Venetian government, 15 Dec. 1521, Sanuto, Diarii, xxxii. 260; Zorzi to J. Contarini, 21 Dec. 1521, ibid. xxxii. 288; Ferrajoli, La congiura, 134–5.
99 A. Gradenigo to Venetian government, 2 Feb. 1522, Sanuto, Diarii, xxxii. 442–3; Ferrajoli, La congiura, 136 n. 1; Lowe, Church and politics, 125.
100 Ferrajoli, La congiura, 6, 137, 350–1.
101 Winspeare, La congiura, 186–7.
102 Gradenigo to Venetian government, 13 July 1522, Sanuto, Diarii, xxxiii. 367.
103 Vat. Lat. 11172, fos 31r–32r.
104 Ibid. fos 31v, 32r; Notai del Tribunale, AC 7156, fo. 270, 17 June 1517; Lowe, Church and politics, 241.
105 Notai Antichi, 1288, no. 278, 21 Nov. 1521.

Rome in January 1522, presumably to see the election of a new pope and to seek a review, but their stay was short-lived: by 13 February he was back in Genoa.[106] He was once again in Rome by 3 March and again by 14 May when de Longueil wrote to Sauli that he was concerned for his safety during the *interregnum* and when faced with powerful enemies.[107] On 13 September Stefano and Soderini are mentioned together for the first time as agitating for a review of the trial. Adrian had agreed to look at the trial documents and to pass them to two other cardinals. Sauli had apparently told the ambassador Gianmaria della Porta that 'the trial documents show the invalidity and falseness of the trial', but as della Porta notes, others believed it valid.[108] Two weeks later Peracchia was freed. Little then happened. Gambarana was charged on 10 February 1523, but nothing came of this and he flourished under Clement VII.[109] As Alessandro Ferrajoli notes, all further investigation probably ended when, on 26 April 1523, Soderini was imprisoned for involvement in another conspiracy.[110]

Why did Soderini and Stefano Sauli press for a retrial? The former, as Ferrajoli suggests, probably resented the pardon, which in itself implied guilt, and the fine imposed on him. Stefano Sauli, in de Longueil's words, wished to 'avenge his brother's injustice and death, and at the same time attempt to recover the cardinal's lucrative benefices'.[111] But why did Soderini not mention Sauli's innocence and *vice versa*? To what degree, if any, had there been an injustice?

106 Maddison, *Marcantonio Flaminio*, 38–9; Notai Antichi, 1288, nos 6, 36–9.
107 Maddison, *Marcantonio Flaminio*, 40; de Longueil to S. Sauli, 14 May 1517, de Longueil, *Orationes*, cc. 135r–v; de Longueil to N. Dragoni, n.d., cc. 142r–v.
108 Ferrajoli, *La congiura*, 139 n. 1.
109 Venetian orator in Rome to Venetian government, 10 Feb. 1523, Sanuto, *Diarii*, xxxiii. 620; Ferrajoli, *La congiura*, 139, 173.
110 Ferrajoli, *La congiura*, 139; Lowe, *Church and politics*, 133.
111 de Longueil to Dragoni, n.d., de Longueil, *Orationes*, cc. 142r–v.

8

'Vir Bonus et Innocens'?

Was Sauli a 'good and innocent man' or not?[1] Was, there, indeed, a plot at all? Some think that there was and that those implicated were guilty, to whatever degree. These include contemporary observers such as Paris de' Grassis (but with reservations about the involvement of Riario, which are shared by Sebastiano Branca di Tedallini), Cornelius de Fine, Paolo Giovio and Francesco Guicciardini.[2]

Others deny that there was a plot. Alfonso Petrucci's Portuguese manservant regarded Petrucci, Sauli and Riario as innocent victims; in about 1526 Jacob Ziegler blamed everything on Cardinal de' Medici. Girolamo Garimberto, a sixteenth-century writer, believed in the 'innocence (of Sauli) which still survives today in the opinion of many', an opinion shared by some later and present-day commentators. The group's most convincing advocate is Kate Lowe, who discovered an account of the plot in the Vatican Archives allegedly written by the cardinals' supporters.[3]

Arguments for the existence of the plot

The diarists de' Grassis, Tedallini and de Fine were not the only witnesses to the unfolding of events who believed in what they saw and heard. The orators present in Rome also believed in the plot – namely Costabili, Minio and the Portuguese ambassador. Their attitude was eventually shared by the Genoese. Although initially the Genoese government had found it difficult to believe Sauli capable of such a thing, in none of the letters from Tommaso Cattaneo is there any indication that he, present in Rome and in close contact with the Sauli, considered the plot to be a fabrication and Sauli (and Riario) to be innocent. On 30 June Cattaneo wrote that he had

[1]   Pasqua, *Vitae*, 298.
[2]   See Ottob. Lat. 2137, fo. 32r ff; *Diario romano*, 370–4; F. Guicciardini, *La storia d'Italia di Francesco Guicciardini*, ed. A. Gherardi, Florence 1919, iii.187–90; Bacceti, *Abbatis Septiminianae*, 229 (who believed that Severo Varini was innocent); Barb. Lat. 4905, fos 154r–157r. For an anonymous *Life* of Leo in the Vatican (which has proved untraceable) the author of which believed in the plot see Bossi, *Vita*, xii. 175.
[3]   Salazar y Castro, MS 76, fos 221r, 226r; J. Ziegler, 'Clementis Septimi episcopi romani vita', in J. Schellhorn (ed.), *Amoenitates historiae ecclesiasticae et literariae*, Frankfurt–Leipzig 1738–9, ii. 315–28; Garimberto, *La prima parte*, 396; Vat. Lat. 9167, fo. 526; ch. 7 n. 2 above.

requested of the pope 'what it was possible for me to request: namely that His Holiness, since he had put the cardinals on trial, should be merciful and restore the deprived cardinals to the cardinalate'.[4] On 12 July he and the Sauli brothers decided not to forward the letters of 9 July from the Genoese government to the pope in which they requested the full restoration of Sauli to the cardinalate and benefices, 'as it does not seem the right time yet to ask for any favour and we should simply thank the pope for the mercy shown'.[5] The government wrote a less than congratulatory letter to Sauli and there is no further news of Sauli in the surviving letters between orators and government following his release, nor was he consulted on Genoese business. It was as if he had ceased to exist.[6]

Agostino Giustiniani was one of Sauli's *famigliari*, and his presence in Rome at the time means that some weight has to be given to his testimony. However, the passage in the *Castigatissimi annali* dedicated to the plot is somewhat ambiguous. The intimate tones used to describe Sauli earlier in the book – 'my cousin and my lord' – are absent.[7] At no point either in his lengthier discussion of the plot, or in the brief mention of it when he records his own return to Rome in 1516, does Giustiniani clearly state his own personal viewpoint. He (somewhat inaccurately with regard to dates) reports events and the general opinion. He notes that Sauli was found guilty of 'having known, and not told, that the Cardinal of Siena wanted to poison the pope'. He criticises the imposition of the fine, citing the 'common opinion that the cardinal was innocent, and that his sin was of such a kind that punishment deserved to be waived rather than be imposed, but it is impossible to still wagging tongues, especially in the licentious and excessively free city of Rome'.[8] This is the most that he offers. At the time of writing the *Annali* Giustiniani had no retribution to fear – he was not resident in Rome, nor was there a Medici pope to threaten him – so why was he not more definite?

A later Genoese commentator was more explicit and implicated Sauli. Umberto Foglietta, the nephew of Agostino Foglietta, one of Cardinal Sauli's conclavists, noted that Sauli would have become a great priest 'if, moved by spite for whatever reason, he had not lent his support to that wicked conspiracy against the pope's person'.[9]

The trial transcript provides evidence of the existence of a plot, but can it be believed? The transcript of the trial of Petrucci's *famigliari* should,

4 'che ad me fu possibile requedendo: che Sua Santità si degnassi poi che per insino adesso si era processo per justitia usare clementia et misericordia et restituire li detti privati': Cattaneo to Fregoso, 30 June. 1517, Archivio Segreto 2342.
5 'non parendo anchora tempo requerire alcuna gratia et sollamenti rengraciare Soa Santità de la gratia facta': Cattaneo to Fregoso, 9 July 1517, ibid. 2342.
6 See, for example, ibid. 1831, no. 131, fos 41v–42v, 30 Oct. 1517.
7 Giustiniani, *Castigatissimi annali*, c. 224r.
8 Ibid. c. 272v.
9 Folietae, *Clarorum ligurum*, 143.

in theory, be an accurate and factual account of their interrogation and their statements, yet it does, as Giovanni Battista Picotti notes, contain some minor embroideries and embellishments, as well as some evidence of manipulation of the suspects.[10] The manner in which Nini first interprets the incriminating letter which begins 'I spoke with Vercelli' in the interrogation of 28 April smacks of manipulation, and there is inconsistency as regards exactly when the decision to elect a new pope was reached. (Although, at this stage in his interrogations, Nini was still undoubtedly intent on protecting himself.)[11]

It is conceivable, of course, that mass fabrication of evidence may have occurred at an early stage in the making of the transcript, but this seems unlikely. The political negotiations recorded in the transcript are certainly not imaginary. Petrucci's wheelings and dealings with other rulers to regain Siena were complex and real and Sauli, Soderini, Castellesi and Riario were aware of them and supported them to varying degrees.[12] Those few scholars who have read the trial transcript can see that amidst the mass of detail of comings and goings and promises of troops, Peruschi was indeed at times looking for evidence that the pope was in danger (and the involvement of Spain certainly would have meant danger of one sort or another), but can also gradually see the plot emerge, to be seized upon by Peruschi who then dedicated most of his energies to it. A letter of Beltrando Costabili of 21 April, almost a month before Petrucci's arrest, shows that it was already known in Rome that Leo was considering charging Petrucci with *lèse majesté* because of his political dealings, and this was before Nini was interrogated about Petrucci's interest in Leo's health. Petrucci was thus already in trouble and his situation merely deteriorated as the plot emerged.[13] Nor was his antagonism towards Leo which emerges in the transcript imaginary or invented: it is confirmed by a surviving letter from Lorenzo Suares to Petrucci of 27 October 1516 in which Leo's health problems are discussed with relish.[14]

There are also convincing circumstantial details: the conversations in which Petrucci informs Nini of the plot and the involvement of the other cardinals are held in his bedroom, at a window overlooking the street. Words are placed in Sauli's mouth when he talks with Nini in his antechamber which it would take an ingenious mind – whose would it have been: that of Peruschi, or perhaps Cardinal de' Medici? – to invent. The settings referred

[10] Picotti, 'La congiura', 256.
[11] Ibid. 258. Picotti's objections (pp. 260–1) to the further evidence provided by Nini are far from conclusive.
[12] Ferrajoli, *La congiura*, 144; Pastor, *History of the popes*, vii. 185–6. Cardinal Petrucci to S. Petrucci, 28 Jan. 1517, Cod. Reg. Lat. 387, fo. 26r.
[13] Pastor, *History of the popes*, vii. 173, confirmed by A.A. Arm. I-XVIII, 2243, fos 52r–54v.
[14] L. Suares to Cardinal Petrucci, 27 Oct. 1516, Cod. Reg. Lat. 387, fo. 186r.

to have been criticised as hardly suitable for such secret discussions, but by their nature tend to support the thesis that Nini was telling the truth.[15]

Letters that contained incriminating evidence were in code, which is suggestive. Furthermore, they convinced the Portuguese orator.[16] Picotti's suggestion that they may have been incorrectly interpreted is possible, but does this not then invalidate Nini's interpretations of the letters dealing with political news? Apparently not.[17]

Do Peruschi's initial promptings, Nini's inconsistency and, especially, the use of torture render the confessions of the *famigliari* invalid as some believe?[18] In the case of Nini, Scipione Petrucci and Pochintesta, the trial minutes hide nothing: every transfer to the torture chamber, the time spent on torture, the state of the prisoner afterwards and any retractions he made are noted. The confessions clearly suggest that a plan to place Vercelli close to Leo – for whatever purpose – existed, but the evil intentions of which he boasted, and to which Nini confessed under torture and then retracted, are perhaps more questionable. But why then did Nini declare himself ready to face Vercelli and Petrucci to confirm his confessions? Furthermore, Bernardino da Perugia and Scipione Petrucci independently confirmed Nini's testimony and in August 1517 Scipione, who, given his almost immediate pardon and return to Siena, had probably turned 'queen's evidence' (or had he agreed to be the prosecutor's mouthpiece?), confirmed the existence of the plot and his own role in egging on Vercelli to the Sienese historian Tizio (an enemy of the Petrucci, but by no means a supporter of Leo).[19]

Perhaps most importantly there is evidence that on one significant point Nini was certainly telling the truth, namely the matter of Sauli's loan to Petrucci of 1,000 ducats. There is a gap in the details of Sauli's bank withdrawals from 30 March to 22 May 1517 and from that date onwards they almost exclusively detail the expenses incurred during the cardinal's incarceration. However, on 1 August 1517, just a day after Sauli's release and almost a month after Petrucci's death, an entry details that 1,000 ducats were paid on Cardinal Sauli's orders to the Cardinal of Siena (Petrucci). The money had been lent by Giovanni Sauli and the entry was obviously only entered later.[20] There can thus be no doubt that, certainly in this detail, neither torture nor Peruschi were leading Nini to make things up, and if he

15 Picotti, 'La congiura', 259.

16 *Corpo diplomatico portuguez*, 469.

17 For the one surviving coded letter dated 12 Aug. 1516 see Cod. Reg. Lat. 387, fo. 182r; Picotti, 'La congiura', 257.

18 Lowe, *Church and politics*, 104; Setton, *The papacy and the Levant*, iii. 168.

19 Ferrajoli, *La congiura*, 35, 40, 146–7; Winspeare, *La congiura*, 133, 166, 201–2; Chigi G II 38, fo. 93r; cf. Picotti, 'La congiura', 264. The answer lies in the transcript: A.A. Arm. I–XVIII, 2243, fo. 71r–v.

20 'Item die prima augusti in ducatos 1000 auri de camera solutos pro ordine sue reverendissime domini reverendissimo domino cardinali de senis': Archivio Sauli, no. 731, fo. 46v.

was telling the truth about this, then he may have been telling the truth about other things.

Leo himself was consistent in demonstrating his conviction that the plot existed. From the beginning he affected surprise at Sauli's involvement: on 20 May he told Minio that he found Sauli's actions difficult to understand because three months earlier he had given him 6,000 ducats in income from benefices, seemingly referring to the division of the benefices of the late Cardinal Sisto Gara della Rovere.[21] His surprise then developed into a relentless *froideur* which continued until Sauli's death, perhaps because of what he saw as Sauli's abuse of their previous intimacy.[22] Some of Sauli's high-profile *famigliari* suffered by association: Agostino Giustiniani remained in Rome in the house of Cardinal Ferrero, waiting in vain for a sign of the pope's benevolence which he had been promised before the plot. In 1520 the Ferrarese orator wrote of the visit to Naples by Alberto Pio da Carpi to consult a famous doctor who had also served Sauli 'and it seems that he knew about the business and immediately left [Rome] and he has been summoned several times by signor Alberto with briefs from the pope and much has been offered to him, but he has never risked returning'.[23] Two years after Sauli's death was there really a risk of recriminations against the *famigliare* of an innocent person? The cardinal's other doctor, Paolo Giovio, was in Rome until 19 August 1517 but then he too fled: on 28 August Jacopo Sadoleto wrote to Francisco Victorio that Giovio, 'to avoid any trace of suspicion had left Rome. We will forward your letters to him'.[24] Giovio himself believed that his own advancement might have been swifter if it had not been for Cardinal Sauli's disgrace. If Sauli had really been innocent, why would Giovio still be suffering three years later? Giovanni Antonio Marostica also left Rome and in September 1517 was lucky enough to be offered the post of Reader in Greek at the University of Padua which he held until 1519. Piero Valeriano's comment that, by the time of his death in 1523, he 'was just then imagining that he had achieved a long-awaited tranquillity for his studies' is also suggestive.[25]

Why, however, would the cardinals have plotted to murder Leo and have agreed on the identity of the new pope? Petrucci's motive – the recovery of Siena – requires no explanation; Soderini, as the brother of the ex-*gonfaloniere* of Florence, undoubtedly regarded Leo as a political enemy; Riario was known to covet the papacy; Castellesi is supposed to have believed in a false

---

[21] I was unable to find confirmation of this in the Vatican Archives but support is found in Minio to Venetian government, 22 Mar. 1517, Sanuto, *Diarii*, xxiv. 14.

[22] Guicciardini, *Storia d'Italia*, iii. 189.

[23] Ferrajoli, *La congiura*, 65 n. 1.

[24] Archivio Sauli, no. 731, fo. 46v. 'Jovius ob contagionis suspitionem quamdam secesserat. Curabimus tamen tuas litteras ad eum perferendas': J. Sadoleto to Francisco Victorio, in *Jacobi Sadoleti SRE cardinalis epistolae quotquot extant proprio nome scriptae nunc primum duplo auctiores in lucem editae: pars prima*, Rome 1760, no. 9 at p. 27.

[25] Marangoni, 'Lazzaro Buonamico', 131; Haig Gaisser, *Piero Valeriano*, 107.

prophecy that he would be the next pope, in which case it seems odd that he should promise to support Riario.[26] Perhaps, as emerged during Nini's interrrogation, he was simply worried about the state of the Church under Leo?[27] There are further discrepancies: in the conclave which elected Leo, Soderini had supported Medici, and Castellesi had not wanted to see Riario pope.[28] Assuming that the plot existed, had the intervening years led them to change their minds? Or had Castellesi's friendship with Petrucci persuaded him? According to Petrucci's Portuguese servant, Castellesi was the cardinal's 'neighbour and great friend' and his *famigliari* accompanied Petrucci to the *palazzo apostolico* on 19 May because many of Petrucci's *famiglia* were absent.[29]

And what of Sauli's motives? They have puzzled many. De' Grassis believed that Sauli took part because the pope did not reward him sufficiently.[30] Guicciardini and Giovio give further clues: the former believed that he took part because of his intimacy with Petrucci and because Cardinal de' Medici had gained some benefices that he wanted. Giovio believed that Sauli was also sufficiently gullible to have believed in a prophecy that named him as a future pope.[31] He then adds that Sauli 'had been offended and become a secret enemy of the pope' and continues that Leo had at the beginning of his reign been forced to concede to relatives or to new men benefices which he had promised to those who had elected him, thus causing complaint amongst the cardinals, the most 'intemperate' of whom had been Sauli.[32] This seems possible: it is unlikely that the cardinal and the Sauli brothers who held the post of *depositarii generali* viewed the transfer of this position to Filippo Strozzi in late 1515 with any great enthusiasm. This is one possible motive for Sauli's enmity. Giovio goes further: he says that when Cardinal de' Medici was granted the see of Marseilles Sauli had sworn that he would never forget it.[33]

However, Giovio was writing more than twenty years after the event and had confused matters: de' Medici was never bishop of Marseilles. It was safely in the hands of Claude de Seyssel from December 1511 and when he did resign it, on 11 May 1517, it was in an exchange with Cardinal Cibo for the bishopric of Turin.[34] There is, nevertheless, one surviving example of Sauli

---

26 Giovio, *Le vite*, 268–9. For Castellesi and the false prophecy see Ferrajoli, *La congiura*, 73; Ottob. Lat. 2137, fo. 34r; *Corpo diplomatico portuguez*, 470; *Relazioni degli ambasciatori*, iii. 55.

27 A.A. Arm. I–XVIII , 2243, fo. 19r; Ferrajoli, *La congiura*, 243.

28 Pastor, *History of the popes*, vii. 23.

29 'seu vezinho e grande amiyno': Salazar y Castro, MS 76, fo. 221v.

30 'tamen quia Papa non forte retribuit ei ut sperabat': Barb. Lat. 2683, fo. 269r–v.

31 Giovio, *Le vite*, 269. This is perhaps also alluded to by de' Grassis who believed Sauli '(ipse) Papa sibi videretur esse': Barb. Lat. 2683, fo. 269r.

32 Giovio, *Le vite*, 270.

33 Ibid.

34 Arch. Consist., Acta Vicecanc. 2, fo. 29r; Eubel, *Hierarchia*, iii. 237.

resenting the preference of de' Medici that is indicative. This dates from 1517 when de' Medici was given the abbey of Clairvaux, which Sauli had coveted. In return Sauli asked Leo to give him the abbey of St Victoire (in the see of Marseilles) which was held by de' Medici, as a recompense. This all began on 9 March and there seems to be a strong possibility that Sauli wrote to Francis I: by 29 March royal approval of the conferral of Clairvaux on de' Medici was looking unlikely, royal distrust of him having been made evident. The situation had not improved by 9 April. By 2 May Cardinal de' Medici had given up hope of taking possession of the benefice and on 14 July a payment was made to Domenico d'Ancona who had been in France at the French court 'regarding the abbey in Marseilles'.[35] Yet, as is obvious, this was after August 1516 when the murder of Leo was supposed to take place, and thus raises another possibility: that there was more than one attempt on the pope's life.

Multiple plotting was certainly what the cardinals were accused of. According to the charges read out in the consistory of 22 June at which they were sentenced, Sauli and Petrucci were accused on four counts: of binding themselves, as soon as Leo had been elected, by faith and by oath to choose the future pope; of meeting and promising to choose Riario as the next pope, informing him of this and promising him their votes; of plotting with Vercelli to infiltrate the surgeon into Leo's household, on the pretext of treating his fistula; and of agreeing that Vercelli would then poison the fistula, and thus kill the pope. This was asserted to have been planned on more than one occasion and to have been communicated to Riario who supported them. Furthermore Sauli and Petrucci were also guilty of treating with Francesco Maria della Rovere and thus breaking the papal *monitorio* against such an act.[36] Thus they all three stood accused of active participation – not just, in the case of Sauli and Riario, of knowing about it – in a plot to murder the pope which was not limited to August 1516 when the pope was ill.

Where did the evidence for these 'multiple plots' come from? On 10 June Nini had been asked if, after the failure of the attempt in August 1516, other attempts to murder Leo had been considered. He replied that he didn't know, although it was possible.[37] Furthermore, Pochintesta, seemingly talking about early 1517, also stated that he believed that Petrucci wanted Leo to restore him to Siena so that the pope could live.[38] The interrogation of Bernardino da Perugia, one of Petrucci's *famigliari*, also supports the hypothesis of several attempts, despite its inconsistencies, and Scipione Petrucci, by his own admission, encouraged Vercelli to poison the fistula about thirty

[35] Cardinal de' Medici to bishop of Bayeux, 8–9 Mar., 29 Mar., 1 Apr., 9 Apr., 2 May, 'Manoscritti Torrigiani', ASI xx (1874), 379, 382–3, 384–5, 389, 1517; 'pro causa abatie marsilie': Archivio Sauli, no. 731, fo. 46r.
[36] Arch. Concist. Acta Vicecanc. 2, fos 37v–38v.
[37] A.A. Arm. I–XVIII, 2243, fo. 36v; Ferrajoli, *La congiura*, 267–8.
[38] A.A. Arm. I–XVIII, 2243, fo. 87v; Ferrajoli, *La congiura*, 308.

days before the cardinal left Rome for the first time, that is in June 1516 and not in August of that year.[39]

Were Leo and his supporters perhaps gilding the lily? Whether true or not, Leo showed that he believed, and wanted others to believe, in the various attempts on his life. The first indication of this is in the consistory of 19 May at which the pope gave some intimation of the nature of the charges. He announced that in the past days he had obtained almost certain proof, via Nini's confession, that the latter had been ordered by Petrucci that he should, by means of Vercelli, infect Leo's fistula with poison, and that Nini had said that he had communicated that wicked plan to Sauli and various others many times.[40]

On 20 May Minio wrote that he had seen the pope and had been told that 'a few days ago' one of Petrucci's *famigliari* had been stopped and a letter from Sauli had been found on him in which he wrote that he had not been able to do what had been agreed. Under interrogation the servant confessed that Sauli had been involved in the business of poisoning the pope.[41] These letters have never been found. Leo's statement perhaps explains the belief that an intercepted letter led to the discovery of the plot and why, although they give the correspondence as that of Petrucci and not of Sauli, Guicciardini, Giovio and others until Ludwig von Pastor, insisted that the plot was discovered almost *in flagrante* while machinations for its completion were continuing. Certainly the use of the phrase 'a few days' shows that the intrigue was, in the eyes of some, not limited to the events of August 1516.[42]

The pope continued to propagate the idea of longstanding hostility: on 29 May Minio wrote that Leo had said that Riario, Petrucci and Sauli were plotting his death four days after his election.[43] The *monitorio* against Castellesi of 15 December 1517 repeated that various negotiations had been held at different times to bring about Leo's death.[44] Yet there are discrepancies: the briefs to the kings of Spain and Portugal that announced the discovery of the plot support the thesis that the plot was ongoing, whilst those to the kings of France and England refer to it as retrospective.[45] Furthermore, on 29 May Costabili reported that in consistory the pope apparently said that 'Petrucci had said that it was true that they had considered poisoning the pope, but that had been a long time ago and that he had given up that idea'.[46]

[39] A.A. Arm. I–XVIII, 2243, fos 71r, 102r–105r; Gattoni, *Leone X*, 192; cf. Picotti, 'La congiura', 251.

[40] Arch. Concist., Acta Vicecanc. 2, fo.11v; cf. Picotti, 'La congiura', 253; Ferrajoli, *La congiura*, 231, 233, 251, 253, 274.

[41] Minio to Venetian government, 20 May 1517, Sanuto, *Diarii*, xxiv. 289.

[42] Giovio, *Le vite*, 265.

[43] Minio to Venetian government, 29 May 1517, Sanuto, *Diarii*, xxiv. 324.

[44] Vat. Lat. 7109, fo. 84.

[45] Ferrajoli, *La congiura*, 33; ASV, Armadio XL, 8, fo. 4r.

[46] Ferrajoli, *La congiura*, 57–8.

As to the instigators of the plot, according to Nini, Petrucci was the chief mover and Sauli, Soderini, Castellesi, Riario and 'Exiguus' knew of it. Soderini and Sauli supported Petrucci financially and with Riario advised Petrucci on various matters. Soderini and Castellesi were accused in the consistory of 8 June of being aware of the plot. According to onlookers, Soderini was in tears and Castellesi looked as if he wished to deny it, but confessed that he had heard Petrucci speak of wishing to kill the pope, but had put it down to childish prattle.[47] Indeed at the time Castellesi was regarded as being the least guilty: Minio wrote, seemingly referring to him, that the 'misdemeanour was of the slightest possible description' and he was merely supposed to have heard Petrucci say in his presence, with reference to Vercelli who was passing by, 'that man will get the college out of trouble'.[48] Does this explain why Leo pardoned them and imposed a relatively small fine? Or was he frightened of public reaction to a harsher punishment of Soderini, an acknowledged political enemy, which would have been put down to personal spite (and thus benefitting Castellesi)?[49] Why did the two cardinals flee and why, if de Fine is to be believed, did Soderini send out a decoy litter to avoid capture?[50] Perhaps, as Tedallini noted, 'they were involved with the cardinals in prison' and knew 'what Cardinal San Giorgio (Riario) knew' or perhaps, innocent or guilty, they did not trust the pope to keep his word that they were pardoned and not to impose a larger fine or imprisonment, a possibility increased by the arrival of Lorenzo de' Medici.[51]

On 25 May Costabili wrote that it was generally reported that 'Sauli was guilty of nothing more than knowing about the plot and not revealing it' and on 1 June Minio wrote that both Riario and Sauli had confessed to knowing about the plot and failing to inform the pope.[52] This would seem to be confirmed by Petrucci's confession, read out in consistory, that he had told Sauli and Riario about the plot to make the latter the new pope, and indeed was the level of guilt apportioned by Agostino Giustiniani.[53] And this is, more or less, what Riario's own relatives admitted to: on 5 June Cesare Riario and others wrote to Henry VIII asking for his intervention after the cardinal's transfer to the Castel Sant'Angelo. Riario had seemingly been imprisoned because of some words Cardinal Petrucci had thoughtlessly spoken in his presence and, perhaps because of Petrucci's youth, Riario had foolishly not referred them to the pope, as he should have done. They did not believe that there had been malice aforethought on Riario's part: he was

---

[47] Barb. Lat. 2683, fo. 205r–v; Ferrajoli, *La congiura*, 69–70.
[48] *Calendar of state papers*, 391, 392–3.
[49] Winspeare, *La congiura*, 143.
[50] Lowe, *Church and politics*, 107.
[51] *Diario romano*, 371–2; Barb. Lat. 2683, fo. 206r.
[52] Capparoni, 'Giov. Battista Vercelli', 33; Winspeare, *La congiura*, 135.
[53] For the dispatch of 25 June 1517 see Sanuto, *Diarii*, xxiv. 419, and Gattoni, *Leone X*, 199 n. 52.

neither to be excused nor condemned in their eyes.[54] Tedallini and Federico
Gonzaga also believed that Riario had heard Petrucci say that he would kill
Leo but had simply not reported it, according to Gonzaga because he had
believed Petrucci's words to be the consequence of passing anger.[55] Does this
seemingly negligible degree of guilt explain why, after the arrest of Petrucci
and Sauli, none of the other cardinal conspirators (but in particular Riario,
as noted by de' Grassis) fled? Or were they simply innocent so that the idea
of fleeing never entered their heads?[56]

According to the trial transcript other cardinals had been aware of Petrucci's dealings and threats. Of the three cardinals named as 'Exiguus', 'Comes'
and 'Sansome' two have been tentatively identified as Marco Cornaro and
Luigi d'Aragona but neither of them, like many of the minor actors in the
plot and in the political negotiations, faced trial or punishment.[57]

The confessions of Petrucci, Sauli and Riario are lost. They may well
have been extracted under torture, given that it was in Peruschi's powers
to use it. Onlookers at the time were far from certain, but rumours were
rife about intimidation, lack of sleep or food and the threat, and perhaps
use, of torture.[58] Guicciardini, followed by Giovio, albeit writing some years
later, believed that the cardinals had been 'harshly examined and confessed
that the plot was devised by Alfonso with Sauli's knowledge'.[59] There are,
furthermore, indications that the confessions were not spontaneous either
with or without the use of torture: both Minio and Costabili reported that
the cardinals had at first denied any involvement, then were asked to read
the others' confessions and then implicated each other.[60]

The lost handwritten confessions were read out at the consistory of 3
June and the cardinals confessed to 'part of their errors'.[61] Their *cedulae*
then formed the part of the transcript of the trial read out on 22 June.
Minio reported that Petrucci had admitted that he had aimed to kill the
pope through Vercelli and that he had told Sauli and Riario. The latter had

[54] BL, MS Cotton Vitellius B III, fo. 182 r–v; Bossi, *Vita*, viii. 102–4.
[55] *Diario romano*, 372; Luzio, 'Isabella d'Este', 71; Gonzaga to I. d'Este, 6 June, Winspeare, *La congiura*, 137.
[56] Barb. Lat. 2683, fo. 203r.
[57] Ferrajoli, *La congiura*, 41, 147, 207, 223; Winspeare, *La congiura*, 79, 172; Barb. Lat. 2137, fo. 32r; Pastor, *History of the popes*, vii. 464–5; cf. D. S. Chambers, 'Isabella d'Este and the travel diary of Antonio De Beatis', *Journal of the Warburg and Courtauld Institute* lxiv (2001), 296–308 at p. 296; *The travel journal of Antonio De Beatis: Germany, Switzerland, the Low Countries, France and Italy, 1517–18*, ed. J. R. Hale, London 1979, 2; Chigi, G II 38, fo. 93r; Garimberto, *La prima parte*, 393; Salazar y Castro, MS 76, fo. 222r.
[58] Capparoni, 'Gio. Battista Vercelli', 33; Costabili, 25 May 1517; Gattoni, *Leone X*, 197 n. 49; Minio, 27 May 1517; Salazar y Castro, MS 76, fo. 224r; Ferrajoli, *La congiura*, 59.
[59] Guicciardini, *Storia d'Italia*, iii. 188; Giovio, *Le vite*, 266.
[60] Capparoni, 'Giov. Battista Vercelli', 34; Pastor, *History of the popes*, vii. 465–6, Costabili, 24 June 1517; Winspeare, *La congiura*, 138–9; Minio to Venetian government, 25 June 1517, Sanuto, *Diarii*, xxiv. 419.
[61] 'partem erroris ipsorum': Arch. Concist., Acta Vicecanc. 2, fo. 33v.

initially denied everything and then said that if the others said it was true then it must be so and that he told Soderini and Castellesi about the plot. On hearing of it Soderini had allegedly said 'do it soon' and Castellesi had laughed.[62] This seems to put the onus on Petrucci and also to indicate that they did not fully confess to the charges officially brought against them. Nor is the puzzle of the degree, if any, of their guilt solved by the public confessions made by Riario and Sauli on the day of their release. Riario, perhaps overly grateful, abased himself and said that his guilt was greater than previously recognised, but without giving further details. But with such public support, why did he need to confess in this manner? On the day of his release Sauli confessed to the charges outlined on 22 June, but the fact that he had been threatened with continued imprisonment if he did not confess in detail must certainly devalue his confession.

After his release Riario reaffirmed that he had been minimally involved. On 28 July he spoke with Minio and played down his own role, saying that he had heard Petrucci talk about killing the pope, but he had not wanted anything to do with it, believing it to be madness and not worthy of his attention. He did not think that the pope should have imprisoned him. Leo later commented to Minio that Riario had been led astray by others.[63] In letters of 9 January and 5 December 1519 to Federico Gonzaga, Alessandro Gabbioneta wrote from Rome that 'the plot to poison His Holiness had indeed existed, thought up by Siena (Petrucci) and by that damned Sauli, the cause and origin of all evil, revealed to San Giorgio who had scorned it and not believed in it'. Riario even admitted that he had made a playful remark about the pope's health in a consistory at which Petrucci and Sauli were present – of February 1517 and hence confirmation of the existence of the 'multiple plots' – and that the pair had reiterated their intentions. He recognised his error in not telling the pope and later in not rebuffing the cardinals when they persisted and acknowledged that he could have suffered the gravest of penalties under the law, but that the pope chose to pardon and free him, albeit leaving him very poor.[64] Was Riario now simply currying favour with the pope and attempting to show his gratitude by admitting that the plot(s) had existed, and also taking advantage of the deaths of Petrucci and Sauli to throw further blame on them?[65] As de' Grassis noted, after his release Riario did 'behave prudently and with humility in everything'.[66] Indeed, when his health began to fail in October 1520 he left for Naples, sailing part of the way to avoid passing through Fondi and arousing Leo's

---

[62] For Minio, 25 June 1517, see Sanuto, *Diarii*, xxiv. 419, and Gattoni, *Leone X*, 199 n. 52.

[63] Minio to Venetian government, 28 July 1517, Sanuto, *Diarii*, xxiv. 543; Ferrajoli, *La congiura*, 66, n. 1.

[64] Luzio, 'Isabella d'Este', 72; Picotti, 'La congiura', 263.

[65] Ibid.

[66] 'prudenter et humiliter in omnibus se exhibet': Barb. Lat. 2683, fo. 224r.

suspicions that he might meet Soderini.[67] On the other hand was Riario simply telling the truth: he knew of a plot, but did not take it seriously?

The evidence seems to indicate that there was indeed a plot. Yet the case is marred by Leo's less than impeccable behaviour on certain points: what seemed to contemporaries to be 'moral black spots'. These pose some uncomfortable questions and have led some to believe that the plot was fabricated for Leo's own purposes. Through it he boosted papal finances through the fines extracted from Sauli, Riario, Soderini and Castellesi, strengthened the college in his favour by the creation of thirty-one new cardinals and rewarded those who examined the cardinals, in what some believe to be an illegal trial, by giving them many of the cardinals' benefices.

It was known to all at the time that papal finances were in a piteous condition due to Leo's prodigality and the war of Urbino.[68] The fines imposed would thus have been very useful: but was Leo moved to impose fines because of his financial needs or did the intervention of foreign powers on the cardinals' behalf mean that he had to show mercy and that a fine represented the best solution?[69] Leo did not need to invent a plot to raise money: he could have imposed the same fines for the coherent, provable and independently confirmed political charges.[70] Nor can Leo be accused of inventing a punishment to suit his needs: there were precedents for the use of fines and they could be applied to men of the Church.[71]

The idea of selling cardinals' hats had already been mooted in late May, but the pope had been unwilling to proceed further, even if it seemed an inevitable step.[72] Throughout June the rumoured numbers of new creations constantly grew – perhaps reflecting Leo's financial needs, or alternatively, after the full extent of the plot had been revealed, demonstrating his increasing sense of vulnerability.[73] Undoubtedly money had changed hands by 1 July, yet given that the *monitorio* issued against dealings with della Rovere meant that the negotiations of Petrucci and the rest were high treason, political treachery on the part of cardinals would in itself have justified the creation of new, more trustworthy, red hats. Leo's trust and authority had been abused

---

[67] Ferrajoli, *La congiura*, 104–5; Lowe, *Church and politics*, 120. Riario died in Naples on 6 July 1521.

[68] M. Giorgi to Venetian government, 9 Feb. 1517, Sanuto, *Diarii*, xxiii. 585; Cardinal de' Medici to bishop of Bayeux, 8 May 1517, 'Manoscritti Torrigiani', *ASI* xx (1874), 389–90.

[69] Winspeare, *La congiura*, 166.

[70] For the accusation of inventing the plot for money see Giovio, *Le vite*, 272, and Winspeare, *La congiura*, 20, 38, 160, 189, 202. See also Ferrajoli, *La congiura*, 141–2.

[71] Ferrajoli, *La congiura*, 89–90; E. Costantini, *Il cardinal di Ravenna al governo d'Ancona e il suo processo sotto Paolo III*, Pesaro 1891, 352–3; *Enciclopedia cattolica*, viii, Vatican City 1952, 1509–11.

[72] L. Guicciardini to F. Guicciardini, 22 May 1517, *Francesco Guicciardini: le lettere*, ii, no. 387 at p. 539.

[73] Minio to Venetian government, 5 June 1517, Sanuto, *Diarii*, xxiv. 354; Barb. Lat. 2683, fo. 208v.

and the plot merely demonstrated further, as Leo said, 'the hatred in which we are held'.[74] It was difficult to justify at the time and remains so today: thirty-one was indeed a very large number, but if the plot were a reality there was some justification for Leo's action, if not for the scale of it.

Rather more difficult to justify is the number of Petrucci's and Sauli's benefices given to those who had helped to prosecute the cardinals.[75] Leo must have been aware of the impression that such rewards would make. If these were rewards for a job well done was this because they had saved Leo's life or had they done his bidding and implicated the innocent?

There is also the question of the legality of the trial. In arresting Sauli and Petrucci without the approval of the majority of the college of cardinals Leo undoubtedly broke his election capitulations; the same can be argued for having them tried by judges other than three cardinals nominated by the college.[76] However, Leo had broken his election capitulations prior to this – in 1515 he had imprisoned Cardinal Sanseverino in the Castel Sant'Angelo – and the cardinals themselves were quick to ignore the capitulations when it suited them.[77] Remolino, Accolti and Farnese were what can be called 'cardinal-advisors' and were appointed by Leo to advise him on further steps to investigate the charges of conspiracy, to read the minutes of the trial and, with the other cardinals, approve the final sentence. Furthermore, they actively consulted with Leo, as reported by the orators and de' Grassis.[78] Ferrajoli, strangely ignored on this point, coherently explains the background to the appointment, and separate non-judicial role of the (on the whole) impartial cardinal-advisors, and also to the hearing of the trial by the *uditore criminale* (Gambarana) instead of by the governor of Rome.[79] Nor were all the defendants refused a defence or witnesses – Pochinesta and Nicolò Masi da Romena spring to mind – and although Nini and the cardinals did not, apparently, enjoy these privileges, the law stated that in crimes against the state the right to a defence rested with the decision of the judges.[80]

[74] Ottob. Lat. 2137, fo. 29; Minio to Venetian government, 4 July 1517, Sanuto, *Diarii*, xxiv. 462; Messer Giorgi to J. Contarini, 21 Dec. 1521, ibid. xxxii. 288; Ferrajoli, *La congiura*, 87–8 n. 3.
[75] Ferrajoli, *La congiura*, 144; Lowe, 'Political crime', 198.
[76] Winspeare, *La congiura*, 120–1; Ferrajoli, *La congiura*, 47; Giovio, *Le vite*, 272.
[77] Pastor, *History of the popes*, vii. 170; Ferrajoli, *La congiura*, 47–8.
[78] Barb. Lat. 2683, fo. 202v; Costabili, 3 June 1517, Ferrajoli, *La congiura*, 58; Minio to Venetian government, 20 June 1517, Sanuto, *Diarii*, xxiv. 403.
[79] Ferrajoli, *La congiura*, 18–19, 46–8; Barb. Lat. 2683, fo. 207v; cf. Lowe, *Church and politics*, 105, although Accolti was in fact made a cardinal in 1511. See Picotti, 'La congiura', 255–6. For reason why the governor of Rome was absent see L. Marini, 'Berruti, Amadeo', *DBI* ix (1967), 410–14 at pp. 411–12, and Minio to Venetian government, 7 July 1517, Sanuto, *Diarii*, xxiv. 464.
[80] A.A. Arm. I–XVIII, 2243, fo. 96v; Ferrajoli, *La congiura*, 32 n. 3, 320. See Ferrajoli, *La congiura*, 68, for a tentative identification of some form of defence allowed to the imprisoned cardinals, which would be seen by the cardinal-advisors only, as based on a passage of a letter of Goro Gheri to Cardinal Bibbiana of 11 June.

Although the moral ambiguities in the handling of the case can, on the whole, be explained when considered in context, it is too easy to concentrate on them and to ignore valid arguments for the existence of a plot. First, Leo did not have to invent a plot in order to raise money: political negotiations with della Rovere would have been enough for that. Second, hostility to the pope on the part of Petrucci and the other cardinals did exist. One might ask whether Leo embroidered this for his own ends, but there was no reason for him to do so, and no concrete evidence of this. The plot, in fact, gradually uncovered itself. Third, Riario never denied either this animus or the existence of a plot, serious or otherwise, nor that Sauli had known about it. Fourth, Sauli continued to be cold-shouldered after his release, not only by Leo but also by his own government. Riario, seemingly less implicated, was rehabilitated and readmitted to papal intimacy. Fifth, Sauli had reasonable grounds for sharing Petrucci's animus towards Leo, grounds which previously have been inexplicable and have supported the case against the plot. Sixth, Giovio was so afraid that he left Rome and a doctor who had served Sauli would not return some three years later: their behaviour is incomprehensible if Sauli were innocent. All the participants had reasons for wanting to eliminate Leo, whether for their own good or for that of others and all were seemingly aware, to some degree, of Petrucci's animus. In the eyes of the law Leo was justified in meting out the punishments that he did: it is their harshness and the opportunism involved, that have somewhat obscured the issue in the eyes of contemporary and later observers.

Arguments against the existence of the plot

If the plot were a fabrication its aim was presumably to rid the pope of enemies, replenish the college of cardinals with men who would support him and refill the papal coffers. It could be argued that no fabrication was necessary in order to create more cardinals and raise more money, so the elimination of papal enemies remains the key motive: were Petrucci, Sauli, Riario, Soderini and Castellesi indeed such?

The case for Petrucci is easy to answer: he had been a thorn in Leo's side since the annexation of Siena and was a cardinal known to have links with Francesco della Rovere. His political alliance with Spain could have proved disastrous for Leo. But was Sauli Leo's enemy? Had the battle over Clairvaux and St Victoire irritated Cardinal de' Medici to the extent that he influenced Leo in the implication of Sauli? Or did the fact that the Sauli family also had links, however tenuous, with della Rovere make him a suitable candidate for elimination? Sauli was living in della Rovere's palace next to Santa Maria in Via Lata and his brother Sebastiano Sauli had bought several castles from della Rovere in 1513.[81] Perhaps, on the other hand, Leo believed not only

---

[81] MS Ferr. 424, fos 52v–53r; Arm. XLIV, 5, fo. 37r–v.

in the prophecy that Sauli would one day be pope but also in that naming Castellesi as the next pope.[82] Or perhaps Castellesi was simply unlucky in being Petrucci's close friend. There is no other conceivable motive for implicating Castellesi, unless there really was a plot. The elimination of Soderini, brother of Leo's political opponent in Florence, would only have been a blessing. Petrucci apart, the reasons for removing Castellesi and Sauli are flimsy, but this seems not to be so for Riario. Tedallini and de' Grassis reported the general suspicion that Leo 'wanted to remind him of the past', that is his alleged involvement in the 1478 Pazzi conspiracy in Florence in which the pope's uncle was murdered and his father injured.[83] But that the then seventeen-year-old Cardinal Riario was in fact an active and willing participant in the Pazzi conspiracy is questionable; as an inexperienced and naïve priest was he simply manipulated by the conspirators?[84] Nor was he eliminated in 1517, merely taught a lesson by being relieved of a large sum of money. Once freed and restored he again enjoyed papal intimacy; he continued to live in Rome and by 10 January 1519 was once again able to vote in secret consistories. Why too, if Tedallini enjoyed Riario's patronage and could perhaps be regarded as hostile to the Medici, did he never proclaim any of the cardinals innocent of any knowledge of Petrucci's, foolish or otherwise, words?[85]

That contemporary public opinion saw the cardinals as victims may also indicate that the plot was a fabrication.[86] Although commentators such as Tedallini, de' Grassis, de Fine and the author of the contemporary anonymous *Life* of Leo reproduced in Bossi believed in the plot, a worried Goro Gheri had his finger on the pulse of popular belief and de' Grassis also reported evidence of sympathy for the cardinals.[87] This was reflected in the *pasquinate* which appeared after Leo's death.[88] In 1517 the climate of disbelief seems to have grown once it was known that fines would be levied as a punishment and that an account of the trial, despite Leo's promise, would never be published. The cardinals' confessions alone were made public – certainly to Francis I – later in the year.[89] Had the promise of publication, seemingly reiterated in early June, been made so that the orators, believing that every-

---

[82] Jungic, 'Prophecies', 365; Lowe, 'An alternative account', 54. The Joachimist prophecy cited by Jungic does not, however, name Sauli personally.

[83] *Diario romano*, 372–3; Barb. Lat. 2683, fo. 203r; Pastor, *History of the popes*, vii. 178.

[84] L. Martines, *April blood: Florence and the plot against the Medici*, London 2003, 168, 117; A. Poliziano, *Della congiura dei Pazzi (Coniurationis commentarium)*, ed. A. Perosa, Padua 1858, 25 n. 7.

[85] Arch. Concist., Acta Misc. 6, fo. 252r; Ferrajoli, *La congiura*, 103. For the 'legami di clientela' between Tedallini and Riario see *Diario romano*, 263.

[86] Lowe, *Church and politics*, 106; E. Rodocannachi, *Histoire de Rome: le pontificat de Léon X, 1513–21*, Paris 1931, 117; Ferrajoli, *La congiura*, 142–3.

[87] Bossi, *Vita*, xii. 175ff; Ferrajoli, *La congiura*, 142 n. 2; Barb. Lat. 2683, fo. 206r.

[88] Cesareo, *Pasquino*, 111–12.

[89] Ferrajoli, *La congiura*, 141–3.

thing would be explained at a later point, would then, like Costabili, 'not bother too much about the details'?[90]

The transcript of the trial is in fact missing and has been for many years. After the events of 1517 it was given to Cardinal Pucci and Cardinal Salviati – Medici favourites – and only re-emerged when it was handed to Cardinal Fieschi for revision. It was then passed to Adrian VI and two other cardinals but then disappeared.[91] In 1893, and again in 1905, Pastor was unable to find the documentation concerning the sentencing of Riario, Sauli and Petrucci, likewise that of Castellesi of 5 July 1518, the transcript and evidence of the *procuratore fiscale* against Riario, Sauli and Petrucci and the transcript of the trial of Petrucci's *famigliari*.[92] Only the latter was located by Ferrajoli. What happened to the rest? Were they misfiled or removed and possibly destroyed?

An alternative account of the plot, apparently written by supporters of the cardinals, lay unidentified in the inventories of the Vatican Archives from at least the late eighteenth century onwards and only appeared with a specific description in inventories compiled after 1925.[93] This document was accurately transcribed and amply analysed by Kate Lowe who notes that it is anonymous and contains neither addressee, title nor date and is written in a hand which was used throughout much of the sixteenth century. It is conceivably a fair copy, given the small number of corrections. This account claims that the plot was a fabrication by Leo to destroy his enemies, to raise money and fill the college with cardinals who would support him.[94] The main points it makes are that Petrucci was tricked into returning to Rome where he was then arrested with Sauli, that torture was used on Nini, that the pope promised to be merciful to the two cardinals, said that he would follow his election capitulations and appointed three cardinals to hear the case ('conoscitori della causa'). This reassured the college and the cardinals' relatives, who did not think of getting outside help. Riario was arrested and threatened with torture and long-term imprisonment if he did not confess. Sauli and Petrucci were tortured and both confessed, as did Vercelli. Their confessions meant that their families and friends could then only try to ensure leniency in carrying out their sentences. Details of the trial were not provided, so the evidence could not be questioned. Sauli regretted having lied and implicated Petrucci and Riario and wished to retract but was persuaded not to do so by Stefano Sauli. The three cardinals were deprived and Petrucci was strangled. Two other cardinals were then accused in consistory and, having been fed their lines, confessed and fled. Sauli, eventually

90 Costabili to A. d'Este, 1 June 1517, Capparoni, 'Giov. Battista Vercelli', 33.
91 Picotti, 'La congiura', 263.
92 Pastor, *History of the popes*, vii. 185.
93 ASV, Inventory, no. 1009, 272–3. Prior to this it was anonymously combined with other documents: Inventory, no. 67, fo. 291.
94 Lowe, 'Alternative account', 53, 55–6; A.A. Arm. I–XVIII, 5042, fo. 2v.

freed and exiled to Monterotondo, returned to Rome and soon died a devout death, repenting of his false confession and urging his confessor, Prierias, to tell a new pope: Prierias later wrote to Adrian VI. The account also posits that if Petrucci had been guilty, Sauli would not have encouraged him to come to Rome and asks why Riario, Soderini and Castellesi did not flee. The account ends leaving it for the reader to decide who is telling the truth.

At first glance the report makes very convincing reading, raising significant questions: why Riario, Soderini and Castellesi did not flee and whether torture invalidated a confession. Furthermore, the details, such as the names and places listed throughout the document, are compelling, as is the use of direct speech.[95] Yet if the details are precise in some areas, they are far from it in others. Why are Domenico Coletta, the *vicecastellano* of the Castel Sant'Angelo, and Gianpietro Peracchia never named in the document when others are clearly identified? Only their positions are given.[96] Why does the account state that nobody knew with any certainty where Castellesi went and what happened to him after he left Rome?[97] Anybody who was present in Rome during and after the plot would have known from the consistorial discussions and the *monitorio* against Castellesi that he was in Venice. Furthermore, no details are given about what happened to Riario after his release, nor does the author mention his rapturous reception by the Curia and the Roman public which would only have strengthened his case. It is also very obviously a biased account: Cardinal Petrucci is painted as whiter than white, a long-suffering and docile victim. His political crimes are glossed over, as is the treaty with Spain. Sauli is a hero, albeit late in the day, a man who recognised his sin and did his best to make amends.

The major difficulty lies in errors of chronology in the document. The first concerns Petrucci's move from Naples to Genazzano, when in fact it happened the other way round: in July 1516 Petrucci went to Genazzano and in December 1516 to Naples, then returning to Genazzano.[98] A careless omission? The author also telescopes dates alarmingly: he states that the first consistory was that in which Leo explained to the cardinals why Sauli and Petrucci had been arrested and that Petrucci had involved Sauli, Riario, Soderini and Castellesi. Other cardinals were in fact publicly implicated more gradually than this. No mention is made of the days Riario spent in the Vatican as guest of Cardinal de' Medici, until his transfer to the Castel Sant'Angelo.[99] Sauli seemingly goes straight from prison to Monterotondo, without his period in disgrace in the Vatican. When he returns, sick, he dies 'shortly afterwards' when in fact he lingered for more than three months.[100]

95 Lowe, 'Alternative account', 58.
96 A.A. Arm. I–XVIII, 5042, fo. 5r; Lowe, 'Alternative account', 55, 58.
97 A.A. Arm. I–XVIII, 5042, fo. 10v; Lowe, 'Alternative account', 56.
98 A.A. Arm. I–XVIII, 5042, fo. 2r.
99 Ibid. fo. 5r.
100 Ibid. fo. 10v.

Gambarana is named as receiving the bishopric of Albenga, without mention of the fact that Cardinal de' Medici held it first.[101] The worst error concerns the consistory at which Soderini and Castellesi 'confess'. According to this account, it came after the deprivation of Riario, Sauli and Petrucci and the execution of Nini and Vercelli.[102] Yet Soderini and Castellesi confessed at the consistory of 8 June, several days before the execution of Nini and Vercelli and the deprivation of the other three cardinals. Has the author deliberately confused the chronology to strengthen his case? A similar mistake is found when discussing their flight: they fled on 20 June, again before any executions and any deprivations.[103]

The author also says that Leo's reported talk of mercy soothed the anxieties of the cardinals' relatives who did not look for 'external remedies', feeling that there was nothing to fear.[104] The involvement of Giovanni Gioacchino da Passano, Domenico d'Ancona and Jacopo Sauli in France on behalf of Cardinal Sauli clearly contradicts this. Furthermore, according to the account the two cardinals resisted their interrogators and refused to confess until Riario did so and Sauli was then tortured.[105] Again the dates do not coincide: the orators' reports give the two cardinals as having confessed before Riario's arrest: that was why he was arrested. Were the orators merely recycling information fed to them by the pope and his supporters?

The Genoese orator was in close contact with the Sauli brothers in Rome: why is there no mention of the cardinal's retraction or protestations of his innocence in Cattaneo's letters? This, and his deathbed confession, are two of the main props which the author of the account uses to show that the cardinals were innocent. Did Sauli try to retract and then meet his brother? The incident takes up more than two sides of the document and is immensely detailed. The blow-by-blow account could only have been written by someone who had been present or had talked to one of the Sauli or, possibly, somebody with a fertile imagination.

Kate Lowe believes that the author can probably be identified as a relative of one of the five cardinals implicated in the plot or as someone acting in a legal capacity on behalf of one of them.[106] She suggests Stefano Sauli, possibly with Cardinal Soderini. Yet it seems unlikely that it is some sort of legal document: it is too imprecise in its lack of dates and too familiar – the use of the words 'I say', noted by Lowe, make it a verbal, intimate, account, perhaps for posterity, but who was meant to read it? It is extremely unlikely that Soderini had anything to do with the document: he, of all people, should have known the date of the consistory in which he confessed to his

---

101 Ibid. fo. 11v.
102 Ibid. fo. 9r.
103 Ibid. fo. 10v.
104 Ibid. fo. 4v.
105 Ibid. fo. 5v.
106 Lowe, 'Alternative account', 57.

involvement (and indeed the dating of the document renders this hypothesis invalid). Stefano Sauli can also be excluded as there is some confusion over the fine paid by Sauli. The author seems to know the final amount paid (25,000 ducats), but implies that this was to release Sauli from the dreadful cell into which he had been moved. No mention is made of the figure Sauli paid as a caution. Who better to have known the exact details than Stefano? And would Stefano have made the mistake of referring to 'he [Stefano] and his brother' when all three brothers, Sebastiano, Stefano and Giovanni were in Rome at the time?[107] The knowledge displayed by the author of the Curia and curial positions may well point to an office-holder, but it is unlikely to have been Stefano as Lowe suggests.[108] He was a learned Ciceronian whose only surviving correspondence in Italian is business correspondence to his family or architects. In a document of such supposed importance, one which found its way, whether by accident or design, into the papal archives, would he have used Italian and in such a familiar style?

It has been suggested that the document is datable to soon after the election of Adrian VI (9 January 1522), given that he is cited in the account, that no news was known of Castellesi's fate, and that it was perhaps 'part of a campaign to press for a revision of the trial'.[109] However, the document must be dated later than that: Adrian is referred to as 'the successor of Leo who *was* pope Adrian' and Sauli 'called for his confessor called Frate Silvestro di Prierio and *at that time* master of the sacred palace, a man of virtuous habits and great authority' (italics added). In both cases the past tense is used. Prierias was master of the sacred palace from late 1515 until his death in 1527, thus providing a *terminus post quem* for the account.[110] This then raises the question as to why there is no mention of the attempt of Stefano Sauli and Soderini to obtain a revision of the trial, a revision which was ultimately abandoned. Was the author unaware of it (which again discounts Stefano Sauli) or did he feel that to mention it would merely weaken his case?

In the account, Cardinal Sauli is never referred to as 'Bendinello', although Petrucci is named as 'Alfonso', perhaps indicating that the author belonged to the Petrucci camp, (or perhaps to avoid confusing him with other members of the Petrucci family).[111] Or was the author someone who was present in Rome during the plot and was close to the Sauli, thus accounting for the detailed names and places, but left Rome before the release of Riario and Sauli? How can the tortuous and erroneous chronology be explained? Was the document written so long after the plot that time had confused events in the writer's mind? It was written to provide an alternative account, but why, after 1527, when all the dust had settled, would somebody wish to stir

---

[107] 'esso et il fratello': A.A. Arm. I–XVIII, 5042, fo. 8r.
[108] Lowe, 'Alternative account', 59.
[109] Ibid. 56.
[110] For the duration of Prierias's appointment see Tavuzzi, *Prierias*, 75.
[111] Lowe, 'Alternative account', 57.

it up again? The Sauli had no axe to grind: they did not abandon Rome after Cardinal Sauli's death as there was, after all, their banking business to consider.[112] There was thus no immediate or obvious threat to their lives or livelihoods and indeed they continued to prosper as 'mercatores romanam curiam sequentes'.[113] The discrepancies within the document make it difficult to argue that it is genuine.

There can be no such doubts about the authenticity of an account written by Alfonso Petrucci's Portuguese servant, although this document too is problematic. The identity of the author is unclear: although he is addressed in the manuscript as Jacobo, he is now generally referred to as the 'Fidalgo de Chaves'.[114] The author, a member of the household of Duke Jaime of Braganca, was in Siena and then Rome from May 1510 to September 1517. He met Petrucci in Siena and probably accompanied him to Rome as a member of his household on his elevation to the cardinalate in 1511.[115] The manuscript is a mid-sixteenth-century copy and details the author's personal memories, for example of *carnevale*, the sights he saw and his journeys, and is often conversational in tone with many short sentences. It was perhaps written contemporaneously with the events described, although there is some doubt about this. The *terminus ante quem* is probably late 1521.[116]

As Eugenio Asensio notes, 'the most vibrant and personal pages are those which narrate ... the tragic destiny of this church dignitary (Cardinal Petrucci)'.[117] And this is one of the problems: the account is far from objective. Petrucci, and consequently the author, hate the Florentines and view them as greedy; Leo is unscrupulous and wanted to kill Petrucci from the outset; despite the negotiations with Spain to recover Siena, which here are not denied, Petrucci is whiter than white and 'in general esteemed and loved by all'. He was innocent of all blame, 'well-built, beautiful, wise and respectful'.[118] Petrucci's innocence is highlighted by the, seemingly

112 B. Doria to Ufficio del Mare, Genoa, 21 July 1518, Archivio Segreto 1959.

113 McClung Hallman, *Italian cardinals*, 139.

114 Salazar y Castro, MS 76, fo. 220r; S. Deswarte-Rosa, 'The Portuguese in Rome and the Palazzo dei Tribunali', in K. J. P. Lowe (ed.), *Cultural links between Portugal and Italy in the Renaissance*, Oxford 2000, 249–64 at p. 251; L. de Matos, *A corte literaria dos duques de Braganca no Renascimento*, Lisbon 1956, 31; E. Asensio, 'Memorias de un fidalgo de Chaves (1510–17): descripción de la Roma de Julio II y Leon X', *Estudios Portugueses*, Paris 1974, 103–21 at p. 105.

115 Deswarte-Rosa, 'The Portuguese', 251; de Matos, *A corte*, 30; Asensio, 'Memorias', 106. Deswarte-Rosa (p. 252 n. 5) notes that a transcription of the manuscript was in preparation in 2000, but enquiries of the publisher (the University of Coimbra) went unanswered.

116 Asensio, 'Memorias', 105, 120; S. Deswarte, 'Uno sguardo venuto da lontano: tra Roma antica e Roma cristiana', in M. Fagiolo (ed.), *Roma e l'antico nell'arte e nella cultura del cinquecento*, Rome 1985, 489–508 at p. 496.

117 Asensio, 'Memorias', 117.

118 Salazar y Castro, MS 76, fo. 213v; 'tirallo do mundo'(fo. 214v); ibid. fos 218r, 219v;

improbable, number of warnings given to the cardinal that he should not return to Rome or go to the Vatican Palace: Asensio notes the similarities between Petrucci's entry into Rome and that of Christ into Jerusalem.[119] In a confrontation with Domenico Coletta at Petrucci's cell door the cardinal is described as a Christ-like figure.[120] To blacken further the case against Leo both Sauli and Riario are said to have died from poison, which is demonstrably untrue.[121]

There are also some discrepancies: Pochintesta is described as executed in July instead of June; there is confusion about if and when the cardinals' goods were confiscated and a rather puzzling piece which describes how the Sauli brothers fell out over paying the fine (no deposit is mentioned) because Sauli was ill and they feared that if they paid they would only be given his corpse. No evidence whatsoever survives of this in other sources, including the Genoese ambassador's reports.[122] But most alarming of all, no mention is made of the confessions of Soderini and Castellesi in consistory and their subsequent fines and flight. Would this have blackened the case against Petrucci?

However, many of the details of the arrest and imprisonment of the cardinals are convincing and are confirmed by other sources such as Tedallini and Minio. What does this indicate? It shows that the author was present or more or less well-informed about many of the events which occurred between Petrucci's entry into Rome and 11 September 1517 when he left, and that he reported them as he chose. The author shares the view of the Romans that the pope wanted to implicate Petrucci in order to lay hands on Siena and says that it was believed that Sauli was implicated because his relatives and brothers had helped to finance Francesco Maria della Rovere in the war of Urbino and Riario because of his presence in Florence at the time of the Pazzi conspiracy.[123] This is the only source that implicates Sauli on account of his family's financial involvement with della Rovere and remains unconfirmed; if true it was a further example of *lèse majesté* and a very serious crime.

What, then, does this document offer? In truth, as its author did not always accompany his master on his travels, it provides little other than confirmation of some of the events after Petrucci's return to Rome and his arrest. For example he was with Vercelli in Rome when Petrucci was at Genazzano (and when much of the plot was supposedly hatched) and he

---

'era mui quisto e amado de todos em general': ibid. fo. 218v; ibid. fo. 221r; 'e de grando corpo e mui fermoso e bom juizo e saber. E de reaes respeitos': ibid. fo. 225r.
[119] Ibid. fo. 221r–v; Asensio, 'Memorias', 118.
[120] Salazar y Castro, MS 76, fo. 222r.
[121] Ibid. fo. 225r–v.
[122] Ibid. fos 222v–223r.
[123] Ibid. fo. 226r.

was in Rome prior to the return of Petrucci in May 1517.[124] Thus he was not privy to Petrucci's more confidential dealings. The Portuguese ambassador believed in the plot and the author of the manuscript spent time with other Portuguese in Rome. It is difficult to avoid the conclusion that his unshakable loyalty to Petrucci, partly due to the favours he received from the cardinal, blinded him to other interpretations.[125]

That there was an attempt to procure a revision of the trial indicates that in the eyes of some at least an injustice had occurred, but its outcome gives no clear answer as to whether the plot existed or not. In December 1522 Adrian VI restored Lattanzio Petrucci to the bishopric of Sovana, yet Peruschi remained free.[126] Gambarana was charged in February 1523, but then no further action was taken. This is far from the 'open favour' with which, according to Picotti, Adrian accepted the idea of a revision.[127]

The motives of Soderini and Stefano Sauli in pressing for a retrial are reasonably clear: Soderini, although implicated by Nini in both the political dealings and in the conspiracy, probably bridled under a pardon; Stefano wished to avenge what he considered to be the injustice done to his brother and his death, as well as to recover some of the cardinal's lucrative benefices. Stefano's affection for his brother endured: in his wills of 1548 and 1563 he made provision for the transfer of his bones from Santa Sabina to Santa Maria di Carignano in Genoa, although this never seems to have happened.[128]

However, Stefano's interest in the cardinal's benefices would also have been in character: in a letter from de Longueil to Marcantonio Flaminio we learn that Stefano, although rich, was mean with money and that he lost Lazzaro Buonamico as a tutor for precisely this reason.[129] Perhaps one of these lucrative benefices was the pension of 4,000 ducats on the abbey of San Simpliciano that was to go to Stefano on Bendinello's death. It is interesting that after Soderini's disgrace there is no further evidence that Stefano continued to press for a revision and perhaps the fact that by 1525, if not earlier, he was in receipt of this pension explains why.[130] It should also be asked why, if Cardinal Sauli were innocent, did his cousins Filippo, a highly respected bishop, and Domenico, both intimates of Giberti, the right-hand man of Clement VII, not pursue the matter further. Or did Filippo, who was often with the cardinal in his last months, not feel in all conscience that he could do so?

124 Ibid. fo. 220r–v.
125 Ibid. fo. 218v; Asensio, 'Memorias', 113, 118.
126 Ferrajoli, La congiura, 118; cf. Eubel, Hierarchia, iii. 30.
127 Picotti, 'La congiura', 252.
128 Notai Antichi, 2049, 25 Aug. 1548; 2870, 22 Mar. 1563.
129 de Longueil to Flaminio, n.d., de Longueil, Orationes, cc. 103v–104r.
130 Puccinelli, Zodiaco, 37.

Was Sauli a good and innocent man? Or did the plot as described by Nini exist? Was Nini prompted and manipulated throughout, or just at certain points? Was Sauli an active participant in the plan to murder Leo or did he simply share Petrucci's animus, know of his intentions and not reveal them? Was this what Stefano Sauli regarded as the injustice? None of those implicated in the plot held Leo in any great affection. When faced with Petrucci's angry outbursts, Sauli, Riario, Soderini and Castellesi probably listened, perhaps treating the whole matter as something of a joke and did not report it to the pope.

The answer lies in the account given by Sauli's doctor and *famigliare*, Paolo Giovio. His links with the Medici – for they were later his patrons and his *Life* of Leo, in which the plot was discussed, was dedicated to Alessandro de' Medici – has led to his account of the plot being discredited. Yet it is clearly based on factual evidence. He was correct in stating that Sauli 'had helped Alfonso with money', as proved by the Sauli account books, and may well be correct in the picture he paints of the four cardinals' dislike of the pope and their indifference to Petrucci's threats.[131] He describes Petrucci's hatred of the pope as a result of the annexation of Siena and how, in fury, Petrucci had spoken to the other cardinals and accused Leo of ingratitude and wickedness, saying that he would liberate the college. He states that Riario, Soderini, Castellesi and Sauli laughed and made fun of him, refusing to take him seriously, 'although they, with their souls corrupted by ambition and hate, desired nothing other than that he in his madness committed that foul deed either openly or through secret means'.[132] The 'treacherous silence of the others, steeped in wicked ambition' brought about their downfall.[133]

And their downfall was justified. There is reasonable evidence from Nini, Scipione Petrucci, Paolo Giovio and Riario himself to show that Petrucci wanted Leo removed, that Sauli and the others were aware of it, and that they listened with varying degrees of attention. It seems likely that Sauli was the more involved – if not in the plot then certainly in the political negotiations. The loan of 1,000 ducats proclaims a certain degree of intimacy and sympathy. Riario, Soderini and Castellesi may well have listened and laughed. Riario's rehabilitation after his extravagant fine and the lesser punishment of the latter two cardinals would certainly be in line with this. This would also explain Soderini's resentment at the fine and why none of them fled. Yet in canon law 'clerics guilty of involvement in, or with knowledge of, a conspiracy were to be stripped of their rank and dignity and placed

---

[131] For Giovio's patronal links see Jungic, 'Prophecies', 364 n. 85. See also Giovio, *Le vite*, 266.
[132] Giovio, *Le vite*, 267.
[133] Ibid. 273.

in jail'.[134] The fact that the conspiracy came to nothing was not a mitigating factor: intention carried the same penalty.[135] To contemporaries and to later commentators this may seem harsh, but in the eyes of the law Sauli was far from 'innocens'.

---

134 Lowe, 'Political crime', 186, citing E. Friedberg (ed.), *Corpus iuris canonici*, Leipzig 1879, i. 632–3.
135 Lowe, 'Political crime', 194.

Conclusion

Foglietta's epitaph, visible on Sauli's tombstone in Santa Sabina until the late *cinquecento*, makes much of the role of fate in his career, and also of his virtue.[1] This should not be read as a posthumous declaration of his innocence: an epitaph has to provide as positive an account as possible of a person's life and rarely has anybody, however badly behaved in life, had their sins recounted on their tombstone. Indeed, in his book Foglietta condemned Sauli for his actions, blaming his acquiescence in Petrucci's machinations on spite or bad advice. It was surely kinder for Foglietta to say that fate (or Petrucci and a combination of tertiary fever and dropsy) brought a swift end to Sauli's career and life.

The epitaph does, however, highlight the fact that now that Sauli was in heaven he 'despise[s] riches, quantities of gold, kingdoms and glory'. This was far from the case when he was still on earth: he had avidly collected benefices, had been keen on money and the spending of it, glorying in the eminence he had attained. He was clearly an ambitious cardinal, but his ambition was dependent on patronage. The patronage encountered in this book has been twofold: that bestowed by the pope and that bestowed by Sauli himself. Unless a cardinal had substantial personal wealth one could not exist without the other, and in order for Sauli to be a lavish patron with a large *famiglia*, to decorate his palace and his churches and to reward humanists for their promotion of him in print he needed money, which was in turn derived from benefices which were in the gift of the pope.

Papal patronage

Papal favour was thus essential and could depend on many factors: a cardinal's birthplace; his usefulness as a papal mouthpiece in local politics; his influence with foreign powers when the international situation proved threatening to the papacy; shared interests such as hunting and socialising but also, as in Sauli's case, the provision by the *depositarii generali* of essential credit. Money

---

[1] 'Invida virtuti mala sors cum cerneret in te/ Ingenium ac dotes eximias animi./ Non tulit, atque tuis successibus obstitit, auso/ Ac decus intentum continuisse gradum./ Felix, si quo coepisti dare vela per altum/ Hoc ires cursu tuque tuumque decus./ Nam virtus cum purpureo te ornavit amictu/ Promisit triplex tum diadema tibi./ At sors, quae meritos olim subtraxit honores/ Non potuit superis te prohibere choris. / Hic tu Caelestes inter sanctumque senatum/ Spernis opes, auri pondera, regna, decus': Folietae, *Clarorum ligurum*, 144.

got the Sauli into papal finances, at long last secured Bendinello's elevation to the purple, and was apparently more important than a cardinal's political clout: it can be no coincidence that even though Sauli played an important diplomatic role in the encounter between Leo and Francis I at Bologna in 1515, his career and his accumulation of benefices were already beginning to falter because his family was no longer in control of papal finances.

The potential political influence of a cardinal illustrates the nature of the papacy in this period: caught between the forces of France, the Holy Roman Empire and Spain, the temporal concerns of an independent Church had assumed an importance equal to its spiritual concerns. Appointments to the cardinalate were made to satisfy the demands of the most important foreign power of the moment, and Sauli's unsteady trajectory under Julius II amply demonstrates the pros and cons of the foreign allegiances of a cardinal and his family. The pro-French Sauli continued to receive papal favour, even when the pope was virulently anti-French; this must mean that Julius was certain of Sauli's loyalty to himself, for the Sauli were not the only bankers in Rome and he could easily have removed them from their position had he so wanted. In fact Sauli continued to demonstrate his personal loyalty, and perhaps affection, after Julius' death when in 1516 he asked Sebastiano del Piombo to echo the papal pose of Raphael's *Julius II*.

Loyalty to the della Rovere pope meant that when Leo X was elected, Sauli's chances of continued favour should have been diminished: there were, as far as it is possible to tell, no special grounds for intimacy with the Medici. But Sauli must have been on reasonable terms with Giovanni de' Medici before 1513: he and the younger cardinals ensured that he was the next pope and Leo proved suitably grateful. Such was his continued intimacy that in 1517, when the plot was discovered, both Cardinal de' Medici and the pope were surprised that Sauli, 'one of us', should have been implicated.[2]

The division of the college of cardinals into 'younger' and 'older' group-ings during the conclave of 1513 is indicative of the nature of the college: opposing groups formed. There were those cardinals who were close to the pope, whether because they were relatives, politically useful or with polit-ical and/or social interests in common; those who felt a loyalty to a past pope; those from the same *patria*; and those who were simply friends such as Petrucci and Sauli. Indeed, it was friendship that caused Sauli's downfall when he partly turned a deaf ear, or, as Italians aptly call it, his *orecchi da mercante* to Petrucci's plans. His adherence to, or perhaps tacit acceptance of, the plot indicates the strength of such ties within the college and the resentment at the power and patronage, not just within the Curia but also on a national and international level, which the pope possessed. It was politics which had nurtured the seeds of Petrucci's political machinations against

---

[2] 'et maxime Sauli, ... (che) lo reputava come uno di noi': Cardinal de' Medici to bishop of Bayeux, 19 May 1517, 'Manoscritti Torrigiani', *ASI* xx (1874), 394.

Leo and then the plot: if Leo had not wanted to extend papal and Medici influence to include Siena and Urbino, thus upsetting Spain and France, then Petrucci would not have treated with other rulers against the pope and Sauli would not have given him financial help and listened to his further plans without informing his (indeed, their) own patron, the pope. In turn Petrucci's *famigliari* would not have been arrested and the plot would not have been uncovered.

Yet the very nature of this plot, that one pope could theoretically be removed and another, already selected, be put in his place, demonstrates the potential instability of the papacy and the problematic nature of a system which allowed certain cardinals to gain power and influence amongst their peers. But as the fate of Petrucci and Sauli also illustrates, a cardinal's individual influence, and that of his family, whether in Rome or in his hometown, was as nothing when compared to that of the pope. The events of 1517 underline the extent of the pope's power and how he was able to act as he felt, his feelings and decisions often changing on a daily basis.

In contradistinction there was a clear dichotomy between the perception and the reality of a cardinal's power. As was the case with Sauli, governments of the diverse Italian states pushed strongly for the elevation of one of their own to the cardinalate, believing that it would bring important influence with the pope. The Sauli themselves undoubtedly entered papal finance hoping for profit, prestige and influence, either through their own money or through the bestowal of the cardinalate on one of their own. Yet their treatment at the hands of Alexander VI when repayments on the *appalto* began at only 45 per cent should have sounded a warning bell: whatever the rights or wrongs of a given situation, the pope had the final say. Indeed, the influence of an individual cardinal was in essence negligible: the pope listened to his favourite advisors amongst the cardinals, but almost inevitably had a papal favourite (often a member of his family) to whom he lent his ear and patronage more readily. Giulio de' Medici became a cardinal in 1513 and only eight years later his income stood at 20,000 ducats: almost a third more than that of Sauli after six years as a cardinal. The pope held the reins of power and if a cardinal did not succeed in ingratiating his way into papal favour, then he risked at worst having no influence at all and little income, and at best merely bringing honour to his *patria* by trotting out his *famiglia* when ambassadors visited Rome. Although cardinals were men revered within Rome for their patronal largesse and influence, they were, essentially, pawns on the papal chessboard and utterly dependent on papal goodwill. If this were withdrawn their careers could alter for the worse.

Of course links with foreign powers could also be brought into play to exert influence on the pope and improve a cardinal's career prospects: and in Sauli's case to save his life. These demonstrate papal susceptibility to external political pressure. The Sauli had helped to finance the French invasion of 1494 and as French subjects loaned Francis I large sums in 1516. The pro-French inclinations of Sauli and his family are a theme which runs throughout his career: French approval of Sauli ensured that there were no obstacles to his gaining important benefices in French-held Milanese territory and that Francis I agitated strongly for mercy on Sauli's behalf in 1517, even sending an orator to Rome. Nor was Sauli alone in benefiting from the support of foreign powers: Henry VIII, the emperor and Venice all spoke up for Cardinal Riario.

A cardinal also had strong ties with his *patria*: he would try, when possible, to promote the political interests of his home town, and also intervene to expedite spiritual concerns such as the reform of convents. There was obviously a sense of common feeling between cardinals from the same state: the two other Genoese cardinals, Fieschi and Cibo, pleaded for Sauli with Leo in 1517. In Rome the cardinal represented his birthplace and while the Genoese government still believed in Sauli's innocence and hoped that it could be proved, they wrote numerous letters to anybody whom they believed could help them, including Franceschetto Cibo whom they obviously regarded not just as the pope's brother-in-law but also as a good Genoese. When they realised that Sauli had disgraced both Genoa and himself it is not difficult to understand why they ignored him. Yet within Genoa the Sauli family continued to prosper: the family eventually proved to be more important than one single member. They were one of only five *popolari* families to head an *albergo* in the reforms of 1528, Santa Maria di Carignano began to be built in the mid-*cinquecento*, and three members of the family became doge in the *seicento*.[3] The self-promotion of the Sauli, at least in this city, achieved long-lasting success, demonstrating that although perceived influence in Rome was deemed to be important, it was not essential in the eyes of fellow Genoese.

Patronage

As a cardinal-patron within Rome, Sauli himself had a well-defined role and public image to sustain and project. He was expected to reflect the *dignitas* of his position and of the Church and there can be little doubt that cardinals were expected to put on a good show for the outside world. But how important in fact was self-promotion? Was it not also a question of personal taste and finances? Cardinal Riario and Cardinal Carafa were ostentatious patrons of palaces, churches and humanists but were well-established cardinals when they undertook such large-scale patronage. Other cardinals, such as Soderini, seem to have been sufficiently sure of their position, or perhaps sufficiently tight-fisted, not to feel the need to spend their money on such things: only

[3] For Giulio (grandson of Sebastiano Sauli), doge 1656–8; Lorenzo *quondam* Ottaviani (grandson of Antonio Sauli), doge 1599–1601; and Francesco Maria Sauli, doge 1697–9, see Bologna, 'L'Archivio della famiglia Sauli', 639.

two humanist works were dedicated to Soderini during his long cardinalate.[4] Sauli seems to have become a patron with some gusto, and obviously had the means at his disposal to allow him to do so. Perhaps he also had a sense of pride in being the first member of a Genoese *popolare* family to become a cardinal. The year 1511, the year of his elevation, marks a turning point in his patronage: he immediately started to celebrate his success. Raphael's *Portrait of a cardinal* can be dated to this year, and although Cattaneo was already a member of his household, Giovio, Giustiniani and Marostica only joined it after that date. In 1515 Sauli moved to a palatial residence which had been admired by his former patron Julius II, a palace large enough to house his sizeable *famiglia* and to host the entertainment which must have contributed to his expenditure. He obviously regarded all this as a good investment of the income from his benefices.

In addition to the more ephemeral patronage of a large and expensive *famiglia*, Sauli also ensured that his own name was glorified through unique, and more durable, works. Cattaneo's *Genua* perpetuated his, and Sauli's, fame amongst later writers and the innovatory *Cardinal Bendinello Sauli and three companions* proved to be an influential memorial. Such was Sauli's pride in his own patronage that, for the first time, and in a uniquely large painting, members of his household were included in a cardinal portrait; Sauli was depicted not just as a cardinal, as had been the case in the earlier Raphael portrait, but also as a ruler and patron. So proud was he of his patronage of Cattaneo and Giovio that he even compared them in paint to Plato and Aristotle. The choice of Raphael and Sebastiano also speaks for itself: they were the most influential painters in Rome, so using them reflected Sauli's sense of prestige and wealth: both were popular and would have been expensive. His liking for the new and innovatory is indicative of a self-importance which may have astounded and unsettled the rest of the Curia: this would certainly explain the tone of the remarks made by Paris de' Grassis in this context.

Yet Sauli also favoured more traditional patronal routes, not forgetting to include his fellow countrymen in his patronage: as Da Vigo underlined, Sauli favoured Ligurians and many featured in his *famiglia*. He also gave generously to the *Arcispedale di San Giacomo degli Incurabili* which had been reformed by the Genoese Vernazza. One of the foremost Genoese humanists, Agostino Giustiniani, was part of Sauli's household and was granted a bishopric at his behest, and Sauli may also have been a participant in the plan to launch a Greek printing press in Genoa.

Cardinalitial patronage was an exchange of favours: in artistic and literary patronage the patron gave money and the fame of association in exchange for the glorification of his name and status. This also had negative implications. While the cardinal-patron was alive and enjoyed the pope's own patronage

---

[4] Lowe, *Church and politics*, 261.

then those who were in his service flourished, but when, as in Sauli's case, disgrace and worse beckoned, then the association proved dangerous and many of those in his service either fled when he was imprisoned or suffered in their later careers. The patronage system as a whole was fragile and finely balanced: ill-health or ill-temper on the part of the patron, whether it was the pope or Sauli, had widespread ramifications for many people.

Sauli the cardinal

Was Sauli a typical renaissance cardinal? It is impossible to say as, despite the traditional picture of wine-swilling lovers of courtesans that has come down to us through novels, films and the somewhat more sensational historians, there is, of course, no cardinal prototype. It is perhaps easier to define what he was not: namely a papal *nipote* or relative, a member of a great Italian ruling family or an ecclesiastic promoted on his own merits, despite Foglietta's emphasis on his virtues. His elevation to the cardinalate was a mutually convenient arrangement for both the pope and the Sauli and like so many similar creations came about through politics, influence and money.

Yet if it is accepted that cardinals were expected to favour certain interests, whether they were politics, religion, artistic and/or humanistic patronage or sheer *joie de vivre*, then he seems to have dabbled in all of these. His presence at a riotous dinner in 1513 may well indicate that he had a love of fun, but it is an isolated incident and one from which it is impossible to draw firm conclusions.[5] It seems more likely, given his multifarious patronal activities in such a short career, that he was intent on setting himself up as a great patron, and that Leo, on the discovery of the plot, was determined to put an end to this ambition. The swift redistribution of Sauli's benefices and the proposed annual income of 2,000 ducats would have meant that if Sauli had lived he would have struggled to survive, let alone maintain a large *famiglia* and commission innovatory celebratory works. Yet it is also difficult not to conclude that he wanted to be a good churchman. Becoming a cardinal did not mean an immediate infusion of religious zeal or a spontaneous burgeoning of interest in one's benefices, but Sauli was a far from disinterested ecclesiastic, rather a man who came from a pious family and who did his best not to forget the ecclesiastical aspect of his role. Julius seems to have recognised this in him and Sauli duly features in the *Stanza della segnatura* in the *Disputa*, a fresco dedicated to theology. He is also clearly depicted as a priest in *Cardinal Bendinello Sauli and three companions*. Archival evidence shows that he benefited his bishopric of Gerace considerably in his short reign and tried to protect the interests of those souls under his care in

---

[5] A. Luzio, 'Federico Gonzaga ostaggio alla corte di Giulio II', *ASRSP* ix (1886), 509–82 at pp. 550–1.

his other benefices. He was also the first link in the chain of Sauli family members with an interest in reform within the Church: he supported Ettore Vernazza and the *Compagnia del divino amore*, was intimate with the ardent friar Agostino Giustiniani and was the patron of a reforming bishop, his cousin Filippo Sauli. Whether his discussions on theology held with Severo Varini and others centred on reform will never be known. Sauli was almost operating in a vacuum, one which was filled some few years later when Filippo and then Stefano Sauli became part of a network of reformers which included such influential figures as Giberti and Pole. Yet he was also a pragmatic ecclesiastical patron, using smaller benefices to reward his *famigliari* and often making sure that if they resigned them they were returned either to himself or his family.

Sauli the man

Years spent researching a man and his family lead to a degree of attachment; but archival evidence has radically altered an original perception that Sauli was a much wronged and unfortunate Genoese, made a scapegoat by the Florentine Medici in order to fill Leo's empty coffers. He emerges as an interesting and strong character. If Brandolini is to be believed, he adapted well to life in the Curia, managing Julius with some skill, gaining benefices when and where possible and widening his own academic interests. From a Genoese background where family came first, after 1515 he became the foremost representative of the Sauli in Rome. To judge from the letters written by the Genoese government before the plot and the discovery of his guilt, he was essentially a decent man, one who served his *patria* and his family well. He was the junior Genoese cardinal, but was also a young man who was determined to promote himself successfully both as a cardinal and as a Sauli, through his lifestyle and his patronage, attracting some of the foremost humanists and artists of the day. Something, somewhere, went wrong. Perhaps the cardinalate, the panegyrics written by humanists and the influence and patronage he exerted over his *famiglia* went to his head, as the printer Iacomo Mazzocchi had feared in his dedication of 1514. In Genoa any glory gained was a family rather than an individual triumph and Sauli was unused to personal power, in whatever context, and to the dynamics of power. Or perhaps the concentration of power and money in the hands of the pope left him frustrated. Sauli was neither an angel nor a demon, simply a misguided prince of the Church who ignored the basic rules and the delicate nature of patronage: namely that the recipient was to be grateful and return, not betray, the patron's trust. He succoured Petrucci when he merely had to tell the pope what he knew was happening. He thus badly underestimated the pope's power and disgrace, ill-health, poverty and death followed, cutting short what could have been a brilliant career.

Bibliography

Unpublished primary sources

Albenga, Archivio Storico Ingauno (ASI)
Archivio Comunale di Albenga, I, consilium 1514
Archivio Raimondi 10, 40

Genoa, Archivio Durazzo Giustiniani (ADGG)
Archivio Sauli, nos 13, 299, 315, 704–5, 707, 712, 714, 719–23, 730–1, 1568

Genoa, Archivio Parrochiale di Santa Maria di Castello
Colonne di San Giorgio S. Maria di Castello

Genoa, Archivio di Stato (ASG)
Archivio del Banco di San Giorgio, Colonne San Lorenzo, 1516, 610
Archivio Segreto, 1830–1, 1958 bis, 1959, 2177, 2342, 2707/C, 2805, 2816,
    2822
Archivio Segreto, Abbazia di San Siro, Pergamena di San Siro, 692–3
Archivio Segreto, Litterarum Fogliazzi, 1959
MSS 10, 494, 798, 839
Notai Antichi, 950, 1004, 1158–67, 1281, 1283–9, 1353 ter, 1394, 1406, 1413,
    1477, 1483, 1488, 1522 bis, 1532, 1830, 1947, 2049, 2870

Genoa, Biblioteca Civica Berio, sezione conservazione, raccolta locale
MSS m. r. III. 1, 19; m. r. V. 4. 1. (1–9); m. r. VIII, 2, 28–32; m. r. IX, 2, 24\25;
    m. r. IX. 5, 2; m. r. XV. 3.1 (1–5); m. r. i. C. 2,25, ii

Genoa, Biblioteca Universitaria (BUG)
MSS B VIII 13; C. IX. 19\21

Locri, Archivio di Stato (ASL)
Fondo Gerace, Fondo del Tufo, 1, 1 bis

London, British Library
MS Cotton Vitellius B. III

Madrid, Real Accademia de la Historia
Salazar y Castro, MS 76, fos 136r–230v

Rome, Archivio Capitolino di Roma (ACR)
Archivio Urbano, sezione 66, protocollo 13–14, 19–21, 23, 25, 28

Rome, Archivio di Stato (ASR)
Camerale I, app. 15–18
Camerale I, mandati camerali 851–5, 857–8
Camerale I, Tesoreria di Perugia e Umbria, 29
Collegio de' Notai Capitolini, 60, 92, 1914
Notai del Tribunale, AC 7151, 7153, 7156, 7157
Ospedale di San Giacomo degli Incurabili, 1145, 1146

Rome, Biblioteca Angelica
MSS 252, 1826

Rome, Biblioteca Nazionale Vittorio Emanuele
Fondo Autografi, A 97/41

Siena, Archivio di Stato (ASS)
Balia, 52
Concistoro, 2426
Notarile Ante-Cosimiano, 1002

Siena, Biblioteca Comunale degli Intronati di Siena (BCIS)
MS K VI 73

Vatican City, Archivio Segreto Vaticano (ASV)
Archivum Arcis, Armadio I–XVIII, 1443, 1903, 2243, 4770, 5042
Archivio Concistoriale, Acta Miscellanea, 3, 6, 31
Archivio Concistoriale, Acta Vicecancellarii, 2
Armadio XXXIV, 27
Armadio XXXIX, 19, 24–6, 28, 39
Armadio XL, 8
Armadio XLIV, 5
Camera Apostolica, Diversa Cameralia, 44–5, 47, 49, 50, 58, 62–3, 65, 67
Camera Apostolica, Introitus et Exitus, 504, 512, 514, 516, 522, 524–5, 535–6, 538, 543, 546–51
Camera Apostolica, Resignationes, 10–13, 15–18, 20
Inventories, nos 67, 347, 1009
Registra Lateranensi, 1129A, 1158, 1161, 1172, 1186A, 1190, 1195, 1200, 1253, 1258, 1276, 1281, 1283, 1293, 1301, 1333, 1363
Registra Vaticana, 889, 913, 917, 943, 960, 969, 971, 975, 990, 994, 997–1000, 1003–4, 1007, 1016, 1029, 1037–8, 1047, 1051, 1066, 1070, 1080, 1105, 1206, 1214

Vatican City, Biblioteca Apostolica Vaticana (BAV)
Codici Registri Latini 387
MSS Barberini Latini 2273, 2683
MS Chigiana G. II. 38
MS Ferrajoli 424
MSS Ottoboniani Latini 2137, 3552

MSS Vaticani Latini 1173, 3570, 3920, 4104, 5664, 7109, 9167, 9451, 11172, 11985

Published primary sources

Acta graduum academicorum ab anno 1501 ad annum 1525, ed. E. Martellozzo Forin, Padua 1969

Armellini, M., Un censimento della città di Roma sotto il pontificato di Leone X: tratto da un codice inedito dell'Archivio Vaticano, Rome 1882

Bologna, M. (ed.), 'L'archivio della famiglia Sauli di Genova', ASLSP n.s. xl/2 (2001), 11–661

Burckhard, J., Liber notarum ab anno MCCCCLXXXIII usque ad annum MDVI, ed. E. Celani, RIS xxxii/1, Città di Castello 1906

Calendar of state papers and manuscripts relating to English affairs, existing in the archives and collections of Venice, and in other libraries of northern Italy, ed. L. Rawdon Brown, London 1864

Cesareo, G. A., Pasquino e pasquinate nella Roma di Leone X: miscellanea della R. Deputazione romana di storia patria, xi (1938)

Chroniques de Jean d'Auton, ed. P. L. Jacob, Paris 1834

Corpo diplomatico Portuguez contendo os actos e relacoes politicas e diplomaticas de Portugal com as diversas potencias do mundo, desde o seculo XVI at, nosso dias, ed. L. A. Rebello da Silva, Lisbon 1862–91

Descriptio urbis: the Roman census of 1527, ed. E. Lee, Rome 1985

di Branca Tedallini, S., Diario romano 3 Maggio 1485 al 6 Giugno 1524, ed. P. Piccolomini, RIS xxxiii/3, Città di Castello 1907

'Le due spedizioni militari di Giulio II tratte dal diario di Paride Grassi bolognese', ed. L. Frati, R. Deputazione di storia patria per le provincie di Romagna i (1886), pp. xxiii–363

Epistolario di Bernardo Dovizi da Bibbiena, ed. G. L. Moncallero, Florence 1955–65

F. Guicciardini: le lettere, ed. P. Jodogne, Rome 1987–2005

F. Ubaldini, 'Vita di Mons. Angelo Colocci': edizione del testo originale italiano: Barb. Lat. 4882, ed. V. Fanelli, Vatican City 1969

Giovio, P., 'Dialogus de viris et foeminis aetate nostra florentibus', in Pauli Iovii opera, ix. 167–321

Gnoli, D., 'Descriptio urbis o censimento della popolazione di Roma avanti il sacco borbonico', ASRSP xvii (1898), 375–520

Gregorii Cortesii Monachi Casinatis SRE Cardinalis omnia quae huc usque colligi potuerunt, sive ab eo scripta, sive ad illum spectantia, Padua 1774

Guicciardini, F., La storia d'Italia di Francesco Guicciardini, ed. A. Gherardi, Florence 1919

Haig Gaisser, J., Piero Valeriano on the ill fortune of learned men: a Renaissance humanist and his world, Anne Arbor, MI 1999

Jacobi Sadoleti SRE Cardinalis epistolae quotquot extant proprio nome scriptae nunc primum duplo auctiores in lucem editae: pars prima, Rome 1760

Lanciani, R., 'Il codice Barberiniano XXX, 89 contenente frammenti di una descrizione di Roma del secolo XVI', ASRSP vi (1883), 223–40, 445–96

Lettere inedite di P. Giovio tratte dall'Archivio Gonzaga, ed. E. Luzio, Mantua 1885

Lettere: Pietro Bembo, ed. E. Travi, Bologna 1987–93

'I manoscritti Torrigiani donati al R. Archivio Centrale di Stato di Firenze: descrizione e saggio', ed. C. Guasti, *ASI* xx (1874), 19–50, 228–55, 367–408; xxi (1874), 16–76, 221–53

Mansi, G. D., *Sacrorum conciliorum nova et amplissima collectio*, anastatic edn, Graz 1960–1

Marcantonio Flaminio: lettere, ed. A. Pastore, Rome 1978

Memoirs of Philip de Commines, lord of Argenton, ed. A. R. Scobie, London 1855

Nicolai Baccetii Fiorentini ex ordine Cistercensi, *Abbatis Septimianae historiae libri VII: hanc notis, variis observationibus, et praefatione illustravit, necnon a temporis ludibriis vindicabit editor*, Rome 1724

Opus epistolarum Des. Erasmi Roterodami, ed. P. S. Allen, Oxford, 1906–47

Paolo Giovio: lettere, ed. G. G. Ferrero, Rome 1956

Pasqua, O., *Vitae episcoporum ecclesiae Hieracensis*, Naples 1754

Pauli Iovii opera, ed. E. Travi and M. Penco, Rome 1984

Poesie latine di Francesco Arsilli medico e poeta senigallese del secolo XVI: tratte da un codice autografo, ed. R. Francolini, Senigallia 1837

Poliziano, A., *Della congiura dei Pazzi ('Coniurationis commentarium')*, ed. A. Perosa, Padua 1858

Priscianese, F., *Del governo della corte d'un signore in Roma dove si ragiona di tutto quello che al signore e a' suoi cortigiani si appartiene di fare, opera non manco bella, che utile e necessario*, 2nd edn, Città di Castello, 1883

Relazioni degli ambasciatori veneti al senato, ed. E. Alberi, ser. ii, volume iii, Florence 1846

Russo, F., *Regesto Vaticano per la Calabria*, Rome 1977

Sanuto, M., *I diarii di Marino Sanuto (1496–1533)*, ed. M. Allegri, N. Barozzi, G. Berchet, R. Fulin and F. Stefani, Bologna 1879–1902

Senaregae, B., *De rebus genuensibus commentaria ab anno MCDLXXXVIII usque ad annum MDXIV*, ed. E. Pandiani, *RIS* xxiv/8, Bologna 1937

Travel journal of Antonio De Beatis: Germany, Switzerland, the Low Countries, France and Italy, 1517–18, ed. J. R. Hale, London 1979

Tutte le opera di Matteo Bandello, ed. F. Flora, Milan 1934

Vasari, G., *The lives of the painters, sculptors and architects*, trans. A. Hinds, rev. edn, New York 1963

Vernazza, B., *Opere spirituali*, Verona 1602

Ziegler, J., 'Clementis Septimi episcopi romani vita', in J. Schellhorn (ed.), *Amoenitates historiae ecclesiasticae et literariae*, Frankfurt–Leipzig 1738–9

Contemporary books and articles

Aenae Platonici Greci Christianissimi: De immortalitate animorum, deque corporum resurrectione, aureus libellus, cui titulus est Theophrastus, ed. A. Giustiniani, Venice 1513

Ariosto, L., *Orlando furioso di M. Lodovico Ariosto con cinque nuovi canti del medesimo*, Venice 1566

Cattaneo, G. M., *Genua*, Rome 1514

Ciaconii, A., *Vitae et res gestae pontificum romanorum et SRE cardinalium*, Rome 1630

Cortese, P., *De cardinalatu*, Rome 1510

Da Vigo, G., *Pratica in chirurgia copiosa in arte chirurgica nuper edita a Ioanne de Vigo Iulii secondi Pon. Max. olim chirurgico que infrascripta novem continet volumina*, Bologna 1514

de Longueil, C., *Orationes duae pro defensione sua in crimen lesae maiestatis, longe ex actiori quam ante iudicio perscriptae, ac nunc primum ex ipsius authoris sententia in lucem editae*, Florence 1524

Epistolarum Pauli Manutii libri XII uno nuper addito: eiusdem quae praefationes appellantur, Venice 1590

Fausto da Longiano, S., *Orationi di M. T. Cicerone di latine fatte italiane*, Venice 1556

Folietae, U., *Clarorum ligurum elogia*, Rome 1574

Fornari, S., *La spositione di M. Simon Fornari da Rheggio sopra l'Orlando Furioso di M. Ludovico Ariosto*, Florence 1549

Garimberto, G., *La prima parte delle vite, overo fatti memorabili d'alcuni papi, et di tutti i cardinali passati*, Venice 1567

Gesner, C., *Bibliotheca universalis, sive catalogus omnium scriptorum locupletissimus, in tribus linguis, Latina, Graeca ac Hebraica: extantium et non extantium, veterum et recentiorum in hunc usq diem, doctorum et indoctorum, publicatorum et in bibliothecis latentium: opus novum, et non bibliothecis tantum publicis privatisve instituendis necessarium, sed studiosis omnibus cuiuscunq artis aut scientiae ad studia melius formanda utilissimum*, Tiguri 1545

Giovio, P., *Le vite di Leone Decimo, et d'Adriano Sesto sommi pontefici, et del Cardinal Pompeo Colonna, scritte per Mons. Paolo Giovio vescovo di Nocera, e tradotte per M. Lodovico Domenichi*, Florence 1549

—— *Le iscrittioni poste sotto le vere imagini degli huomini famosi in lettere*, trans. H. Ohio, Venice 1558

Giustiniani, A., *Castigatissimi annali con la loro copiosa tavola della eccelsa e illustrissima repubblica di Genoa, da fideli e approvati scrittori, per el reverendo Monsignore Agostino Giustiniano genoese vescovo di Nebio accuratamente racolti*, Genoa 1537, 1981

Jongelinus, G., *Notizia abbatiarum ordinis Cistertiensis per orbem universum: libros X completa*, Coloniae Agrippinae 1640

Laurenzio, J., *Plutarchi Libellus aureus quomodo ab adulatore discernatur amicus: Joanne Laurenzio Veneto viro doctissimo interprete nuper ad utilitatem legentium summa diligentia publicatus*, Rome 1514

Penni, G. G., *Croniche delle magnifiche e honorate pompe fatte in Roma per la creatione et incoronatione di Papa Leone X. Pont. Opt. Max.*, Florence 1513

Puccinelli, P., *Zodiaco della chiesa milanese*, Milan 1650

Ruscelli, G., *Delle lettere di principi, le quali si scrivono da principi, o a principi, o ragionano di principi*, Venice 1581

Sauli, P., *Opus noviter editum pro sacerdotibus animarum curarum habentibus*, Milan 1521

—— *Euthymii Monachi Zigaboni Commentationes in omnes psalmos de Greco in Latinum conversae per R. D. Philippum Saulum Episcopum Brugnatensem*, Verona 1530

Staffetti, L., 'Il "Libro di ricordi" della famiglia Cybo pubblicato con introduzione, appendice di documenti inediti, note illustrative e indice analatico da Luigi Staffetti', *ASLSP* o.s. xxxviii (1908), pp. vii–615

Ughelli, F., *Italia sacra sive de episcopis Italiae et insularum adiacentium*, Rome 1644–62

Ugonio, P., *Historia delle stationi di Roma che si celebrano la quadragesima di Pompeo Ugonio: all'illustrissima et eccell. Sig. Camilla Peretti dove oltre le vite de santi alle chiese de quali e' statione, si tratta delle origini, fondazioni, siti, restaurazioni, ornamenti, reliquie, et memorie di esse chiese, antiche e moderne*, Rome 1588

Secondary sources

Abbondanza, R., 'Alciato, Andrea', *DBI* ii, Rome 1960, 69–77

Anon., 'Ritratto di Cesare Borgia il Valentino e Niccolò Macchiavelli in conversazione davanti al cardinale Pedro Loys Borgia e al segretario don Micheletto Corella', in *I Borgia*, Rome 2002, 215

Armellini, M., *Le chiese di Roma dalle loro origini sino al secolo XVI*, Rome 1887

Ascarelli, F., *Annali tipografici di Giacomo Mazzocchi*, Florence 1961

Asensio, E., 'Memorias de un fidalgo de Chaves (1510–17): descripciòn de la Roma de Julio II y Leon X', *Estudios Portugueses*, Paris 1974, 103–21

Avesani, R., 'Buonamico, Lazzaro', *DBI* xi, Rome 1969, 533–40

Ballistreri, G., 'Brandolini, Raffaele Lippo', *DBI* xiv, Rome 1972, 40–2

—— 'Cattaneo, Giovanni Maria', *DBI* xxii, Rome 1979, 468–71

Barberi, F., 'Le edizioni romane di Francesco Minizio Calvo', *Miscellanea di scritti di bibliografia ed erudizione in memoria di Luigi Ferrari*, Florence 1952, 57–98

—— 'Calvo, Francesco', *DBI* xvii, Rome 1974, 38–41

Baroni, C., *S. Simpliciano abbazia Benedettina*, Milan 1934

Bataillon, M., *Erasme et l'Espagne*, 2nd edn, Geneva 1991

Bauer, C., *Studi per la storia delle finanze papali durante il pontificato di Sisto IV*, Rome 1928

Belgrano, L., *Vita privata dei genovesi*, Genoa 1880

Beny, R. and P. Gunn, *The churches of Rome*, London 1981

Berthier, J., *L'Eglise de Sainte-Sabine à Rome*, Rome 1910

—— *Le Couvent de Sainte-Sabine à Rome*, Rome 1912

Bertolotto, G., 'Il codice greco Sauliano di S. Anastasio scoperto ed illustrato', *ASLSP* o.s. xxxv (1892), 7–48

—— 'Genua poemetto di Giovanni Maria Cataneo con introduzione e appendice storica a cura del socio Girolamo Bertolotto', *ASLSP* xxiv (1894), 729–818

Bianconi, A., *L'opera delle Compagnie del 'Divino Amore' nella Riforma Cattolica*, Città di Castello 1914

Bietenholtz, T. (ed.), *Contemporaries of Erasmus: a biographical register of the Renaissance and Reformation*, Toronto 1985–7

Black, C. F., *Italian confraternities in the sixteenth century*, Cambridge 1989

Boccardo, P. and L. Magnani, *Il Palazzo dell'università di Genova: il collegio dei Gesuiti nella strada dei Balbi*, Savona 1987

Bonino, G. G., *Biografia medica Piemontese*, Turin 1824

Borenius, T., 'A portrait group by Sebastiano del Piombo', *Burlington Magazine* xxxvii (1920), 169–70

Borlandi, A., '"Janua, janua italiae": uno sguardo al quattrocento genovese', *ASI* cxliii (1985), 15–38

Bossi, L., *Vita e pontificato di Leone X di Guglielmo Roscoe: tradotto e corredata di annotazioni e di alcuni documenti inediti dal conte Cav. Luigi Bossi*, Milan 1816–17

Brouette, E., A. Dimier and E. Manning (eds), *Dictionnaire des auteurs cisterciens*, i, Rochefort 1975

Brunelli, G., 'Fregoso, Federico', *DBI* l, Rome 1998, 396–9

Bullard, M., *Filippo Strozzi and the Medici*, Cambridge 1980

—— 'Farming spiritual revenues: Innocent VIII's "appalto" of 1486', in A. Morrogh (ed.), *Renaissance studies in honor of Craig Hugh Smyth*, Florence 1985, 29–42

—— 'Fortuna della banca Medicea a Roma nel tardo quattrocento', in Gensini, *Roma capitale*, 235–52

—— 'Raising capital and funding the pope's debt', in J. Monfasani and R. Musto (eds), *Renaissance society and culture: essays in honor of Eugene F. Rice Jr.*, New York 1991, 23–32

Calvini, N., 'Biblioteche rinascimentali in Liguria', *Atti e Memorie della Società Savonese di Storia Patria* x (1976), 97–107

Camajani, G. G., *Il 'Liber nobilitatis Genuensis' e il governo della repubblica di Genova fino all'anno 1797*, Florence 1966

Camasca, E. (ed.), *Tutta la pittura di Raffaello: i quadri*, Milan 1956

Cambiaso, D., 'I vicari generali degli arcivescovi di Genova', *ASLSP* n.s. xii (1972), 11–70

Capparoni, P., *Paolo Giovio archiatra di papa Clemente VII*, Grottaferrata 1913

—— 'Giov. Battista da Vercelli, sifilioatra squartato sotto Leone X', *Bollettino dell'Istituto Storico Italiano dell'Arte Sanitaria* i (1921), 3–36

Cappelletti, F., 'Le origini cinquecentesche: dal Palazzo Fazio Santoro al Palazzo Aldobrandini al Corso', in A. G. De Marchi (ed.), *Il Palazzo Doria Pamphilij al Corso e le sue collezioni*, Florence 1999, 13–29

Carandente, G., *Il Palazzo Doria Pamphilij*, Milan 1975

Caravale, M., *La finanza pontificia nel cinquecento: le province del Lazio*, Camerino 1974

Cardella, L., *Memorie storiche de' cardinali della santa Romana Chiesa*, Rome 1793

Cassandro, M., 'I banchieri pontifici nel XV secolo', in Gensini, *Roma capitale*, 207–34

Castiglioni, A., *A history of medicine*, New York 1947

Cataldi Palau, A., 'Un gruppo di manoscritti greci del primo quarto del XVI secolo appartenenti alla collezione di Filippo Sauli', *Codices Manuscripti* xii (1986), 93–124

—— 'Catalogo dei manoscritti greci della Biblioteca Franzoniana (Genova) (Urbani 2–20)', *Bolletino dei Classici: Accademia dei Lincei* supplement viii (1990), 1–120

—— 'Catalogo dei manoscritti greci della Biblioteca Franzoniana (Genova) (Urbani 21–40), *Bollettino dei Classici: Accademia Nazionale dei Lincei* supplement xvii (1996), 1–235

Cattaneo, E., 'Istituzioni ecclesiastiche milanesi', *Storia di Milano*, ix, Milan 1961, 509–720

Cavanna Ciappina, M., 'Cicero, Andrea', *DBI* xxv, Rome 1981, 386–8

—— 'Fregoso, Paolo', *DBI* l, Rome 1998, 427–32

Cesareo, F. C., *Humanism and Catholic reform: the life and work of Gregorio Cortese (1483–1548)*, New York 1990

Cesari, A., *Severo Varini (frate umanista) ricerche di Augusto Cesari*, Bologna 1894

Cevolotto, A., *Agostino Giustiniani un umanista tra bibbia e cabala*, Genoa 1992

—— 'Fieschi, Battista' *DBI* xlvii, Rome 1997, 433–4

—— 'Fieschi, Nicolò', *DBI* xlvii, Rome 1997, 503–6

—— 'Giustiniani, Agostino', *DBI* lvii, Rome 2001, 301–6

Chabod, F., 'L'epoca di Carlo v', *Storia di Milano*, ix, Milan 1961, 3–506

Chambers, D. S., *Cardinal Bainbridge in the court of Rome 1509 to 1514*, Oxford 1965

—— 'The economic predicament of Renaissance cardinals', in W. M. Bowsky (ed.), *Studies in medieval and Renaissance history*, Lincoln, Nebraska 1966, 289–313

—— *A Renaissance cardinal and his worldly goods: the will and inventory of Francesco Gonzaga (1444–1483)*, London 1992

—— 'Isabella d'Este and the travel diary of Antonio De Beatis', *Journal of the Warburg and Courtauld Institute* lxiv (2001), 296–308

Chastel, A., *Musca depicta*, Milan 1994

Cherubini, P., 'Franciotti della Rovere, Galeotto', *DBI* l, Rome 1998, 165–7

Chiti, A., *Scipione Forteguerri (il Carteromaco): studio biografico con una raccolta di epigrammi, sonetti e lettere di lui o a lui dirette*, Florence 1902

Cole, B., *Italian art, 1250–1500*, New York 1987

Contarino, R., 'Fornari, Simone', *DBI* il, Rome 1997, 80–2

Cosenza, M. E., *Biographical and bibliographical dictionary of the Italian humanists and of the world of classical scholarship in Italy, 1300–1800*, Boston, MA 1962

Costantini, E., *Il Cardinal di Ravenna al governo d'Ancona e il suo processo sotto Paolo III*, Pesaro 1891

D'Achiardi, P., *Sebastiano del Piombo*, Rome 1908

D'Agostino, E., *I vescovi di Gerace-Locri*, Chiaravalle 1981

D'Amico, J. F., *Renaissance humanism in Rome*, Baltimore–London 1983

Da Langasco, C., *Gli ospedali degli incurabili*, Genoa 1938

Da Prato, C., *Genova: chiesa di San Siro: storia e descrizioni*, Genoa 1900

Da Siena, S., *Bibliotheca sancta*, Cologne 1586

Davis, C., 'Un appunto per Sebastiano del Piombo ritrattista', *Mitteilungen des Kunsthistorisches Instituts in Florenz* xxvi (1982), 383–8

De Caro, G., 'Armellini, Francesco', *DBI* iv, Rome 1962, 234–7

De La Garanderie, M.-M., 'Christophe de Longueil', in Bietenholtz, *Contemporaries of Erasmus*, ii. 342–5

De Maio, R., *Riforme e miti nella chiesa del cinquecento*, Naples 1973

De Matos, L., *A corte literaria dos duques de Braganca no Renasicmento*, Lisbon 1956

De Simoni, L., *Le chiese di Genova: storia, arte, folclore*, Genoa 1948

Deswarte, S., 'Uno sguardo venuto da lontano: tra Roma antica e Roma cristiana', in M. Fagiolo (ed.), *Roma e l'antico nell'arte e nella cultura del cinque-cento*, Rome 1985, 489–508

—— 'The Portuguese in Rome and the Palazzo dei Tribunali', in K. J. P. Lowe (ed.), *Cultural links between Portugal and Italy in the Renaissance*, Oxford 2000, 249–64

De Vecchi, P., 'Raffaello e il ritratto "di naturale"', in *Raffaello e il ritratto di Papa Leone*, 9–50

Deutscher, T. B., 'Lazzaro Bonamico', in Bietenholz, *Contemporaries of Erasmus*, i. 166

Enciclopedia cattolica, Vatican City 1948–54

Eubel, C. and G. Van Gulik (eds), *Hierarchia catholica medii et recentioris aevi sive summorum pontificum, SRE cardinalium, ecclesiarum antistitum series*, 2nd edn, Munster 1913–2001

Fanelli, V., 'Il ginnasio greco di Leone X a Roma', *Studi Romani* ix (1961), 379–93

Ferino Pagden, S. and M. A. Zancan, *Raffaello: catalogo completo dei dipinti*, Florence 1989

Ferrajoli, A., 'La congiura dei cardinali', *Miscellanea della Reale Società Romana di Storia Patria*, vii, Rome 1920, i–355

Fidanza, P., *Teste scelte di personaggi illustri in lettere e in armi cavate già dall'antico, o dall'originale e dipinte nel Vaticano da Raffaello di Urbino e da altri valenti pittori ora esattamente disegnate, incise in rame secondo la loro grandezza e divise in due tomi da Paolo Fidanza pittore e incisore romano*, Rome 1757–74

Fiorio, M. T. (ed.), *Le chiese di Milano*, Milan 1985

Fragnito, G., 'Cultura umanistica e riforma religiosa: il "De officio viri boni ac probi episcopi" di Gaspare Contarini', *Studi Veneziani* xi (1969), 1–115

—— 'Carvajal, Bernardino Lopez de', *DBI* xxi, Rome 1978, 28–34

—— 'Castellesi, Adriano', *DBI* xxi, Rome 1978, 665–71

—— 'Cortese, Gregorio', *DBI* xxix, Rome 1983, 733–40

—— 'Il cardinale Gregorio Cortese (1483?–1548) nella crisi religiosa del cinque-cento', *Benedictina* (1983), 129–71

Freedberg, S. J., *Painting of the high Renaissance in Rome and Florence*, Cambridge, MA 1961

Frenz, T., *Die Kanzlei der Päpste der Hochrenaissance (1471–1526)*, Tubingen 1986

Frommel, C. L., *Der romische Palastbau der Hochrenaissance*, Tübingen 1973

Gaeta, F., 'Barozzi, Pietro', *DBI* vi, Rome 1964, 510–12

Garin, E., *Astrology in the Renaissance: the zodiac of life*, trans. C. Jackson, J. Allen and C. Robertson, London 1983

Gattoni, M., *Leone X e la geo-politica dello stato pontificio*, Vatican City 2000

Geanakoplos, D. J., *Greek scholars in Venice: studies in the dissemination of Greek learning from Byzantium to western Europe*, Cambridge, MA 1962

Gensini, S. (ed.), *Roma capitale: (1447–1527), Pisa and San Miniato 1994: atti del IV convegno di studio del centro studi sulla civiltà del tardo medioevo, 27–31 Ottobre 1992, San Miniato (Pisa)*, Pisa 1994

Giacchero, G., 'Frate Angelo da Chivasso padre della casana genovese', *Storia dei genovesi* iii (1988), 179–96

Gigante, M., 'Benigno, Cornelio', *DBI* viii, Rome 1966, 513–14

Gilbert, F., *The pope, his banker and Venice*, London 1980

Giordano, D., *Scritti e discorsi pertinenti alla storia della medicina e ad argomenti diversi*, Milan 1930

Giulia Cavagna, A., 'Tipografia ed editoria d'antico regime a Genova', in D. Puncuh (ed.), *Storia della cultura ligure*, ASLSP xlv/1 (2005) iii. 355–419

Goiffrè, D., *Gênes et les foires de change: de Lyon à Besançon*, Paris 1960

Granero, A., *Albenga sacra*, Albenga 1997

Gualdo Rosa, L., 'Delio, Sebastiano', *DBI* xxxvi, Rome 1988, 650

Guazzoni, V., 'La tradizione della ritrattistica papale nel Rinascimento e il *Leone X* di Raffaello', in *Raffaello e il ritratto di Papa Leone*, 89–133

Guidi Bruscoli, F., *Benvenuto Olivieri: i mercatores fiorentini e la camera apostolica nella Roma di Paolo III Farnese (1534–1549)*, Florence 2000

Haidacher, A., *Geschichte der Päpste in Bildern: eine Dokumentation zur Päpstgeschichte von Ludwig von Pastor*, Heidelberg 1965

Haile, M., *Life of Reginald Pole*, 2nd edn, London 1911

Hay, D., 'The Renaissance cardinals: Church, state, culture', *Synthesis* iii (1976), 35–46

—— *The Church in Italy in the fifteenth century*, Cambridge 1977

Heers, J., *Gênes au XVe siècle: activité économique et problèmes sociaux*, Paris 1961

—— *Le Clan familial au moyen âge*, Paris 1974

Hirst, M., *Sebastiano del Piombo*, Oxford 1981

Hollingsworth, M., *Patronage in Renaissance Italy from 1400 to the early sixteenth century*, London 1994

—— *The cardinal's hat: money, ambition and housekeeping in a Renaissance court*, London 2004

Hurtubise, P., 'L'Implantation d'une famille florentine à Rome au debut du XVI siècle: les Salviati', in Gensini, *Roma capitale*, 253–71

Hyde, H., 'Gerard David's *Cervara altarpiece*: an examination of the commission for the monastery of San Girolamo della Cervara', *Arte cristiana* lxxxv (1997), 245–54

—— 'From devotion to damnation: the Sauli as men of the Church in the early cinquecento', *Devotio* i (2000), 41–72

—— 'Genoa: "urbem … cuius similem non habet orbis universus"', *Bulletin for the Society of Renaissance Studies* xviii (Oct. 2000), 1–7

Jaffé, M., *The Devonshire collection of Italian drawings: Venetian and north Italian schools*, London 1994

Jones, R. and N. Penny, *Raphael*, New Haven 1983

Jourda, P., 'Un Umaniste italien en France: Theocrenus (1480–1536)', *Revue du seizième siècle* xvi (1929), 40–57

Jungic, J., 'Prophecies of the angelic pastor in Sebastiano del Piombo's "Cardinal Bandinello Sauli and three companions"', in M. Reeves (ed.), *Prophetic Rome in the high Renaissance*, Oxford 1992, 345–70

Jungmann, A., *The mass of the Roman rite: its origins and development*, New York 1950

Kempers, B., 'The canonical portrait of a cardinal: Bendinello Sauli, Raphael and Sebastiano del Piombo', in M. Gallo (ed.), *I cardinali di Santa Romana Chiesa: collezionisti e mecenati*, ii, Rome 2001, 7–21

Latuada, S., *Descrizione di Milano, ornata con molti disegni in rame dalle fabbriche più cospicue, che si trovano in questa metropoli*, Milan 1737–8

Lercari, A., 'Da Passano (dei Signori) Giovanni Gioacchino', in W. Piastra (ed.), *Dizionario biografico dei Liguri dalle origini ai nostri giorni*, iv, Genoa 1998, 210–17

Liberti, R., *Diocesi di Oppido-Palmi: i vescovi dal 1050 ad oggi*, Rosarno 1994

Lowe, K. J. P., 'Questions of income and expenditure in Renaissance Rome: a case study of Cardinal Francesco Armellini', in W. J. Sheils and D. Wood (eds), *The Church and wealth* (Studies in Church History xxiv, 1987), 175–88

—— 'Un episcopato non esaminato: analisi delle relazioni tra il vescovo di Volterra e la sua diocesi prima della Riforma', *Rassegna Volterrana* lxv–lxvi (1989–90), 107–25

—— 'A Florentine prelate's real estate in Rome between 1480 and 1524: the residential and speculative property of Cardinal Francesco Soderini', *Papers of the British School at Rome* lix (1991), 259–82

—— *Church and politics in Renaissance Italy: the life and career of Cardinal Francesco Soderini, 1453–1524*, Cambridge 1993

—— 'The political crime of conspiracy in fifteenth- and sixteenth-century Rome', in T. Dean and K. J. P. Lowe (eds), *Crime, society and the law in Renaissance Italy*, Cambridge 1994, 184–203

—— 'An alternative account of the alleged cardinals' conspiracy of 1517 against Pope Leo x', *Roma moderna e contemporanea. Rivista interdisciplinare di storia* xi (2003), 53–77

Lucco, M., 'Catalogo delle opere', in M. Lucco and C. Volpe (eds), *L'opera completa di Sebastiano del Piombo*, Milan 1980, 90–144

—— 'Sebastiano del Piombo', in J. Turner (ed.), *The Grove dictionary of art*, xxviii, New York 1996, 331–6

Luzio, A., 'Federico Gonzaga ostaggio alla corte di Giulio ii', *ASRSP* ix (1886), 509–82

—— 'Isabella d'Este e Leone x dal congresso di Bologna alla presa di Milano (1515–1521), *ASI* xl (1907), 18–97

—— *Isabella d'Este ne' primordi del papato di Leone X e il suo viaggio a Roma nel 1514–15*, Milan 1907

Maccà, G., *Storia del territorio Vicentino*, Caldogno 1812

McClung Hallman, B., *Italian cardinals, reform and the Church as property*, London 1985

Maddison, C., *Marcantonio Flaminio: poet, humanist and reformer*, London 1965

Majanlahti, A., *The families who made Rome: a history and a guide*, London 2005

Malacarne, V., *Delle opere de' medici, e de' ceruschi che nacquero, o fiorirono prima del secolo XVI negli stati della real casa di Savoia*, Turin 1786

Marangoni, G., 'Lazzaro Buonamico e lo studio paduano nella prima metà del cinquecento', *Nuovo Archivio Veneto* n.s. i (1901), 118–51, 301–18

Marini, G., *Degli archiatri pontificii*, Rome 1784

Marini, L., 'Berruti, Amadeo', *DBI* ix, Rome 1967, 410–14

Martines, L., *April blood: Florence and the plot against the Medici*, London 2003

Mauri, C., *Storia e descrizione delle chiese distrutte ed esistenti in Milano e dintorni*, Milan 1857

Mayer, T. F., *Reginald Pole: prince & prophet*, Cambridge 2000

Menotti, M., 'Vannozza Cattanei e i Borgia', *Nuova Antologia* (Nov.–Dec. 1916), 471–86

—— *I Borgia: storia e iconografia*, Rome 1917

Mercati, G., 'Francesco Calvo e Fausto Sabeo alla cerca di codici nell'Europa settentrionale', *Rendiconti della Pontifica Accademia Romana di Archeologia* xiii (1937), 149–78

Miglio, M., 'Brenta, Andrea', *DBI* xiv, Rome 1972, 149–51

Mills, J., *Carpets in paintings*, London 1983

—— 'The coming of the carpet to the West', in D. King and D. Sylvester (eds), *The eastern carpet in the western world from the 15th to the 17th century*, London 1983, 11–23

Minieri Ricci, C., *Biografie degli accademici Alfonsini detti poi Pontaniani dal 1442 al 1543*, Naples 1881

Minnich, N., 'Raphael's portrait *Leo X with Cardinals Giulio de' Medici and Luigi de'Rossi*: a religious interpretation', *Renaissance Quarterly* lvi (2003), 1005–52

Moresco, M., *Le parrocchie gentilizie genovesi*, Turin 1901

Moroni, G., *Dizionario di erudizione storico-ecclesiastica da S. Pietro sino ai nostri giorni compilato dal cavaliere Gaetano Moroni romano primo aiutante di camera di Sua Santità Gregorio XVI*, Venice 1840–61

Mullett, M., *The Catholic Reform*, London 1999

Munoz, A., *Il restauro della basilica di Santa Sabina*, Rome 1938

Museo del Prado: catalogo de las pinturas, Madrid 1985

Musso, G. G., 'La cultura genovese fra il quattrocento e il cinquecento', *Miscellanea di storia ligure*, i, Genoa 1958, 121–87

Musso, R., 'Lo "stato cappellazzo": Genova tra Adorno e Fregoso (1436–1464), *Studi di storia medioevale e di diplomatica* xvii (1998), 223–88

O'Malley, J. W., *Praise and blame in Renaissance Rome: rhetoric, doctrine, and reform in the sacred orators of the papal court c. 1450–1521*, Durham, NC 1979

Occhiato, G., 'Il soccorpo', in S. Gemelli (ed), *La cattedrale di Gerace: il monumento, le funzioni, i corredi*, Cosenza 1986, 101–26

Oldoinus, A., *Athenaeum Ligusticum seu syllabus scriptorum Ligurum nec non Sarzanensium, ac Cyrnensium Reipublicae Genuensis subditorum*, Perugia 1680

Olin, J. C., *The Catholic Reformation: Savonarola to Ignatius Loyola*, New York 1992

Oppedisano, A., *Cronistoria della diocesi di Gerace*, Gerace 1934, 528–9

Origone, S., 'Il patrimonio immobiliare del monastero di San Siro di Genova (secoli X–XIII)', *Studi Genuensi* x (1973–4), 3–14

Orth, P., 'Zur *Solymis* des Giovanni Maria Cattaneo', *Humanistica Lovaniensa; Journal of Neo-Latin Studies* l (2001), 131–41

Pacini, A., 'I presupposti politici del "secolo dei genovesi": la riforma del 1528', *ASLSP* n.s. xxx/1 (1990), 7–422

—— 'Ideali repubblicani, lotta politica e gestione del potere a Genova nella prima metà del cinquecento', in S. Adorni Braccesi and M. Ascheri (eds), *Politica e cultura nelle repubbliche italiane dal medioevo all'età moderna, Firenze, Genova, Lucca, Siena, Venezia: atti del convegno (Siena 1997)*, Rome 2001, 189–236

Pallucchini, R., *Sebastiano Viniziano*, Milan 1944

Partner, P., *Renaissance Rome, 1500–1559: a portrait of a society*, London 1976

—— 'Papal financial policy in the Renaissance and Counter-Reformation', *Past and Present* lxxxviii (1980), 17–62

—— *The pope's men: the papal civil service in the Renaissance*, Oxford 1990

—— 'Il mondo della curia e i suoi rapporti con la città', in *Roma, città dei papi* (Storia d'Italia xvi, 2000), 203–34

Paschini, P., *La beneficenza in Italia e le 'Compagnie del Divino Amore' nei primi decenni del cinquecento: note storiche*, Rome 1925

—— 'Tre illustri prelati del Rinascimento: Ermolao Barbaro, Adriano Castellesi, Giovanni Grimani', *Lateranum* n.s. year xxiii (1957), 11–207 at pp. 45–130

Pastor, L. von, *The history of the popes*, 3rd edn, London, 1949–60

Pastore, A., 'Flaminio, Marcantonio', *DBI* xlviii, Rome 1997, 282–8

—— *Marcantonio Flaminio: fortune e sfortune di un chierico nell'Italia del cinquecento*, Milan 1981

Pellegrini, M., *Ascanio Maria Sforza: la parabola politica di un cardinale-principe del rinascimento*, Rome 2002

Petrucci, F., 'Carafa, Oliviero', *DBI* xix, Rome 1976, 588–96

—— 'Cibo Mari, Lorenzo', *DBI* xxv, Rome 1981, 275–7

Petrucciani, A., 'Il catalogo di una biblioteca genovese del '700', *Accademie e biblioteche d'Italia* liv/ii (1986), 32–43

—— 'Le biblioteche', in D. Puncuh (ed.), 'Storia della cultura ligure', *ASLSP* xlv/1 (2005), iii, 233–345

Petrucelli della Gattina, F., *Histoire diplomatique des conclaves*, Paris 1864–6

Piazza, C. B., *La gerarchia cardinalizia di Carlo Bartolomeo Piazza della Congregazione degli Oblati di Milano*, Rome 1793

Picotti, G. B., 'La congiura dei cardinali contro Leone x', *Rivista Storica Italiana* n.s. i (1923), 249–67

Pigler, A., 'La Mouche peinte: un talisman', *Bulletin des Musées Hongrois des Beaux-Arts* xxiv (1964), 47–64

Piovan, F., 'Forteguerra, Scipione', *DBI* xlix, Rome 1997, 163–7

Pirri, R., *Sicilia sacra*, Palermo 1733

Pope-Hennessy, J., *The portrait in the Renaissance*, New York 1966

Premoli, O., 'Domenico Sauli ed i Gesuiti', *Archivio Storico Lombardo* xv (1911), 147–55

Prosperi, A., 'Note in margine ad un opuscolo di Gian Matteo Ghiberti', *Critica Storica* iii (1965), 367–402

—— 'La figura del vescovo fra quattrocento e cinquecento: persistenze, disagi e novità', in G. Chittolini and G. Miccoli (eds), *La Chiesa e il potere politico dal medioevo all'età contemporanea* (Storia d'Italia ix, 1986), 217–62

—— 'Le visite pastorali del Giberti tra documento e monumento', in A. Fasani (ed.), *Riforma pretridentina della diocesi di Verona: visite pastorali del vescovo G. M. Giberti, 1525–1542*, Vincenza 1989, i, pp. xxxiii–lx

—— 'Le "costituzioni" tra evangelismo e controriforma', in R. Pasquali (ed.), *Le 'costituzioni per il clero' (1542) di Gian Matteo Giberti, vescovo di Verona*, Vincenza 2000, pp. xix–xxvi

Puncuh, D. (ed.), *I manoscritti della raccolta Durazzo*, Genoa 1979

Raffaello e il ritratto di Papa Leone: per il ristauro del 'Leone X con due cardinali' nella Galleria degli Uffizi, Milan 1996

Ramsden, E. H., *Come, take this lute*, Bristol 1983

Reale, G., *Raffaello: la Disputa*, Milan 1998

Renazzi, F. M., *Storia dell'università degli studi di Roma*, Rome 1803–6

Riedl, J. O., *A catalogue of Renaissance philosophers (1350–1650)*, Milwaukee 1940

Rodocanachi, E., *Una cronaca di Santa Sabina sull'Aventino*, Città di Castello 1898

—— *La première Renaissance: Rome au temps de Jules II et de Léon X*, Paris 1912

—— *Histoire de Rome: le pontificat de Jules II, 1503–13*, Paris 1928

—— *Histoire de Rome: le pontificat de Léon X, 1513–21*, Paris 1931

Rossi, V., 'Testamento dell'elefante', in *Scritti di critica letteraria: dal Rinascimento al Risorgimento*, Florence 1930

Rowland, I. D., 'The intellectual background of the "School of Athens": tracking divine wisdom in the Rome of Julius II', in M. Hall (ed.), *Raphael's School of Athens*, Cambridge 1997

Rubio y Balaguer, J., *Las eglogas de Garcilaso de la Vega*, Barcelona 1945

Rusk Shapley, F. *Catalogue of the Italian paintings: National Gallery of Art, Washington*, Washington 1979

Ruysschaert, J., 'Trois Recherches sur le XIVe siècle romain', ASRSP lciv (1971), 10–29

Schenck, W., *Reginald Pole, cardinal of England*, London 1950

Schiavo, A., *Il palazzo della Cancelleria*, Rome 1964

Seidel Menchi, S., 'Passione civile e aneliti Erasmiani di riforma nel patriziato genovese del primo cinquecento: Ludovico Spinola', *Rinascimento* xviii (1978), 87–131

Setton, K. M., *The papacy and the Levant (1204–1571)*, Philadelphia 1976–84

Shaw, C., *Julius II: the warrior pope*, Oxford 1993

Simar, T., *Christophe de Longueil, humaniste: 1488–1522*, Louvain 1911

Simoni, P., 'Appunti sulle opere a stampa del vescovo veronese G. M. Giberti', *Studi storici Luigi Simoni*, xliii (1993), 147–67

Solfaroli Camillocci, D., *I devoti della carità: le Confraternite del Divino Amore nell'Italia del primo cinquecento*, Naples 2002

Soprani, R., *Li scrittori della Liguria e particolarmente della Maritima*, Genoa 1667

Spotorno, G. B., *Della Bibbia poliglotta di Monsignor Agostino Giustiniani vescovo di Nebbio: ragionamento del P. Don Giambattista Spotorno Barnabita*, Genoa 1820

Stabile, G., 'Camillo, Giulio', *DBI* xvii, Rome 1974, 218–30

Suida, W. E., *Paintings and sculptures from the Kress Collection, National Gallery of Art*, Washington, DC, 1951

Symonds, J. A., *Renaissance in Italy: the Catholic reaction*, London 1920

Tabacchi, S., 'Grassi, Achille', *DBI* lviii, Rome 2002, 587–91

Tavuzzi, M., *Prierias: the life and works of Silvestro Mazzolino da Prierio, 1456–1527*, London 1997

Tester, S. J., *A history of western astrology*, Woodbridge 1987

Tiraboschi, G., *Storia della letteratura italiana di Girolamo Tiraboschi*, Milan 1833

Tomaini, P., *Brugnato città abbaziale e vescovile: documenti e notizie*, Città di Castello 1961

—— *Attività pastorale di Filippo Sauli vescovo di Brugnato (1512–1528)*, Città di Castello 1964

Turchini, A. 'Giberti, Gian Matteo', *DBI* liv, Roma 2000, 623–9

Ulianich, B., 'Accolti, Pietro', *DBI* i, Rome 1960, 106–10

Vigna, R. A., *Illustrazione storica, artistica ed epigrafica dell'antichissima chiesa di Santa Maria di Castello in Genova*, Genoa 1864

Whittaker, J., 'Giles of Viterbo as classical scholar', in *Egidio da Viterbo, OSA e il suo tempo: Atti del V convegno dell'Istituto Storico Agostiniano, Roma–Viterbo, 20–23 Ottobre 1982*, Rome 1983, 85–105

Wilson, N. G., *From Byzantium to Italy: Greek studies in the Renaissance*, London 1992

Winspeare, F., *La congiura dei cardinali contro Leone X*, Florence 1957

Yates, F. A., *The art of memory*, 2nd edn, London 1992

Ydema, O., *Carpets and their datings in Netherlandish paintings, 1540–1700*, Woodbridge 1991

Zerbi, C., *Della città, chiesa e diocesi di Oppido Mamertina, e dei suoi vescovi: notizie cronistoriche*, Rome 1876

Zimmerman, T. C. P., *Paolo Giovio: the historian and the crisis of sixteenth-century Italy*, Princeton 1995

Unpublished theses

Boccardo, P., 'Materiali per una storia del collezionismo artistico a Genova nel XVII secolo', PhD, Milan 1989

Hyde, H., 'Early *cinquecento* "popolare" art patronage in Genoa, 1500–1528', PhD, Birkbeck College London 1994

Taviani, C., '"Franza populo e fora lo gatto": una rivolta cittadina nelle guerre d'Italia: Genova 1506', PhD, Perugia 2004

Index